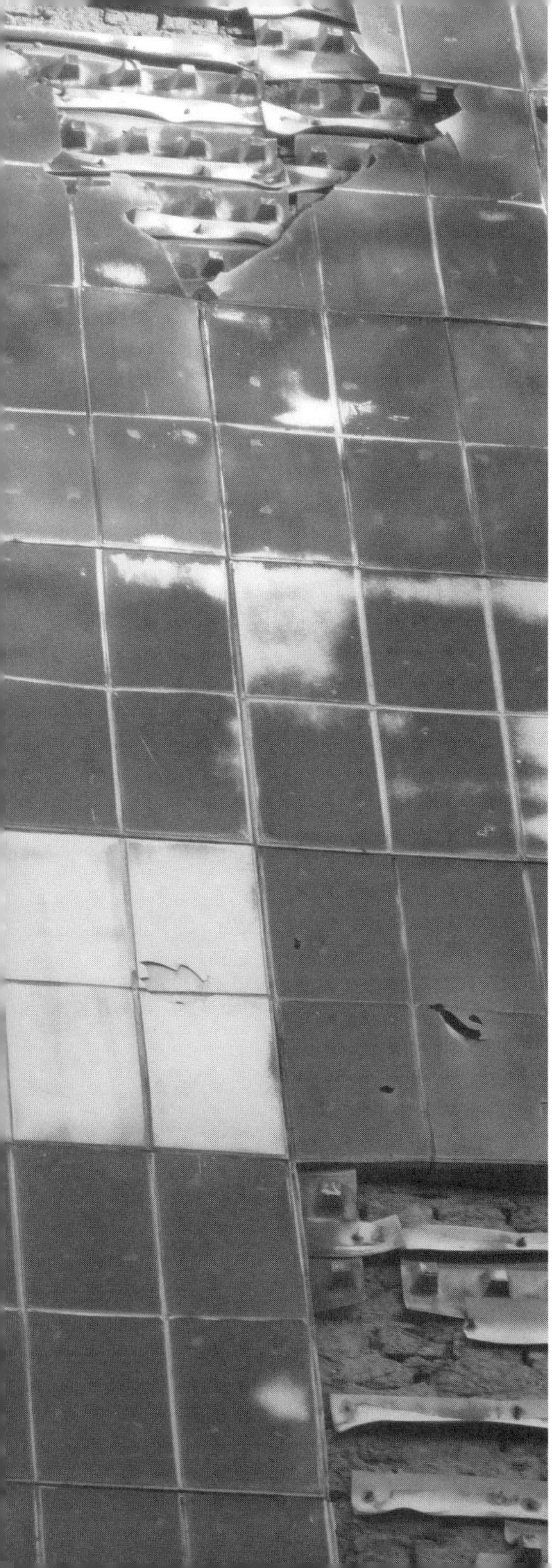

THE WALLS OF BERLIN

URBAN SURFACES : ART : FILM

Stephen Barber

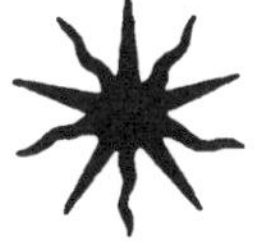

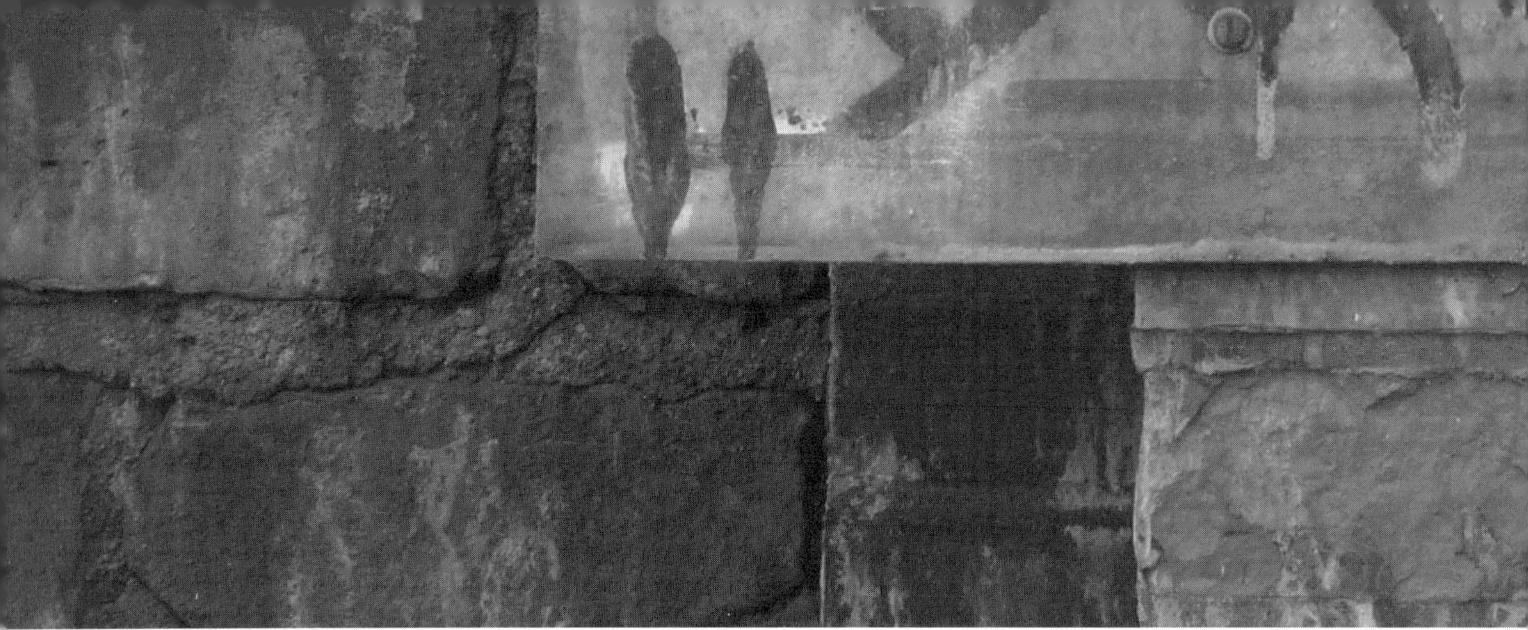

THE WALLS OF BERLIN

Urban Surfaces : Art : Film

Stephen Barber

ISBN 978-0-9820464-6-3
Published 2011 by Solar Books

Solar Art Directives: Seminal Cities
www.solarbooks.org

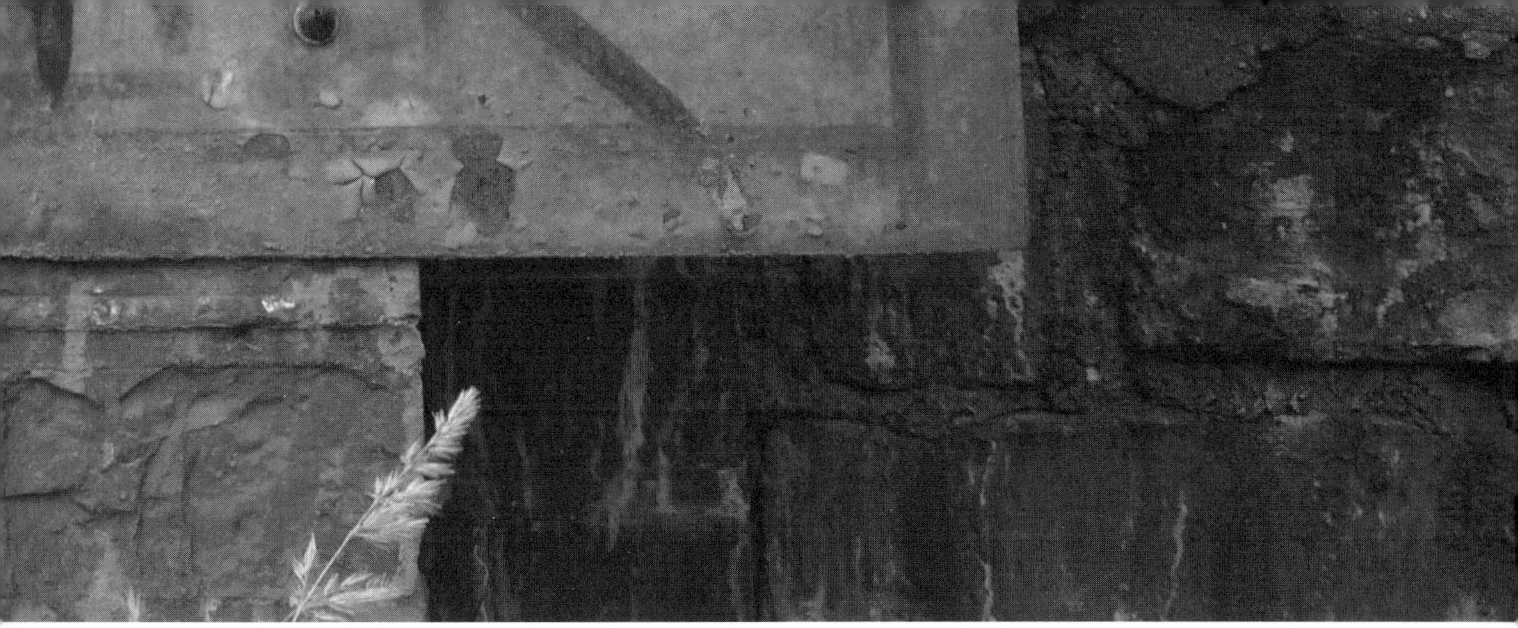

Contents

The Baltic Wall   5

The Skladanowsky Projector   9

40 WALLS OF BERLIN   15

Berlin-by-the-Sea   181

A 'Wall' of Berlin   185

Images   191

Acknowledgements   192

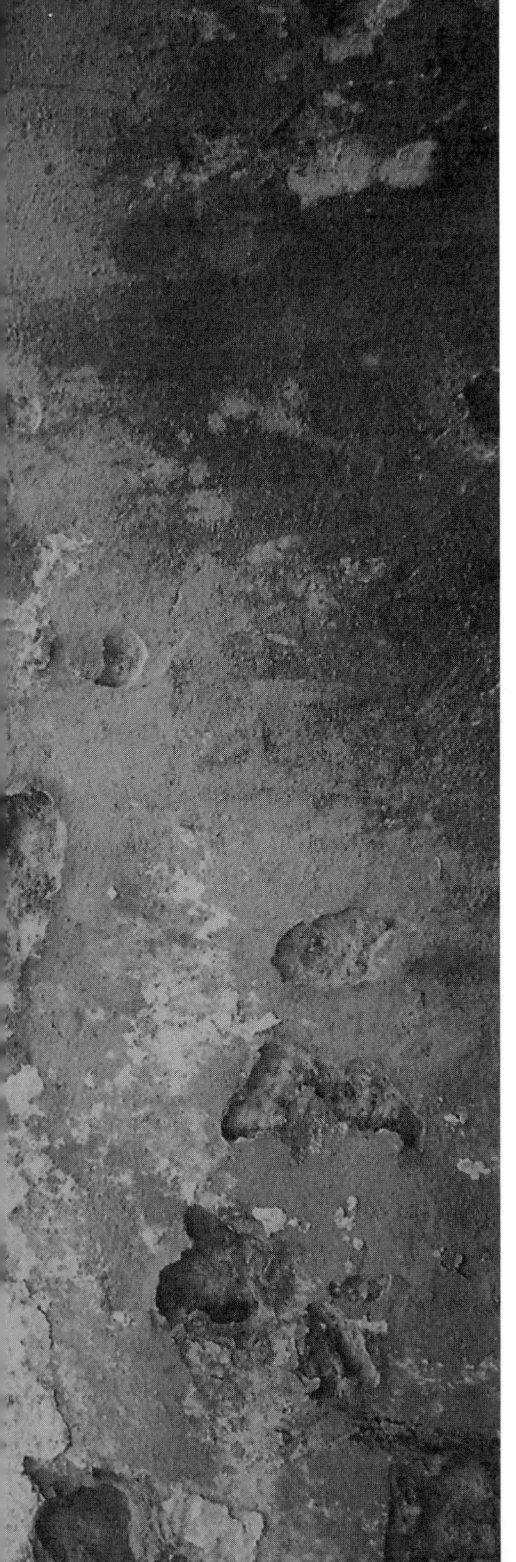

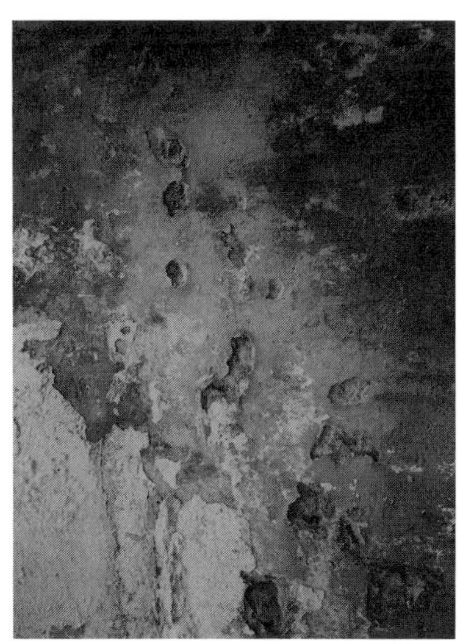

The Baltic Wall

In extremis: all urban surfaces are screens, their strata forming apertures to project out their ineradicable histories and their charges of memory, and to propel the eye that intimately touches them, from immediacy to immediacy. Urban surfaces, vivified both by superficial gestural sweeps and deep tactile embeddings of the eye, manifest their infinite manias and preoccupations, their damagings and scars, non-erasable inscriptions and entrenched derelictions, outlandish markings and graffiti lineages, fractures and fissures and openings, proliferating layers and mutating outgrowths, strange veerings and oscillations across time, pervasive corporeal residues, and mysterious urban vanishings. Urban surfaces comprise the blocked-up mouths of the city, that demand an unleashing in order for their languages and their images to disgorge. And for such transformational memories and obsessions to be released, urban surfaces may also exact a meshing of their preoccupations with those of film and visual art, so that the city instigates and creates its own films and its art-images, at the same time that its filmmakers and artists are provoked and engulfed by those surfaces, entering into the endless narrative abyss of what makes up a city.

While travelling in the Baltic cities, I was stopped-dead by a wall, along an alleyway of derelict, emptied-out sixteenth-century houses, that led to a city's boarded-up film museum. I touched that wall, frozen and damp, dense and open. A ragged scattering of machine-gun bullet-impacts had choreographed its way vertically up or down that surface, during one or other of the numerous conflicts that had assigned that city to Soviet or German empires. A human body had once stood before it, in combat or in readiness for execution, and the constellated gougings had multiple variants, according to the angles of fire, and their penetrations of that surface or their deflected ricochets. Or could some ferocious form of pulverising urban disintegration exactly mirror the impact of a spray of bullets? At the most intensive impact-site, the iridescent algae-green surface appeared to have largely effaced itself, as though in shock, down to a pale primrose hue, while far darker green patches of mutated cement, or whitewash, had amassed around that zone, in places concentrating into a deliquescing near-black, or to blue. At several points, a further layer of wall-coating had once been applied, but had friably cracked and mostly dispersed, and misfired, as though unable to adhere itself to that tumultuous surface. And visible deep within the bullet-impacts, and at the perimeters of that zone, the original brickwork infrastructure was exposed: the manual work utterly irregular, in places made of small rectangular ochre bricks, at others of jagged chunks of stone, with cracked and petrified objects maladroitly thrust into the voids of the

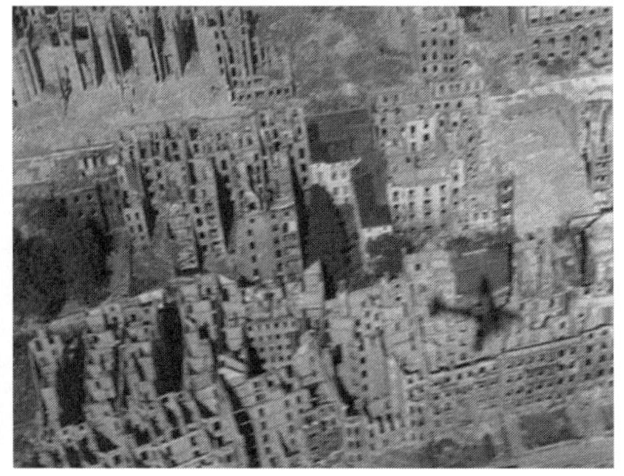

long-gone mortar, against the grain and perhaps in desperation, to somehow maintain the disintegrating building upright, as a disjuncture and a wound, and as a living element of the city, its surface as intense and immediate as that of any image from film or art.

And so, from the point of origin of that seminal Baltic wall, I involuntarily started thinking about Berlin: the supreme, unique site for revelatory urban surfaces. Berlin forms a miraculous city of voluble walls whose profound traumas, ecstasies and obsessions constitute its urban media. And, simultaneously, Berlin holds a vanished, silent city within itself: that of East Berlin, erased from one moment to the next, on 3 October 1990, as an urban conjuring trick whose power exceeded all others, while the figures that had inhabited it continued to live in that vacuumed space. Berlin is a city of protests and political revolutions – almost always failed revolutions – and of consumerist mutations and grandiose corporate architectures, with those two contrary forces pinioned together, unsteadily and deliriously mismatched, with a visual impact like that of a fist that takes two disparate handfuls of ashes, crushes them together, then sweeps that mixed substance across the face of an oblivious urban surface, for which memory is either too glaring or else forgotten. And with that abrupt compulsion to look at, into and through Berlin's urban surfaces, I left the Baltic wall behind, headed for the airport and took a flight to the city.

As the aeroplane made its westward approach into Berlin, through mist and cloud, I tried to catch glimpses of the city, each urban flash filtered and obscured by weather-conditions that delineated and controlled the time and parameters of those visions. The vast artery of the Karl-Marx-Allee materialised for a split-second. Then the entire city disappeared, caught within a last-minute storm. As though to compensate for those limitations and erasures, a sudden rush of film and art images of Berlin filled my eyes, and I realised how, above all other cities, the film and art images of Berlin always collided and intersected with the contemporary city, and were a creation of Berlin, just as they determined its perception, from the first-ever film images of the city conjured by the Skladanowsky Brothers in the 1890s, and the imageries of the then-accelerating, mutating city and its peripheries, painted by its artists, onwards, through digitised media, to the present moment. To look into the urban surfaces of Berlin, and explore their essential emanations, those surfaces need to hold, embedded within them, the film and art of the city.

This book forms a sequence of forty journeys into Berlin, and through its urban surfaces, with those preoccupations with film and art always held close at hand. For every ocular journey that may excoriate and probe the face of the city, a film or an art image (including those from the GDR era) works to delineate and focus whatever is exposed, and to release the vital charge of history, memory, obsession, passion that had been concealed or abandoned there, intentionally or involuntarily. Each exploration of an urban surface is marked by an initiating photographic image – an image always saturated in memory and time, and by corporeality – that serves as a conduit to activate whatever can be discovered, in language, about that surface. A city is nothing, and nowhere, unless it is extreme, and all of the worldwide century-long fascination with Berlin stems from its vital aberrance: its inability to behave as cities habitually do, so that it insurges, is apocalyptically destroyed, creates manically, divides and falls, and sensationally pleasures itself, located in urban excess. Berlin projects its scarred and adorned surfaces, simultaneously profound and capricious, always held in tension and complicity with film and art.

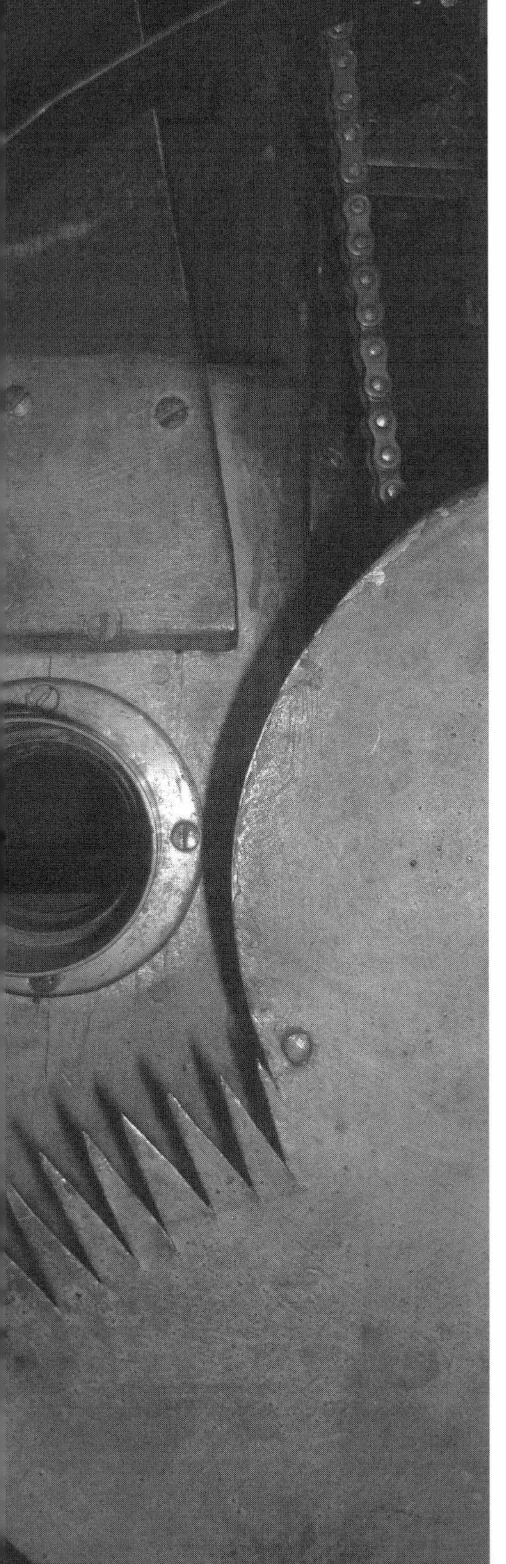

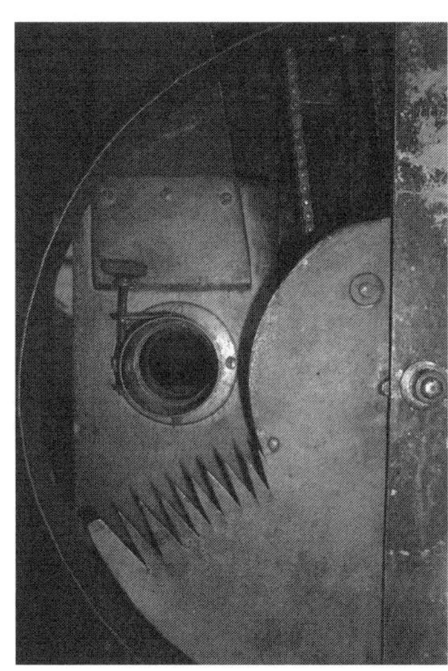

The Skladanowsky Projector

The Skladanowsky projector, the 'Bioskop', constructed by the Berlin magicians Max and Emil Skladanowsky in the summer of 1895, and used for the first-ever screening of films for a public audience, at the Wintergarten Ballroom of the Central Hotel in Berlin's Friedrichstrasse on 1 November 1895, forms the originating vision machine for the memory-seared city, for all of its time and space, and for every urban surface it contains. Since Berlin is a city that generates itself through its projections, pre-eminently those held by its film and art images, and through the intersection of those projections with its urban surfaces, the Skladanowsky projector constitutes the seminal organ of perception able to conjure the city into life. Berlin's art images are located in the urban matter of the city itself, without any unique origin, and their points of contact with the city are indelibly meshed into the walls of Berlin themselves, but its film images, together with those images' materialisation within the face of the city, originate solely in the extravagant dreams and ruined urban obsessions held by the Skladanowsky projector.

From the Berlin airport in the south-east, I took the train straight through the city, as though in oblivion, skimming over its endless transmutations, eyes averted, out to Potsdam, just beyond the south-western perimeter of Berlin. Across the river from the Potsdam station, the Skladanowsky projector stood in the foyer of the town's film museum, confined in a glass case, semi-abandoned and overlooked. Max Skladanowsky had already been experimenting with film cameras for two or three years, shooting films from the roof of a building in the Prenzlauerberg district and in the northern streets of Berlin, when he devised and hand-built his idiosyncratic projector, in order to show those films to public audiences. Possessing none of the technological sophistication or resources of the era's other film-pioneers, he had conceived of his dual-lens 'Bioskop' projector out of the blue, with a sense of urgency, as an outlandishly botched, unprecedented, but still somehow operational device. Not knowing how to build a film projector, he had done it anyway, like the young bell-founder in Tarkovsky's *Andrei Rublev*, and it had miraculously worked. I stood and looked into the one exposed lens of the projector, its counterpart obscured by the serrated mechanism which enabled hand-perforated film-images to be illuminated by each lens in alternation. But once I had looked into that lens, I had allowed an irreparable ocular inhabitation to take hold, from the very origins of film. And I realised that all of the urban surfaces I would explore in Berlin would now be envisioned and impelled directly through the seminal aperture of the Skladanowsky projector's lens – with the film images of Berlin alternating with its art images, just as the projector alternated its own two separate inputs of images – in the

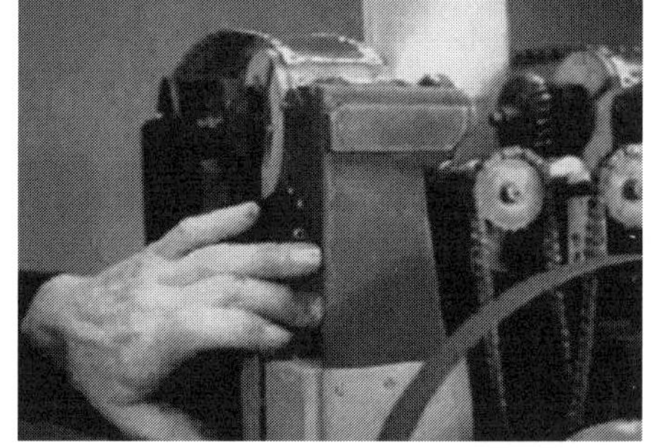

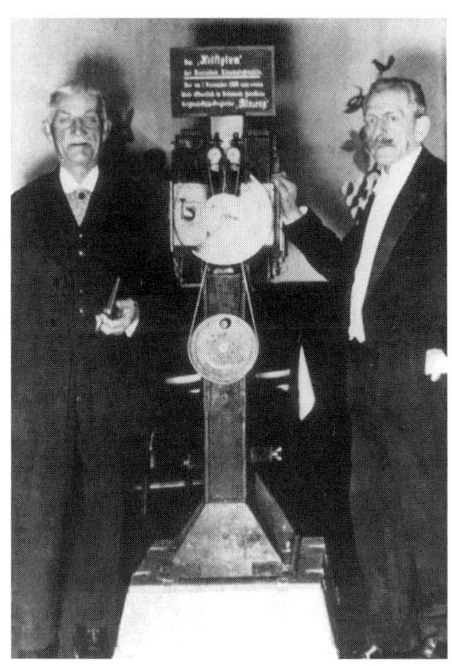

form of visual and textual conjurations of the city.

The first journey undertaken through Berlin, launched and directed by the Skladanowsky projector, was one which tracked the scattered traces within the city of the Skladanowsky Brothers themselves, as near-forgotten and vanished instigators of film. From the immediate tangible contact with the Skladanowsky projector, I left the Potsdam film museum and headed for the centre of Berlin on foot, across the Glienicke bridge and through the dense lake-side forests on the city's south-western expanse, passing by the tiny forest cemetery where the singer Nico – the haunting presence in the films of Philippe Garrel, and the bewitching provocateuse in Fellini's *La Dolce Vita* – had been buried. Finally, I reached the site in the Friedrichstrasse of the Wintergarten Ballroom, where the Skladanowsky projector had unwittingly instigated the all-powerful, worldwide regime of the cinematic spectacle (only a month or so before the Lumière Brothers staged their own first public projections, in Paris's Grand Café), the film-images shown on a side-stage as a minor, subsidiary attraction as part of an evening-long programme of magic-acts and dancers. The vast entertainment palace of the Wintergarten Ballroom, with its ornate glass roof, together with the lavish Central Hotel which enclosed it, had been utterly destroyed by an RAF bombing raid on 21 June 1944; its location, in the multiply-rebuilt Friedrichstrasse, had eventually been taken by the Rossmann pharmacy-supermarket. In Franz Kafka's novel *Der Verschollene* (*The Man who Disappeared/Amerika*), Rossmann is the name of the young outcast who vanishes by train into the interior of America; and during the final winter of his life, 1923-24, living in Berlin at a time of acute economic turmoil with his lover Dora Diamant, the ailing Kafka had frequently visited the Friedrichstrasse in his search for restaurants able to alleviate his tubercular starvation, before finally abandoning Berlin for

Vienna to fade out of existence in a convalescence clinic. But within the contemporary urban surfaces of Berlin's Friedrichstrasse, and the erasure of his cinematic traces, Max Skladanowsky is 'the man who disappeared'.

From the site of the Wintergarten Ballroom in the Friedrichstrasse, I walked to the junction of the Kastanienallee and the Schönhauserallee; on the roof of the nineteenth-century apartment-building at that junction (the 'Ecke Schönhauser'), Max Skladanowsky had shot the first-ever film of Berlin, one second in duration, of his brother Emil dancing, with the innumerable industrial towers, chimneys and spires of northern Berlin visible in the background. Max Skladanowsky had subsequently been so eager to disappear backwards into time, to enhance his status as a film-pioneer, that he had backdated those urban images to 1892, when they had actually been made around two years later. From that roof, high above the city, the panorama of northern Berlin appeared almost identical to the moment of the Skladanowsky Brothers' inhabitation of that space, the chimneys and spires diminished by wartime bombing, but supplemented by the prefabricated housing-towers of the GDR era. A mosaic had been embedded into the paving stones in front of the apartment-building, with the single word 'Skladanowsky' part-submerged by construction debris and a pile of red earth. Further north along the Schönhauserallee, the site of the Café Sello – where the Skladanowsky Brothers had staged experimental test-runs of their projector in the summer of 1895, in front of an oblivious clientele of unsuspecting beer-drinkers, in preparation for their Wintergarten Ballroom film-screening – had been erased and replaced by a neighbourhood cinema and then by a supermarket, its garish facade awrily disconnected in time and space to the now-stranded commemorative mosaic installed on the pavement in front of that site's

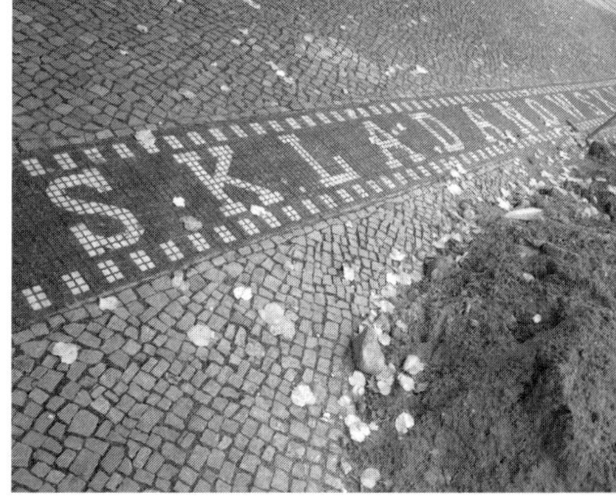

earlier incarnation, with the date and name of the Skladanowsky projector: '1895 Bioskop'. The traces of the Skladanowsky Brothers' presence appeared to be gradually disintegrating in the mutating terrain of Berlin, with only the infinite power of their projector's urban illumination, and its capacity to permeate and reveal the city's surfaces, conversely enduring, and proliferating. The Skladanowsky Brothers' cinematic experiments had collapsed in acrimony only a year after their Wintergarten Ballroom screening; far more technologically adept filmmakers and exhibitors rapidly superseded them, their trade licenses were arbitrarily suspended by the Berlin authorities, and their film-career ended almost before it began. The two brothers, Max and Emil, quarrelled and split-apart, with Emil falling out of history. Heading further north, I finally reached the cemetery of the Pankow district of Berlin, where the gold-engraved word 'Bioskop' led my eye to Max Skladanowsky's tomb. By the end of his life, three months into the Second World War, the Nazi regime, with its own filmic obsessions, had vaunted his innovations of over forty years earlier, and Goebbels sent a wreath to his funeral.

From Max Skladanowsky's tomb in the Pankow cemetery, I walked back through Berlin and its peripheries to the Potsdam film museum and the battered-together projector of serrated metal, glass, nails and wood, and stared back into the lens of that unique medium of urban memory and urban disappearance. From that vital aperture, a sequence of forty walls of Berlin now irresistibly emerged, each of them imprinted with the determining presence and inflection of film and art, together with the compulsive scarifications, ecstasies, voids and effacements of the city; all that remained was to follow the ocular trajectory of that projection of light, into and through the urban surfaces of Berlin.

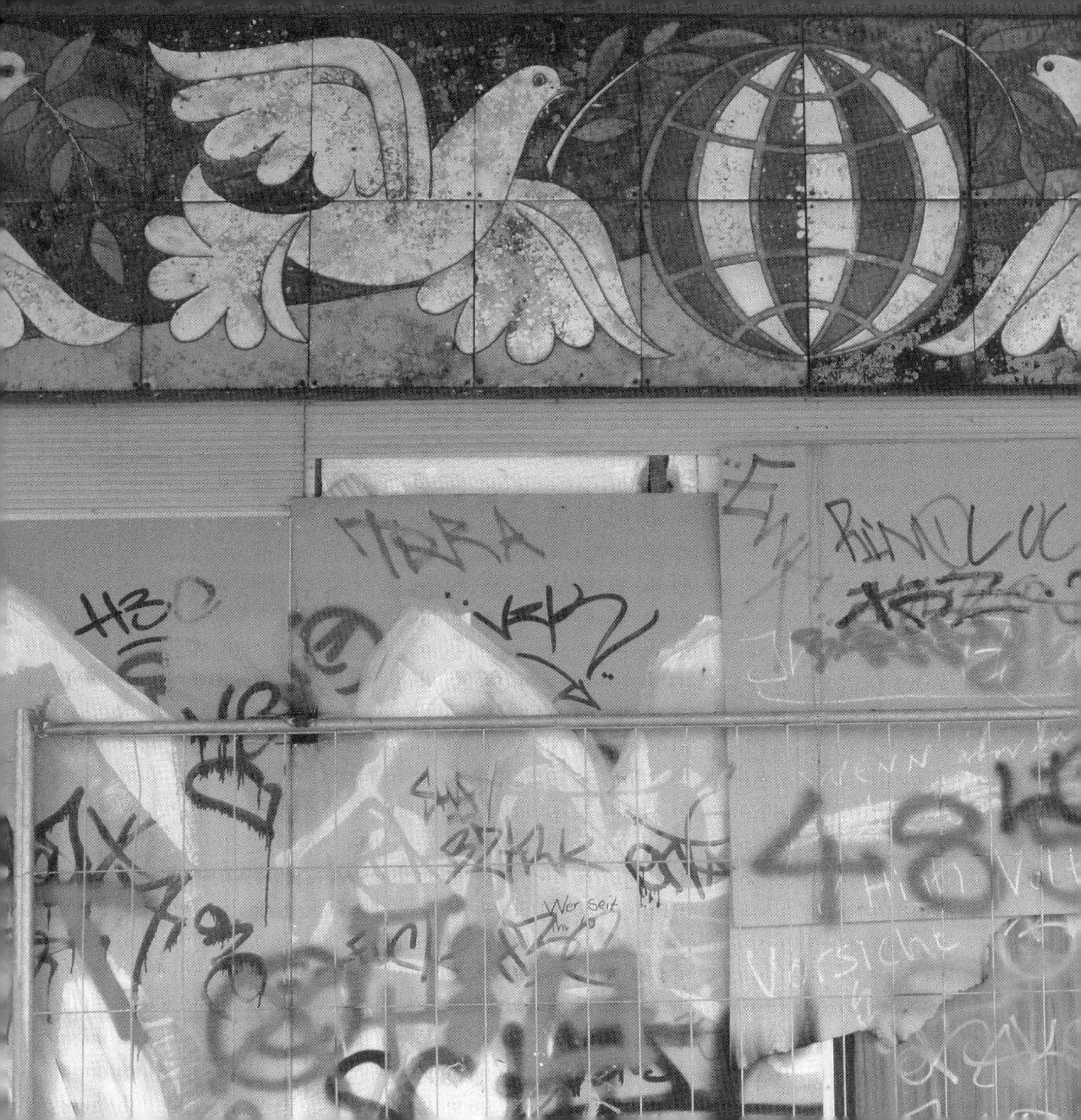

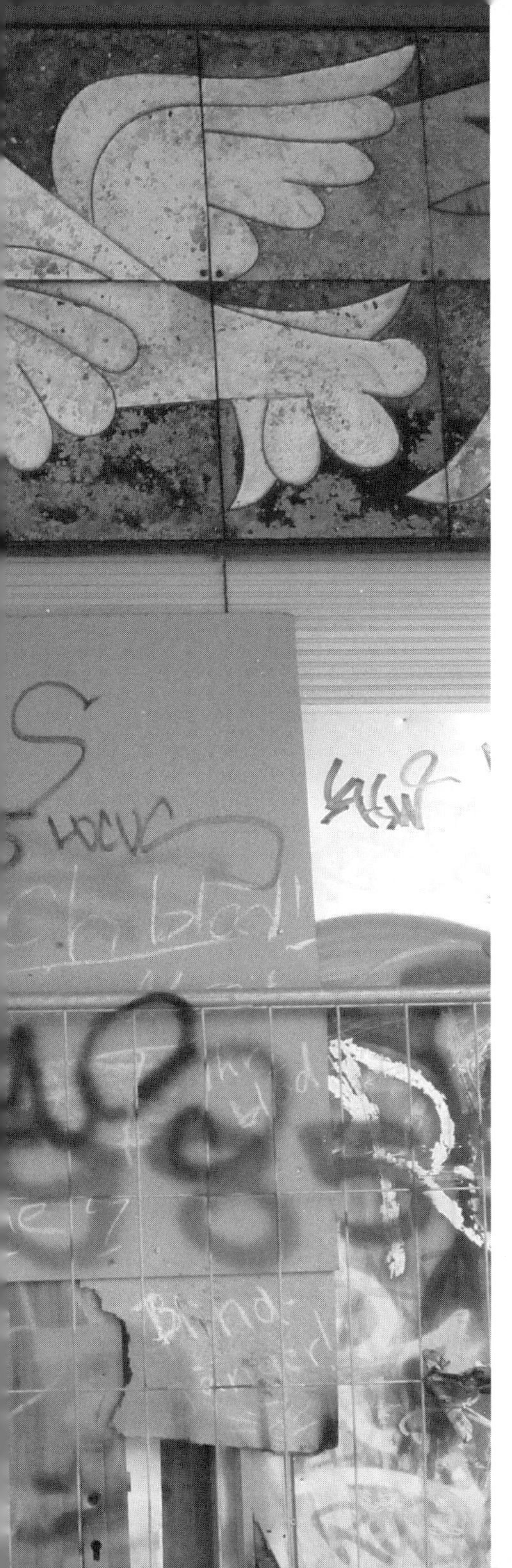

40 WALLS OF BERLIN

'Today I believe that it's not the people who scream in the streets but the streets themselves which are crying out. When they can no longer tolerate their void, they proclaim it. But, in reality, I'm not really certain of this.'
–Siegfried Kracauer, 'Screams in the Street' (1930),
in *Strassen in Berlin und Anderswo* (*Streets in Berlin and Elsewhere*)

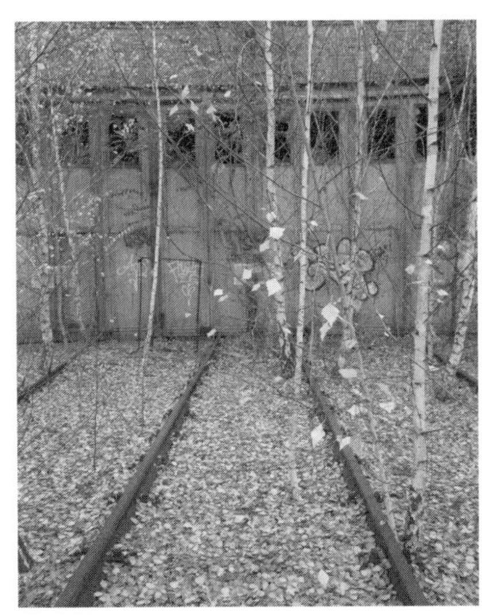

I

In Berlin, each exterior urban surface alternately closes and opens out its projections, against and towards the eye. Alongside an immense and abandoned railway roundhouse in the Pankow district, its disintegrating interior of skeletal iron pillars and precariously ripped flooring accessed covertly from a gap in its walls, an arc-shaped shed used for the nightly storage of trains for the city's transport system had also fallen derelict. From a turntable, railway tracks now overgrown with slender birch trees led to each of the fifteen closed gates of the shed. Every pane of glass of the grey metal gates had been shattered, the surfaces delicately interspersed with outbursts of graffiti, already decades-old, archaic data for the languages of the city. Above the metal gates, the concave brickwork of the shed's exterior surface bore no inscriptions, as oblivious to the passage of time as during the era when the gates below it had rhythmically opened and closed to allow the entry, storage and departure of trains through the course of the Berlin day. The indefinite closure or barricading of those gates intimates a forcible sealing of urban languages and images. But whenever an aperture of the city opens, it starts to flood its volatile content incessantly, image upon image and text upon text.

In the films and art of Berlin, a determining moment is always that of arrival in the city and the instigation of urban movement, from stasis. In films such as Walter Ruttmann's *Berlin: Die Sinfonie der Grossstadt* (*Berlin: Symphony of the Great City*) (1927), and Jacques Tourneur's *Berlin Express* (1948), journeys into Berlin by train precipitate sensations of the imminence and immediacy of the city. In Billy Wilder's *A Foreign Affair* (1948), Mikheil Chiaureli's *The Fall of Berlin* (1949) and Guy Hamilton's *Funeral in Berlin* (1966), arrivals into Berlin by aeroplane – often vertiginously spinning arrivals – work to unseal the city's closure and to tear it open for an act of urban envisioning. Above all, in the first sequence of *Berlin: Die Sinfonie der Grossstadt*, the onrush of the train journey across the Brandenburg plain towards Berlin is signalled as one of exhilarated impatience, the accumulating indicators of the city's growing proximity gradually amassed in order to seize that desired urban opening, finally accomplished with the train's arrival into the Anhalter Bahnhof. Once the city has become visually prised-apart by the moment of arrival, and its facades rendered unhinged, it will remain open for as long as it is ready to transmit its content, into the eye, and into the durations of films or art-works.

In *Berlin: Die Sinfonie der Grossstadt*, the unleashing of the city's closed surfaces is marked by a sequence which shows the gates of Berlin's transport sheds being opened for the day, at dawn. In Ruttmann's film, the gate of the railway shed, identical to the Pankow shed's facade, is released for a train marked with its destination, that of Potsdam, to emerge from the interior space; in adjacent sequences,

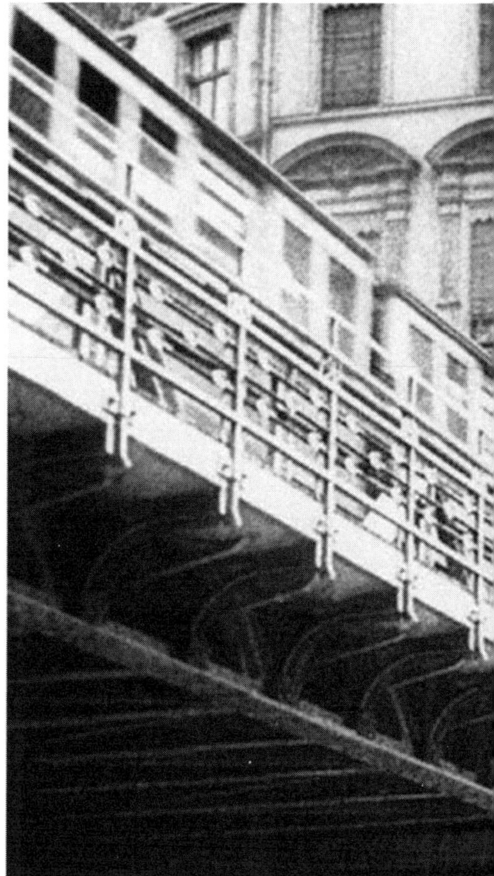

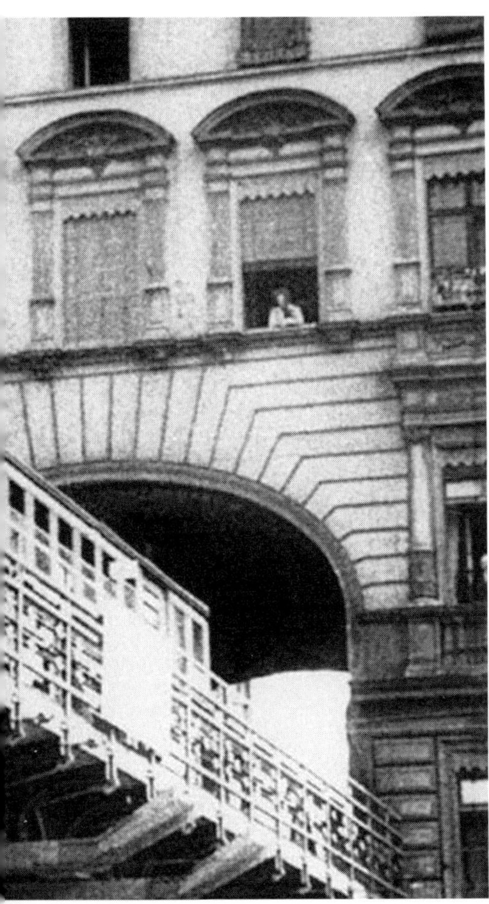

the gates of tram-sheds and of suburban train-sheds open too, so that the city's transport media are expelled for their day's work. The initiation of those urban conduits forms a ritual undertaking in the film; without that opening-out of the city's surfaces and the release of its media, the eye could never penetrate the face of the city, and its time – linear, chronological time in Ruttmann's film, from early dawn until the sexual decadence of the Berlin night – would be annulled. In the revelation of the city carried by its opening, Berlin's transport media appear as its organs of corporeal and ocular movement. But that pervasive visual facilitation can also go deeply askew, in the film and art of Berlin: in Ernst Ludwig Kirchner's lithograph *Das Eisenbahnunglück* (*The Railway Disaster*) (1915), one of his numerous depictions of Berlin's densely entangled transport system, a train has spectacularly plunged from its overground track into the street below, closing down the city's space and imbuing it with calamity and dereliction.

Once the steaming Potsdam-bound train emerging at dawn from the railway shed in *Berlin: Die Sinfonie der Grossstadt* has left its opened gate, it immediately moves onto a vast exterior turntable, on which it can be rotated and then launched, set into its correct trajectory to enter and traverse the city. Such urban turntables form revolving prisms of vision, able both to direct and derail the imageries and memories of the city, intermittently gathering speed in vertiginous rushes of images, and embodying the act of scanning the accelerating, haywire screens and facades of the contemporary digitised city, as well as tracking its decelerating, malfunctioned movements into sclerotic dereliction and stasis. The tree-grown tracks emerging from the abandoned railway shed in Pankow also led directly to their turntable, the structure now corroded and buckled beyond repair, unable any longer to project Berlin's urban media in any direction, closed-down like an eye subject to a disease that irreparably brought about the fall of vision. That turntable, disused for decades and emblazoned with intricate strata of rust, had become marooned and anachronistic; originally created to emit the city's movement, it was now cancelled-out like the one lens of the Skladanowsky 'Bioskop' projector always obscured from view by its serrated mechanism, in order that the other lens could project clearly.

Even in their dereliction, each closed-down lens or image – each obscured surface or eye, of Berlin – forms a vital aperture, in many ways as illuminating as the city's open eyes, in mediating the endemic disorientation in urban perception, its corporeal and sensory turmoil, malfunctions and erasures, eclipses and falls of darkness, ruinations and abandonments, catastrophic political and architectural ambitions, together with the engrained excess of the city which can never be perceived in a linear, chronological way. Such obscured urban surfaces, pre-eminently those traced by film and art images, are ones in which the city reveals itself by falling apart, simultaneously closed and dis-closed. The metal gates of the Pankow railway shed, part-obscured by the trees which had grown between the tracks that led to those gates, emanated a sense of profound calm at their apparently permanent closure, and their status of stranded obsolescence within Berlin's engulfing movements, as though that aura of aberration were, in itself, an ineradicable and essential element of the city.

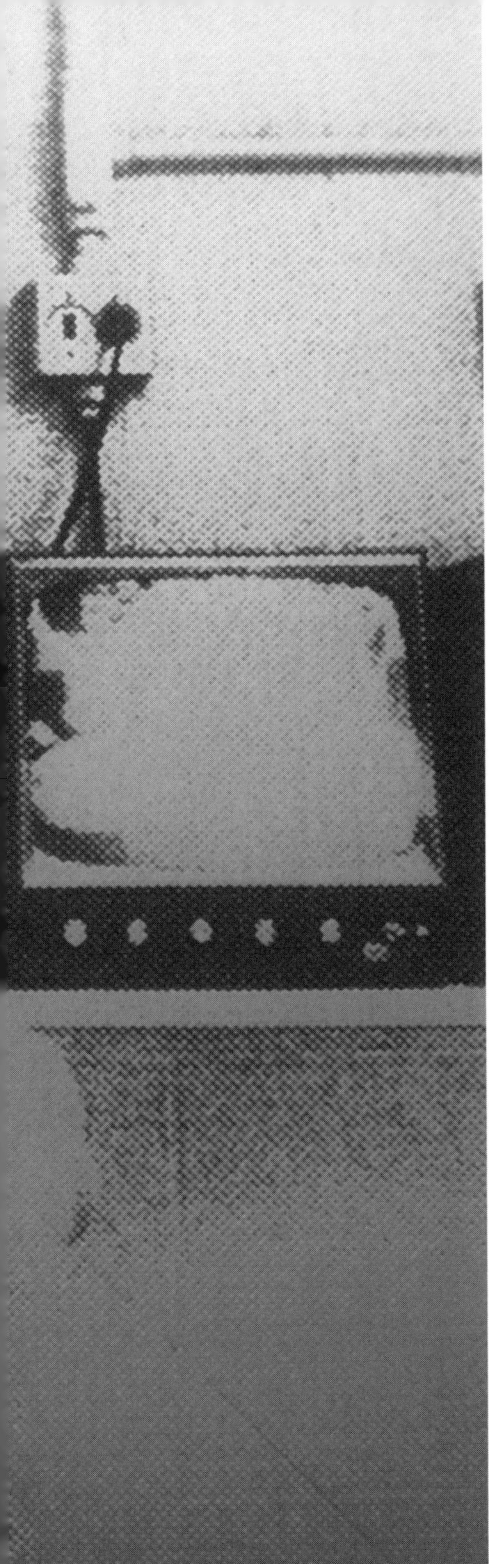

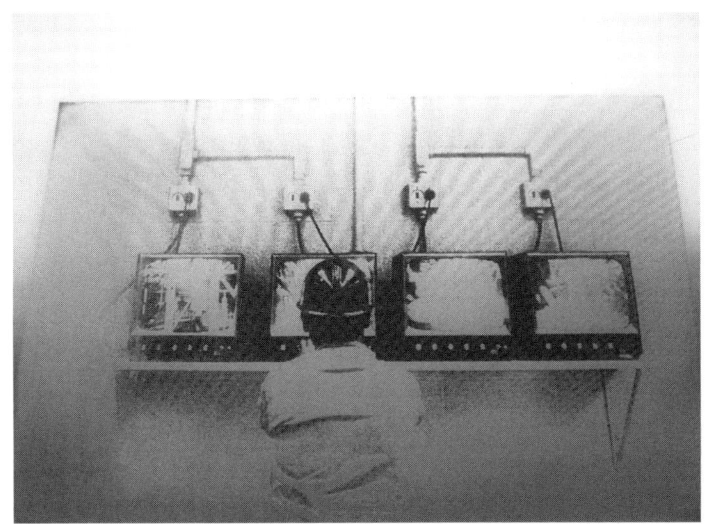

2

On the Karl-Marx-Forum plaza, constructed only three years before the disappearance of the GDR and East Berlin, a mysterious photographic image of a hardhatted man generating or controlling the visual contents of four identical screens, his back to the camera, had been affixed to a metal plinth devoted to the amassing of images of revolutionary violence and urban conflict. That image, adhered to the plinth by a transfer process – alongside many other images, of lipsticked South American revolutionary-women wearing hammer-and-sickle dresses and of Berlin in flames – remained fixed and exposed, while the city around it subsequently transmutated, the adjacent buildings demolished, overhauled or re-faced. The only damage endured by that metallic image, over the decades since its imprintation, and its fall into the archaic along with that of the GDR, were two thin lines of abrupt cancellation, inflicted with a sharpened implement, forming an 'x' exactly at the intersection between the hardhatted controller's head and one of his screens, as though an urban onlooker had been taunted beyond endurance by that image of the arbitrary launching and projection of urban vision, which had impacted directly into the space of the city with the same perverse, engulfing power as that of the Skladanowsky projector, and so had been compelled to negate it, inflicting a mark of erasure precisely at the sensitised juncture between the corporeal and the visual.

The entire terrain within which that urban surface of mysterious vision was located, extending from the Alexanderplatz across to the Schlossplatz on the far side of the river Spree channel, had been incessantly reconstructed and destroyed since the beginning of the 1930s, when Piel Jutzi's film *Berlin Alexanderplatz* (1931) was shot in the Alexanderplatz, its sequences showing the square's transformation into the great axis of eastern Berlin, with tramtracks poised over voids as gangs of workers excavated new subway lines or subterranean annexes for its department stores and arcades. The area of dense streets was then largely obliterated by wartime bombing. In films from the early GDR era, such as Slatan Dudow's *Frauenschicksale* (*The Destiny of Women*) (1952), journeys into the city always irresistibly converge on the Alexanderplatz, its buildings newly propelled into reconstruction, while the districts to the east remained scorched-earth wastelands. That frenzy of reconstruction demanded the summary subtraction of previously ineradicable urban elements, above all the vast Prussian castle, dynamited in 1950 in the Schlossplatz, whose name then changed to the Marx-Engels-Platz. In a painting by Ronald Paris from 1962, *Regenbogen über dem Marx-Engels-Platz* (*Rainbows over the Marx-Engels-Platz*), the area is caught in the turmoil of its early reconfiguration, which would continue until the mid-1980s, as though that immense, decades-long process were explicitly conceived with its own imminent annulling in mind. In

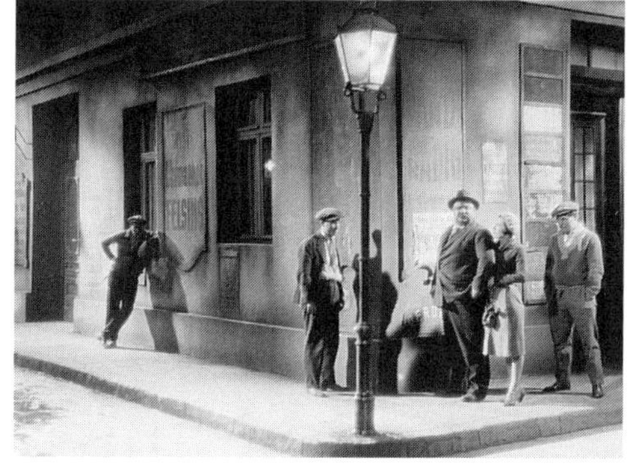

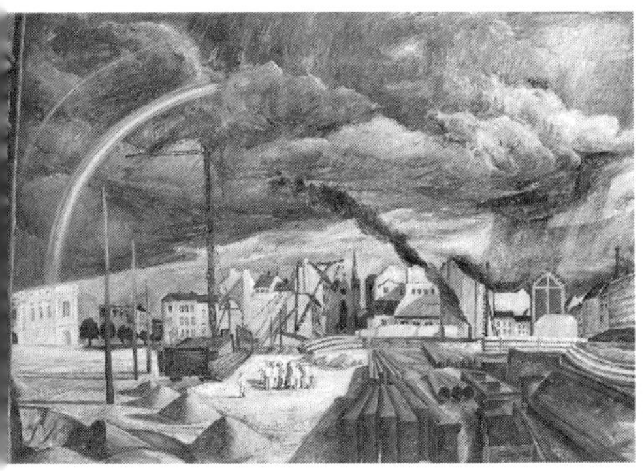

that painting, the all-consuming reconstruction of the Marx-Engels-Platz takes place as though a terrible natural disaster is ongoing, belied by the oblivious rainbow surmounting the city; groups of concentrated workers are surrounded by desultory traces of old ruined buildings as they amass the materials – pipes, frames, metal components – with which to materialise the new city. The most glaring materialisation of that reconstruction would be the 365-metre-high Television Tower, completed in 1969 and visible from almost every point in the city. Archival film-footage of the tower's fraught construction, extending throughout the second half of the 1960s, shows its stranded base poised for years like a great exposed nail embedded between the Alexanderplatz and the Karl-Marx-Forum, as though emulating the construction strategies of the Japanese architect Arata Isozaki, who worked under the ethos that 'the city of the future lies in ruins' and battered nails into maps of Tokyo to visualise his designs. Further archival footage, shot from the tower's pinnacle as it eventually neared completion, shows workers poised vertiginously against its surfaces as they riveted it together, with Berlin spinning below.

The image of the Marx-Engels-Forum's hardhatted vision-controller, working in his overalls to generate the dreams or hallucinations of Berlin, across four equally-sized screens, intimates the power of 'public' urban media, when they insurge from the city's surfaces, in order to infiltrate, activate or contaminate the spaces and eyes around them. The vision-controller is working intently on adjusting the dials below one of his four screens, which show an indistinct content of industrial machinery or technology, apparently on fire, and gradually imploding across the four screens, remaining intact on the screen to the man's left but disintegrating into flames on his far right. The content of that urban surface remains enigmatic – if this hardhatted man is the great visualiser of Berlin, controlling and fine-tuning its images, he appears to be determinedly propelling it into calamity, despite the low-grade technological means at his disposal, with the shoddy screens arranged on a wooden shelf, and the danger he himself faces, signalled by the hardhat he wears, of some lethal eruption from the screens above his head. As an insoluble image-surface that reveals Berlin's fractures and mutations, emanating outwards from its metal plinth into the Marx-Engels-Forum and into the eyes of its urban spectators, that mystery of the city projects its own obsessional vision.

All of the colossal urban ambition that relentlessly reconfigured the Marx-Engels-Forum and its adjacent terrain, across many decades, is tangible in the images from film and art that seize it, from the film-sequences of the Alexanderplatz's early-1930s overhaul to its postwar reconstruction from ashen zero, through to the officially-sanctioned paintings of the area's reconstruction, and finally to the film-footage of the ceremony at which the GDR's head of state, Erich Honecker, smilingly inaugurated the 1986 manifestation of that space – including its leaden statues of Marx and Engels, and the enigmatic silver plinths that held the image of the great urban visualiser with his four screens – as though acting in ecstatic anticipation of that vast ambition's sudden vanishing, into the parallel world of the reunified, post-1989 city. All of the furious determination to conceive, amend or upend urban space, in a multiplicity of variants, is momentarily legible in that redundant but prescient urban image-surface of the hardhatted, overalled man with his four screens. One screen will not suffice: such screens must virally proliferate, to expand and intensify their visions, and in the contemporary city of Berlin, those four ramshackle screens of the Marx-Engels-Forum plinth mutate into the infinite digital image-screens that now constellate the present city, with its corporate imperatives and new ambitions, as implosive as those generated by the hardhatted, revolutionary man.

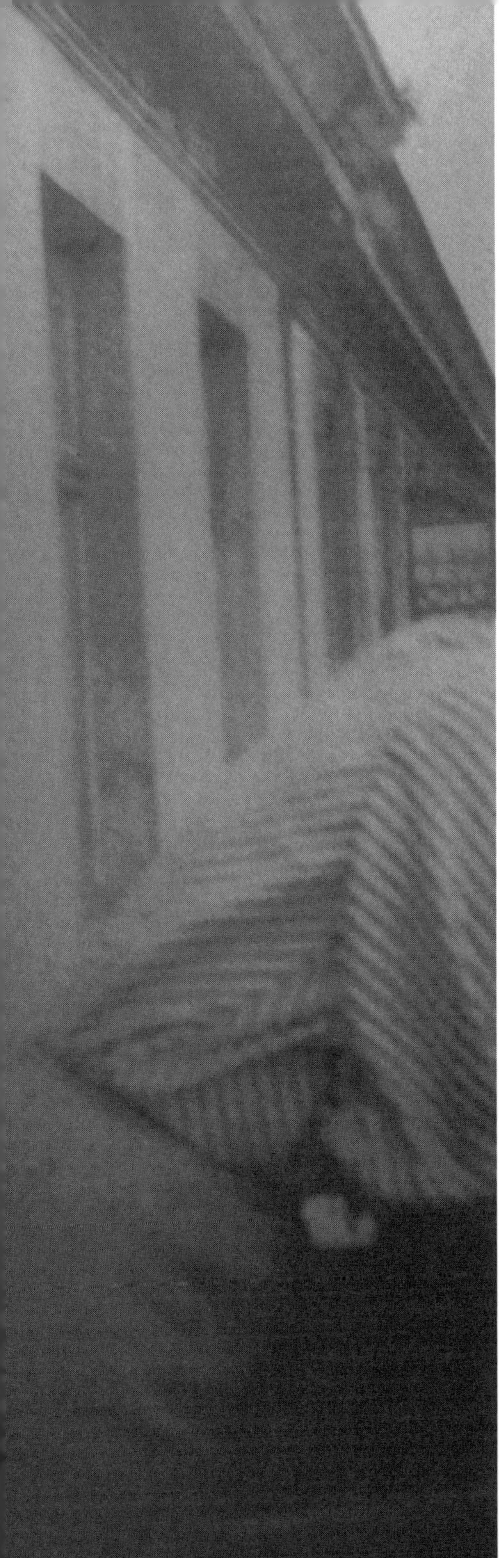

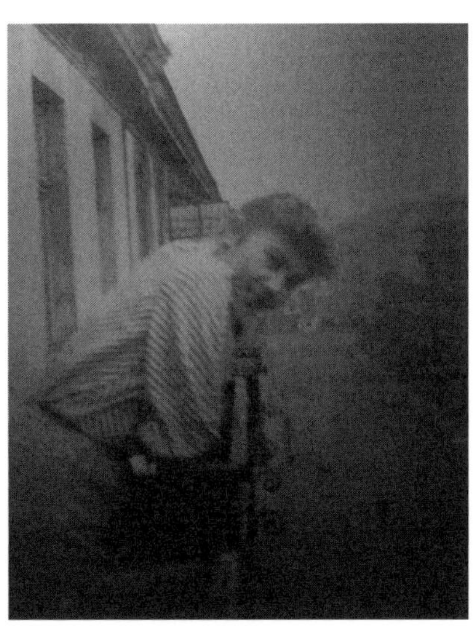

3

Alongside the public emanations of Berlin's awry urban visions – pre-eminently mediated by the mysterious, hardhatted image-generator to his four screens, and then projected outwards, into the space and eyes of the Marx-Engels-Forum, from the beguiling surface of its metal plinth – other visions leak more covertly and intimately from the city's revealing facades. In the rear-courtyard of a nineteenth century apartment building in the once-decrepit district of Prenzlauerberg, earmarked for wholesale erasure by the GDR authorities in the 1980s and reprieved from demolition only by the depth of its own neglect and by the erasure, instead, of the GDR itself, a photographic image had been affixed to a blank firewall by a transfer process apparently identical to that used to adhere the photograph of the great urban visualiser and his screens to the Marx-Engels-Forum plinth. The photograph, imprinted onto that wall as a fragile and secretive transmission of memory, showed a young woman in a skirt and blouse, standing on the concrete balcony of a top-storey apartment, leaning towards the street against a windowbox, and smiling at the camera. The street below – the Schliemannstrasse – appears strangely voided of almost all human traces: a lone elderly woman in a dark coat is walking down the middle of the street, while a black dog has traversed it and has almost reached the kerbside. One or two blurs half-indicate other figures that may be walking the far pavement, and a single car is parked on the far side of the road, as though a car were an aberration whose presence could only be exempted from the prevailing urban emptiness as an exceptional case. Above the apartment-building facades, on the far side of the street, the spire of a school complex is just barely gathered into visibility from the deteriorated pixels that form the sky above the street's vanishing-point. The only addition to the photograph, in its adhering to exterior urban space, was a date carefully scratched into the wall beside it: '1954'.

Within the mutating zones of urban surfaces, such intimate images, apparently destined for privacy, can irresistibly detach themselves from their intended neglect or oblivion, to resurge into the city as revelatory apparitions on its facades, through the compulsions or obsessions of memory. The body of the young woman, photographed directly against Berlin's exterior surfaces, leans out into the street as though to actively assert her presence against those voided facades, so that her face is positioned as the central axis of the image, simultaneously supplanting and vivifying the city; but once consigned to the photographic image, that act's jostling encounter between corporeality and the urban takes on inverse dimensions, in which the woman's body abruptly plummets into the infinite abyss of the urban image and into its unmarked time and space (the photograph consigned for decades to a drawer, or lost), from which only its projection back onto a sensitised urban surface releases it, forming a new exhalation that meshes the urban and the corporeal. Like the plinth-image of the overalled image-generator and his screens, the photograph of the smiling young woman is integrally enigmatic; her re-apparition, on the walls of Berlin, may be the result of the haunted memory of a family-member or friend, or else of a counterfeited memory of someone who has simply chanced upon the forgotten or abandoned photograph, and felt compelled to materialise that woman's presence, even intimately and covertly. The ocular act of viewing that photograph – now transferred entirely into an urban medium (of the original paper photograph itself, no remnant subsists), as a kind of corporeal wall-graffiti, made of human and street-surface traces rather than words or tags – is one of skinning that photographic membrane away from the wall which now holds it, in order to internally absorb that excoriated image, wrested from its place in the city.

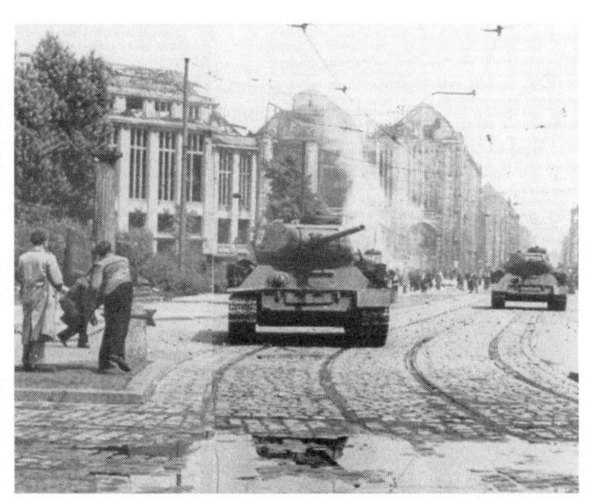

The year of the photograph, 1954, formed an open aperture in East Berlin allowing the inhabitation of its streets by an onrush of voided calm, which the image emanates, in its profound urban emptiness, located down on the street below the young woman's smiling face; that moment of calm was pinioned between far more tumultuous periods, from the recently past and violently suppressed workers' street-riots of 16-17 June 1953 that began on the Stalinallee (later to become the Karl-Marx-Allee) and spread into the heart of East Berlin, to the oncoming upheavals and new suppressions of the later 1950s, which would eventually lead to the neglected, fallen-apart courtyards of the Prenzlauerberg district becoming a centre for covert dissident activity against the GDR regime, and for experimental film and art works, shot on 8mm home-movie stock and painted on cardboard or other to-hand materials, shared clandestinely between small groups of activist-artists, and possessing an aura of intimacy like that of the young woman leaning out against the face of the city from her balcony. An essential illicit tension always exists somewhere within the act of surveying the urban, in the resolutely scarred terrain of Berlin, even when that viewing forms an intimate or private one, and a parallel, vital tension is deeply embedded into the volatile rapport between the corporeal, the visual and the urban.

In 1957, three years after the smiling young woman was photographed and in close proximity to that same site in the Prenzlauerberg district, Gerhard Klein shot a pivotal sequence of his feature film about disabused East Berlin teenagers, *Berlin Ecke Schönhauser* (*Berlin Schönhauser Corner*); the sequence was set under the elevated subway line at the street-junction directly above which, more than sixty years earlier, the Skladanowsky Brothers had filmed Berlin's urban surfaces for the first time, from their roof-top vantage-point. The opening shot of Klein's film is of the Skladanowsky Brothers' building, as though compulsively drawn to it, in order to initiate a seminal film of Berlin's streets. A gang of nihilistic, no-future East Berlin youths spend their time in an archway below the subway tracks, wondering whether to try to make their move over to West Berlin; obsessed with rock music but lacking any records or any medium to play them, they dance between themselves, enclosed in a zone of tenuous intimacy within the busy urban space surrounding them, as they conjure up the soundtrack to their dance by vocally improvising a score for it. For the brief duration of the dance, that implosive, self-directed intimacy remains intact, as a perverse enigma within the city. But finally, as though such private compulsions within urban space can never sustain themselves more than momentarily, that intimacy blows open, as one of the gang-members turns outwards, throwing stones which shatter a streetlight to shower passers-by in shards of glass; police-squads immediately arrive to break that gang apart.

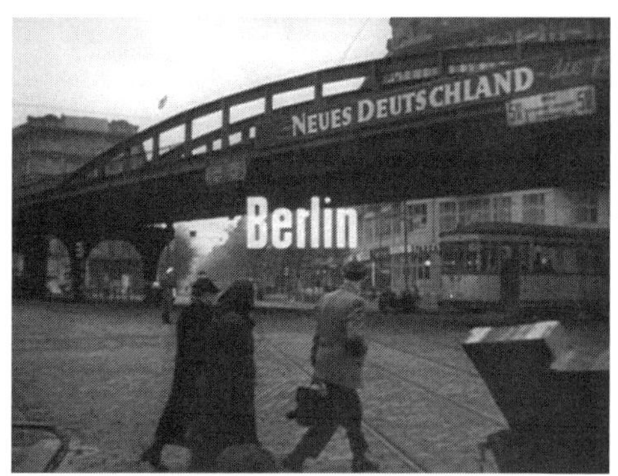

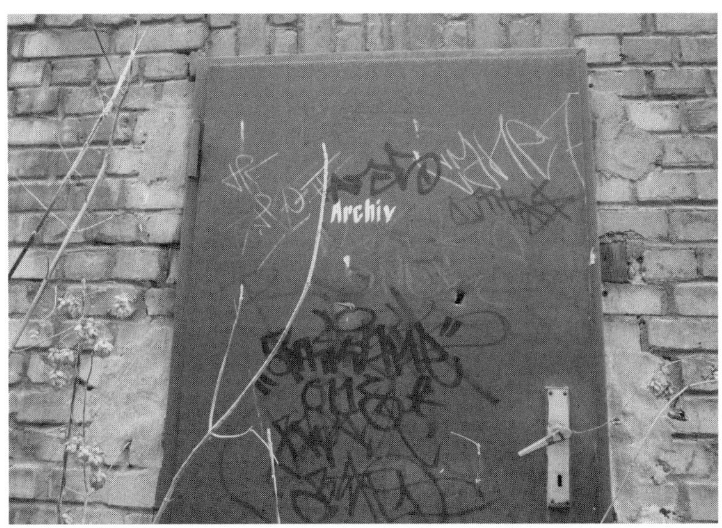

4

Berlin forms an infinite archive of memories, gestures and voices: an ashen, destroyed archive, hidden behind closed doors, or else glaringly evident, assembled on its urban surfaces, as a projected archive of meshed sensations, images and texts. On the edge of Berlin, among a miniature factory-city of long-abandoned buildings, whose purpose has leaked out and become opaque (the only, unreliable indicator is the presence nearby of a cigarette factory, also derelict, of which this assemblage of buildings could comprise an annex), the blue-painted door of a brick hut bears a stencilled inscription in white: 'Archive', poised within multiple graffiti inscriptions, including one written in black immediately above the door's original designation, as though the marker-penned graffiti tag had supplanted the building's formal role, and the name 'Archive' had become only the tenuous, superseded translation of that transformed, vitally illegible new status. A window next to the door is covered with wire mesh, though its glass is gone; apart from a few voided shelves and a terminal moraine of ground-down brick, ashes and debris, the dark interior of the archive has been comprehensively emptied-out, like the archive-buildings that stand beside the Khmer temple-cities, whose contents, documenting those grandiose cities' origins and glories, utterly vanished (looted, or deteriorated by moisture), leaving behind only the intact archive-shells. Even so, a determined but short-lived attempt has been made to enter and ransack that archive; mid-way between its handle and its name's inscription, the door bears the trace of an implement that has violently penetrated its surface, as the first stage of a revelatory peeling-open that has itself been definitively abandoned. Through that jagged aperture, a beam of light, like that of a cinema-projector, illuminates the archive's ashes and dust.

Whenever an archive materialises in Berlin, whether it forms an alien presence or one which attempts explicitly to embody particular histories or memories of the city, it becomes transfigured into an imminently erased and incendiary body, with its integral destructiveness escalating in intimate rapport with the grandiosity of its ambitions; archives in Berlin – whether documenting genocide, population movements, the secret police of the GDR or other, innumerable and uncountable agencies of urban suppression – appear always bound into a movement of compulsive expansion that renders them colossal architectural monoliths, subject to petrifaction and fissuration. In 1991, the artist Anselm Kiefer, who has never lived in Berlin, exhibited his immense archive of lead books, known both by the German title *Zweistromland* (*Land Between Two Rivers*) and the English title *The High Priestess*, together with its accompanying archive of lead film-reels, at the Neue Nationalgalerie in Berlin, close to the then still-derelict Potsdamerplatz. That momentary inhabitation of the city, by a vastly all-encompassing archive of text and image – an

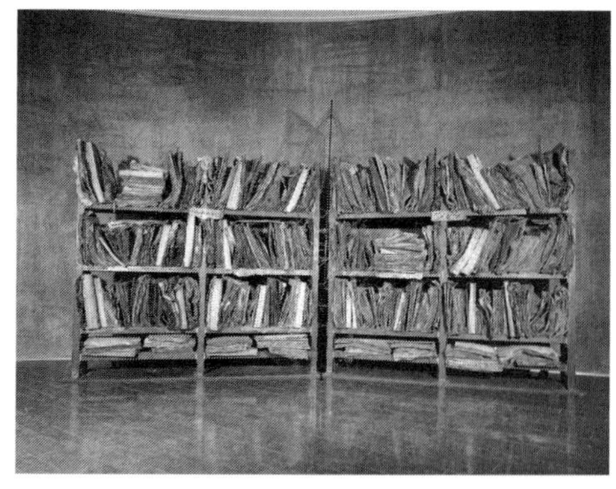

alien presence permeated with its own final unreadability, and unviewability, through its construction in lead – delineated the entire future status of all urban knowledge in Berlin: compulsive, excessive, and inflected by its incipient descent into ash. In many ways, the entire terrain of Berlin's urban surfaces may resemble one of Kiefer's immense paintings showing ruined landscapes of debris, ash and blackened earth, interspersed with vivid poppies and askew inscriptions of text (according to Kiefer, often-flawed citations from his memories of books, rather than exact transcriptions), and open to their viewer's gaze and perception.

Four years back in time, before Berlin's determining transmutation into Kiefer's *Zweistromland* (many of the city's most intensively amassed memories, as well as its museum-collections of the Tigris-Euphrates region, are enclosed in the scarred buildings of its own 'land between two rivers': the Museuminsel, located between the two channels of the Spree river), Wim Wenders had shot the library-sequences of his film *Der Himmel über Berlin* (*Wings of Desire*), in the Staatsbibliothek, directly across the Potsdamerstrasse from the Neue Nationalgalerie. In Wenders' film, the camera explores the library's surfaces and spatial dimensions while the multiplied internal voices of its inhabitants fill that space to excess, as they absorb and simultaneously articulate its components. That massed vocal sound causes intermittent pain to the angels, Damiel and Cassiel, who patrol and scan the archive – as much West Berlin secret police as angelic comforters – in order to locate interesting human 'cases', and are drawn to one or another of its occupants, largely oblivious to the actual content of the archive (which forms another variant of the all-engulfing 'knowledges' of Berlin) and engaged primarily with how those occupants internalise and project its elements; Damiel seizes a pencil from one of those occupants, as an instrument of that projection. The voices of the archive's inhabitants are also those that literally form an

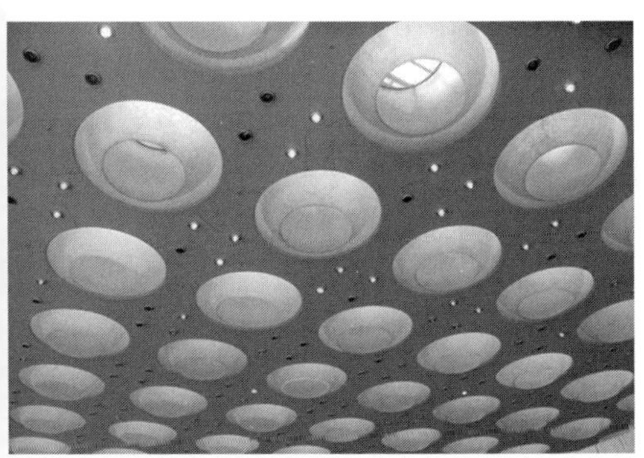

urban 'medium' to spectrally conjure the dead of Berlin, enumerating and recording and reciting what has already vanished, but still forms a focus of ineradicable obsession, that finds a way to manifest itself through the voice, as well as through languages, images and urban surfaces.

Museums and national libraries, along with other institutions where languages and images amass, constitute the powerfully dominant archives of the the city. However, an aberrantly minuscule archive, such as the abandoned, blue-doored hut marooned on the city's edge – a world away from Berlin's institutional and memorial archival-forms – remains in many ways identical to them, as though, instead of constituting an entirely surpassed and 'ended' building, it were actually an archive still in formulation, poised at its moment of origin. An archive cannot pass over fully into a condition of erasure until it has taken on the grandiose and excessive urban dimensions which those dominant manifestations of the city's knowledge hold, and which are intimated through works of art and through film, in whose images the urban archive is seized through the multiple compacting and accumulation of ocular and sensory perceptions. The resistant exterior surface of that neglected, blue-doored archive appeared indestructible, though its contents, glimpsed through the openings in that surface, had already been reduced to debris and ashes, and even its name, announced on the building's graffiti-strewn door, had been overtaken and itself consigned to dereliction.

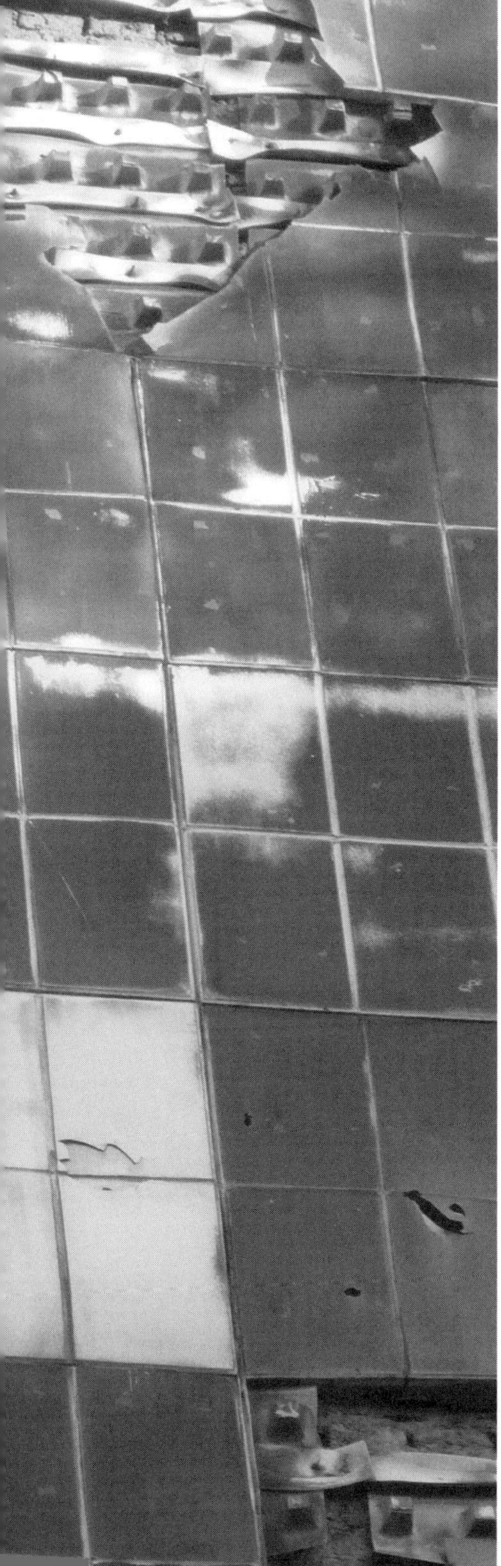

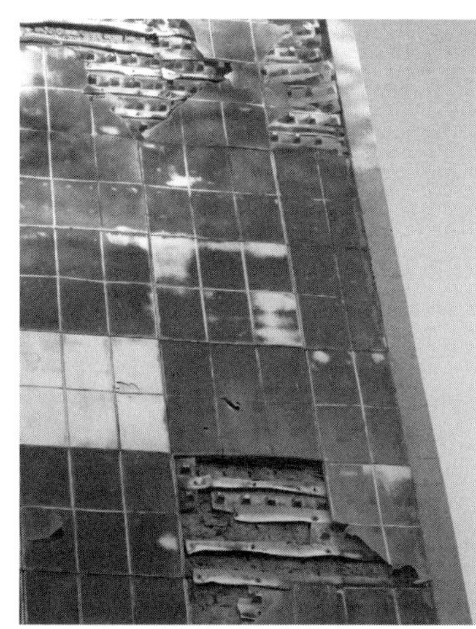

5

Urban facades in Berlin are often pitched at their last-ditch moment, secured to their profound or subterranean underpinning only by a tenuous adhesive of memory. At the eastern end, or origin, of the Karl-Marx-Allee – the vast and ornate arterial avenue constructed as the Stalinallee, conceived in 1949, and conjured out of the decimated wasteland that had been created four years earlier by the invading Soviet army's transit through it, supplemented by bombing and shelling – the rear facade of one of the apartment buildings had come unstuck. At some point in the terminal decades of the GDR, the original and indestructible stone cladding which formed the predominant surface of the Karl-Marx-Allee had been mysteriously replaced here by a celluloid casing, as though intended as a screen for outdoor film projections, in which the film's own celluloid had unaccountably been confounded with the surface on which it was to be projected, resulting in an ultimately awry, film-inflected urban surface.

That celluloid casing, as though protesting its mishap, had then warped, split apart, and peeled, entire chunks vanishing into the street below. In some sections, where the celluloid had gone, the concrete layers and rusted metal wall-brackets below could be seen, though the concrete had grown as friably eroded as the surface of a Kiefer painting, and the wall-brackets had themselves warped like the original celluloid, expelling their nails, as though jostling for position and visibility in the city, projecting themselves outwards, even if it meant tearing themselves away from the building's surface. In other places, a further internal layer of the facade had been unearthed, within jagged patches of exposure: perforated, plastic channels, running horizontally within the facade, installed for no other reason than to await the moment to burst through it. At the building's edge, those unsecured channels had no choice but to turn outwards, and point directly into the Karl-Marx-Allee's exterior space. That surface appeared anomalous within the remainder of the avenue's facades, which had been comprehensively renovated in the 2000s in a great homogenising endeavour, so that the uniquely unpeeled and revelatory celluloid casing on that building constituted the very last unreconstructed facade that had miraculously eluded a corporatised urban re-surfacing.

Equally, that botched and wounded surface of Berlin could have been created intentionally as the very first trace of a new manifestation of the avenue's existence: as embodying a seminal engulfing into decay, in which all of the avenue's buildings (and those of all of Berlin) violently unscreened their internal layers to expose and disclose their memories, obsessions and histories. The original construction of the avenue, as the Stalinallee, had been a significant event for the consolidation of the then still-formative GDR state, demonstrating that East Berlin was no longer a precarious, blackened terrain and could eventually possess the prestigious solidity and permanence of the avenues of Moscow. Many artists documented the building of the Stalinallee, which, at that time, arose out of a vast zone of flattened,

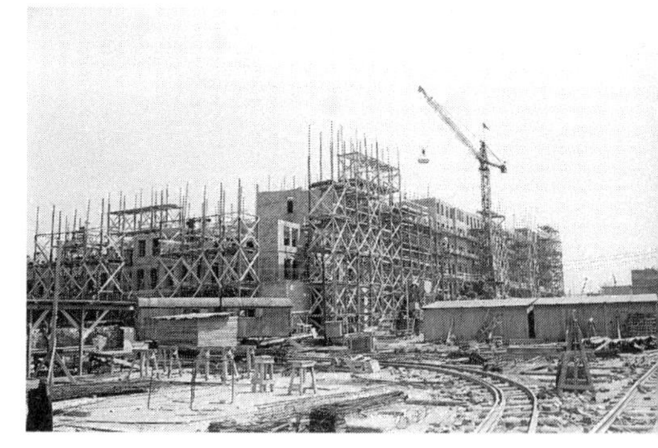

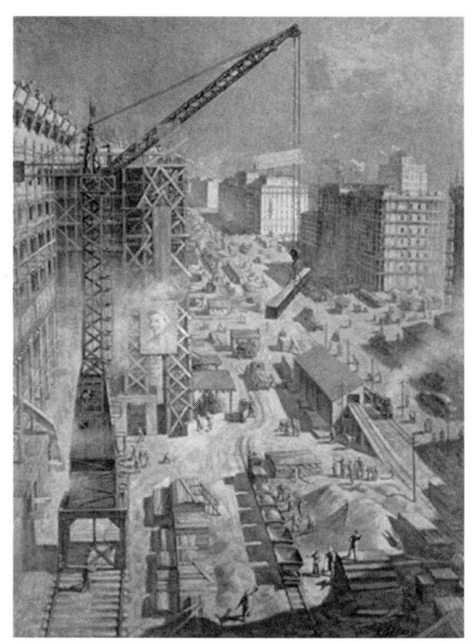

irreparable ruins which was only later filled by many hundreds of other, far lower-grade apartment blocks. Heinz Löffler's painting *Aufbau der Stalinallee* (*Construction of the Stalinallee*), from 1953, shows the massive construction complexity ongoing at ground level, with many cranes and networks of miniature railways needed to transport its elements into place; the painting's urban viewpoint is an omniscient one, poised high on the still-raw but palatial buildings, looking down at the intensive but ordered activity required to bring that avenue into existence. The corporeal dimension of that urban activity was highlighted in Otto Nagel's painting *Junger Maurer* (*Young Bricklayer*), in which the figure of a grinning Stalinallee super-quota worker-hero stands directly in front of the stone-faced edifices he has just completed; the painting was made during the year of the death of Stalin, to whom the avenue had already been dedicated and named (before being snatched away in 1961, with its renaming as the Karl-Marx-Allee, together with the statue of Stalin that occupied a key site on the avenue and was erased, along with those in other Soviet-Bloc cities, such as Prague, once it suited Stalin's successors in the USSR to reveal and revile the infinite scale of his death-dealing strategies).

Stalin had been a pre-eminent obsession for Berlin ever since the city's fall to the Soviet army in 1945, as though the city could not be restarted from zero without his presence; in the Soviet director Mikheil Chiaureli's 1949 film *The Fall of Berlin*, the fighting has barely finished and the Reichstag has only just been captured, on 30 April, when an aeroplane abruptly appears in the sky, skids to a halt nearby, and Stalin himself has already landed in the city, to universal acclaim, as though compulsively drawn to begin slicing Berlin apart and incorporating it through his own presence (Stalin's postwar manifestation in Berlin had actually taken place several months on, in July, for the Potsdam Conference, but when he later saw Chiaureli's film of his arrival, he exclaimed: 'I should have arrived like that!'). The avenue's entire process of construction resonated with that determining, hallucinated presence of Stalin; Kurt Maetzig's 1952 film *Roman einer Jungen Ehe* (*Story of a Young Marriage*) features a prominent sequence in which a celebration is held by the Stalinallee's constructers, sited between its still in-progress facades, to dedicate the avenue to the glory of Stalin; an actress performs a grandiose text, written by the GDR state-poet Kurt Barthel, that positions Stalin as the sole originator of Berlin's resuscitation from ashes. In that text, Stalin re-activates Berlin's hopeless urban inhabitants, infuses life into the voided city, and instils it with a new momentum: one vitally propelled by his own all-overruling compulsions with death and power, and which, almost as a negligent afterthought, materialises that palatial, scarred avenue as his own embodiment.

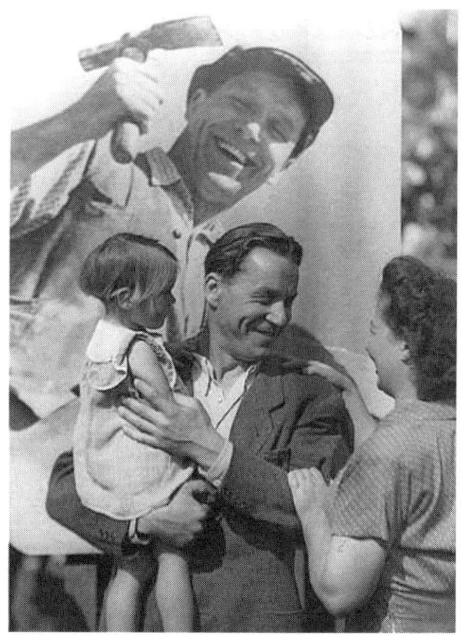

The torn ochre celluloid casing of the avenue's extremities emanates that memorial scarification and its temporal sites of focus, across the past and the future, among them the workers' street-riots that originated from the Stalinallee in June 1953, three months after Stalin's death, and flared through East Berlin before being lethally suppressed, as though (in addition to protesting working-conditions and the very existence of the GDR) they had transmitted an involuntary response, of negation, towards that aura of death and power, infused by its naming into the essential fabric of the avenue from which those riots emerged; in Nagel's painting of that same year, the young Stalinist super-quota bricklayer, seemingly proud of his achievements, must simultaneously be dreaming too about those riots, and the conflagration of his just-accomplished urban work. The ripped-open, celluloid-panelled facade of the Karl-Marx-Allee – in exposing a sliding, transmutating terrain of disintegration, within the multiple layers of its interior space – mediates a pivotal urban fascination and attraction for those unique instances in which buildings irresistibly open their apertures, to make their revelations, as urban and corporeal acts that envision the city, but also intimate the process of the future annulling of that vision.

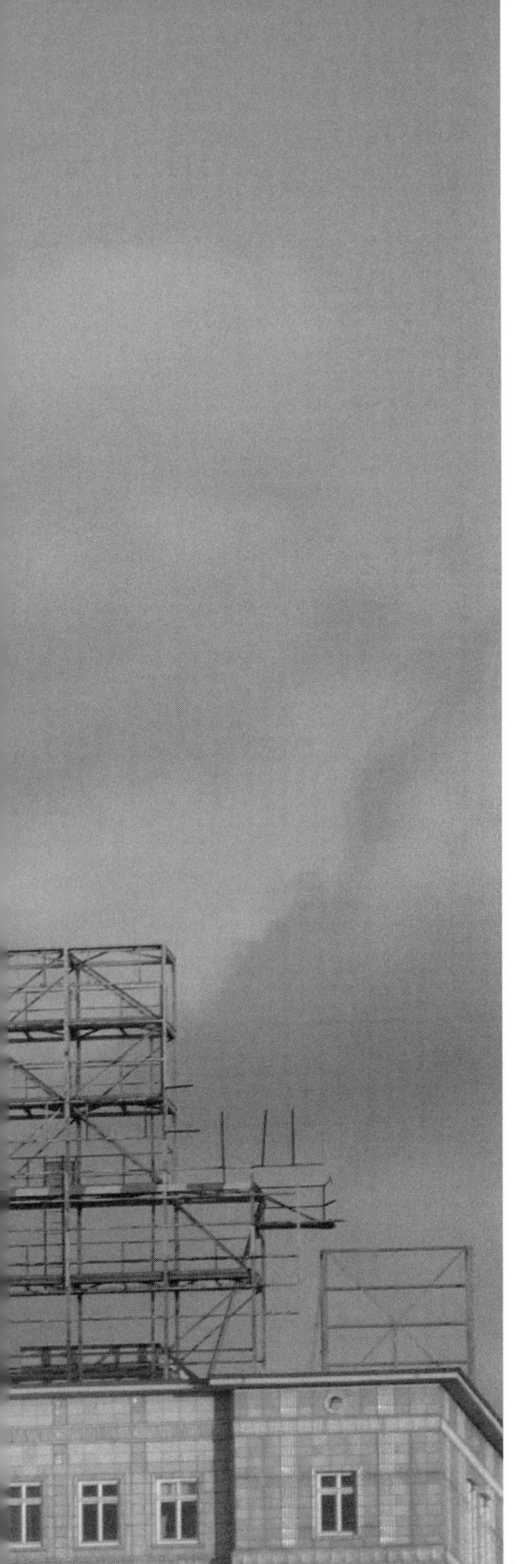

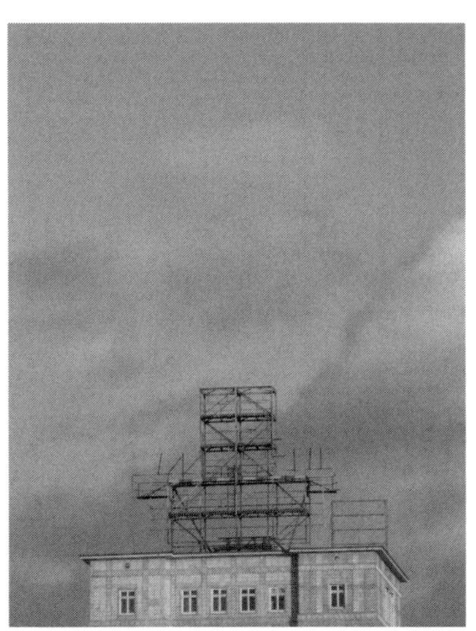

6

At the opposite end of the Karl-Marx-Allee, poised on the rooftop of one of the ornate apartment towers which circled the Strausbergerplatz, an assemblage of scaffolding had been constructed to display a vast hoarding or image-screen, with five levels of ascending metal struts, and several additional struts pointing vertically upwards from the second level, to which a ladder was attached, allowing for the installation of whatever content needed to be exclaimed from that pinnacle of the city. During the GDR era, the site had been used for the manifestation of images and texts of state power, or for the glorification of toxic chemical and plastics industries, such as those of the lethally-blighted towns of Bitterfeld and Zwickau; over the subsequent decades, after the GDR's vanishing, it had exclaimed corporate endorsements. But that hoarding-site, as a pre-eminent urban surface for the incessant transmission of essential images and texts into the city below, had now been utterly voided, the scaffolding rendered idle; it transmitted the vital transparency of terminal messages, against the sky of Berlin, into thin air. But that dereliction in itself held elements of irrepressible memory and forcible oblivion: alongside the main assemblage of scaffolding, a subsidiary construction, intended to support a secondary screen but now equally voided and transparent, had its space obliquely traversed by two narrow struts forming an 'x' of negation, identical to the two marks of erasure incised across the photograph of the hardhatted, image-generating man on the metal plinth by the Alexanderplatz. The Karl-Marx-Allee remained indelibly infused by its origin in Stalin's death-and-power presence, along with the street-riot furore and subsequent upheavals with their focal point in that avenue, so that the projection-zone constructed high above it, in levels of scaffolding, appeared as a uniquely sensitised site for the transmission of urban data, memories, maledictions or images. The capricious cancellation and voiding of that site's content imparted an inverse emphasis to the scaffolding which held it, as though that construction could now be inhabited by resonances, across time, of other seminal urban scaffolds, such as that used to publicly hang and display the upside-down corpse of Mussolini, in the Piazzale Loreto in Milan.

In order to legibly display and project the contents of their buildings' exterior surfaces into the surrounding spaces, for purposes of maintaining a consistent urban equilibrium, cities must allow an immediate identification of those contents, for the eyes of the inhabitants that glimpse and absorb them, in transit through those cities' avenues, so that such contents serve to collect and consolidate urban memories and simultaneously create a salutary focus for whatever preoccupations need to be emphasised for the contemporary moment. But in Berlin, that process of display and projection is

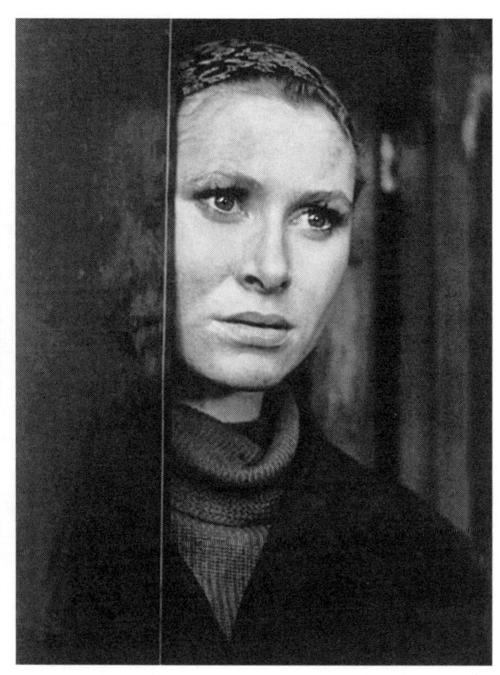

profoundly awry. Urban surfaces have undergone such an intensive experience of scarification and multiple inter-layering that only a corrosive ocular scanning of those surfaces will release and reveal their contents; irresoluble elements of the urban texture have become so tumultuously compacted together that every surface holds contrary, self-cancelling strata. And when a primary site for the legible consolidation of urban memory has been created, as with the hoarding above the Karl-Marx-Allee, poised high above the city's teeming surfaces as though intentionally to shake off their presence, it is an aberrantly emptied-out one, in which memory can only deliquesce in the gaps between the hoarding's metal struts, and all extremes of sensation are rendered equivalent as they escape, through the hoarding's transparency, into the sky beyond it.

End-to-end transits of the Karl-Marx-Allee reveal the extreme ambitions and fractures of its presence within the city, which the voided screen above the Strausbergerplatz intimates. Whereas paintings, such as those by Nagel and Löffler of the avenue's process of construction, pinpoint instants at which time has become stilled, film has the capacity to dynamically sweep through that avenue. In the final sequence of Dudow's 1952 film *Frauenschicksale*, a foundry worker and a woman just released from prison transit the Karl-Marx-Allee (still the Stalinallee at that moment); they enter the avenue in a truck, moving from their point of origin at the prison, on the city's eastern edge, to traverse areas of blackened ruins as they approach the avenue, on their way towards the Alexanderplatz, where a vast festival-event is taking place, vacuuming East Berlin's population towards it. Their transit of the avenue, east to west, forms an interval of exhilaration for the vehicle's mesmerised occupants: the avenue's gleaming, untainted surfaces and joyful inhabitants emanate an aura of urban resuscitation, together with that of acute architectural aspiration mediated by the facades of the grandiose buildings along its course, such as that of the gigantic Deutsche Sporthalle (eventually demolished, to leave a gap in the avenue, like that created by the removal of Stalin's statue, since its over-rapid construction had been shoddily executed), and the vehicle's occupants become increasingly ecstatic as they accomplish their transit between the avenue's compelling surfaces.

Alongside the ripped celluloid building and the voided rooftop hoarding which form the two extreme points of an end-to-end contemporary transit through the Karl-Marx-Allee, its two cinemas, both constructed in the early 1960s, the Kino Kosmos and the Kino International, are also pitched at its opposite parameters, as though constituting two omniscient eyes for that avenue ('kino-eyes', like those which the Soviet filmmaker Dziga Vertov dreamed of, to blow-open cities through enhanced forms of vision), thereby forming its uniquely revealing media. At the avenue's eastern end, the ocular status of the Kosmos as a cinema is erased through the building's downgrading into that of a moribund venue for corporate events such as jewellery fairs, while at the western end, the Kino International, its architectural form pitched-forward into the avenue as though to assail the eyes of passers-by, maintains its cinematic status intact, by a hairsbreadth. Those two cinemas operate like the dual lens of the Skladanowsky 'Bioskop' projector, in which one aperture of vision must close in order for the other to open. Even at urban sites from whose surfaces it appears that nothing further can be transmitted or displayed – such as the Kino Kosmos's darkened screen, or the voided hoarding poised transparently above the Karl-Marx-Allee – the contrary projections of Berlin remain relentlessly at work.

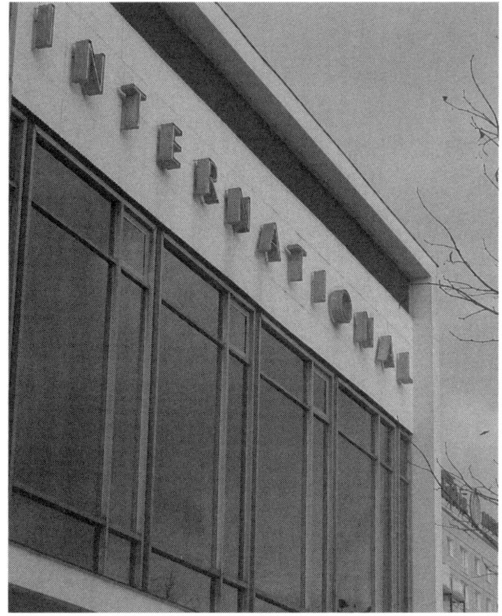

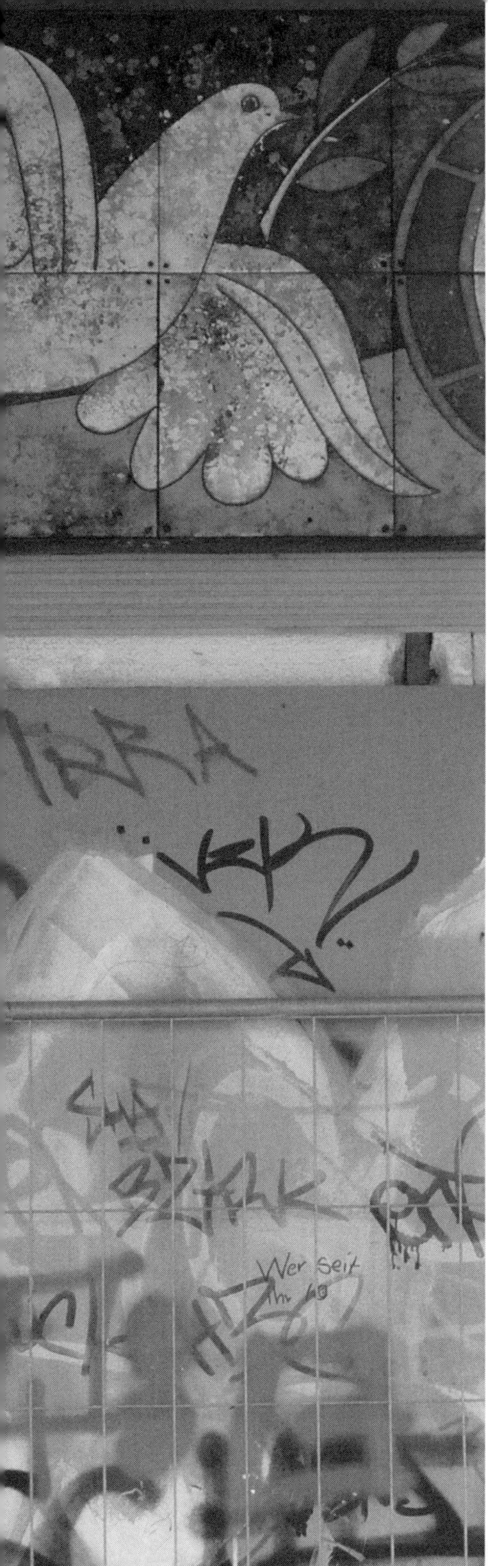

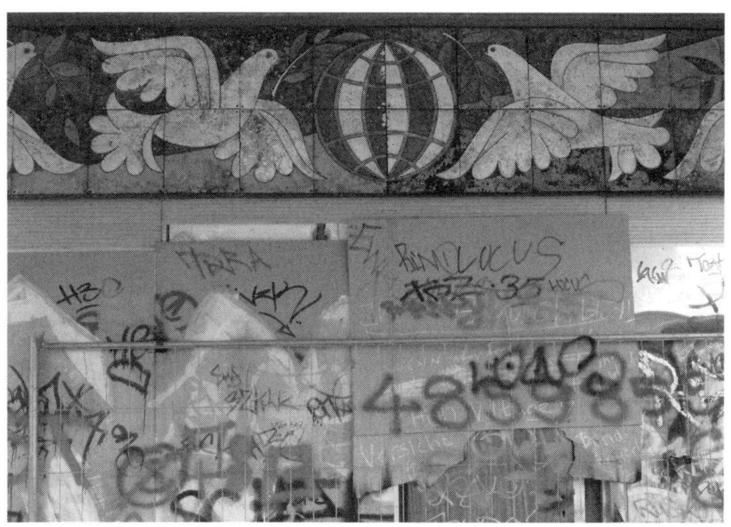

7

Beyond the grounds of the eighteenth-century Schönhausen palace, where state guests of the GDR regime such as Gorbachev and Castro once stayed in luxurious surroundings, a shoddy pre-fabricated hotel had been constructed for the overspill of those guests' entourages, prior to being abandoned at the abrupt cessation of the GDR, and falling into dereliction, its hazardous interior spaces infiltrated by drug-addicts and punks before being halfheartedly boarded-up, and its exterior surfaces gradually amassing a vast lineage of graffiti inscriptions, on its broken-glass window facades and fissured grey concrete cladding. The hotel's political elites had entered its grounds through a terrain of flagpoles, now rusted and stripped of their flags, before reaching the building's entrance foyer. Although few visitors now approached that foyer, sealed-shut with plywood and cardboard panels, in its redundancy, those panels displayed an infinite accumulation of fluorescent graffiti images, numbers and texts, as though an obsessive compulsion to excessively inscribe that surface had operated in directly inverse proportion to the scarcity of eyes left to scan it. Above that chaotic surface, the still-vivid tiled mosaic of the hotel's original entrance depicted a succession of doves bringing olive-branches to a blue-and-white striped globe. In defiance of the global peace intimated by that mosaic, many of the graffiti inscriptions seethed with sexual conflicts and exclamations. Although that facade appeared lost in voided time and exiled from all sensorial urgency, spraycanned letters in red and yellow announced: 'Girls for 10 euros for half an hour!', along with the telephone number for any interested passer-by to call to arrange an assignation, with the figure of '10 euros' subsequently devalued by marker-pen amendments to '1 euro' (the zero painstakingly barred-out), as though the accomplishment of the proposed sexual act had now become such a vitally pressing matter that its entire financial rationale could be undercut and debased, as long as that peripheral urban surface could still somehow possess the power to generate its sexual manifestations.

Alongside their strata of memory, loss and oblivion, Berlin's urban surfaces form corporeal screens for intricate sexual data, whose inscription, as with that of the derelict state-hotel's entranceway, simultaneously carries its own devaluation and cancellation, as the immediacy of that sexual exclamation melts away. If the inscription cannot instantly generate an act able to collide the corporeal and the urban, in a sensorial fusing which propels the city into new constellations, that exclamation instantly transforms into one of increasing desperation and isolation, so that the surfaces of Berlin constitute residual archives of misfired, misaligned penetrations, and of sexual acts gone awry. In Frank Ripploh's seminal film of West Berlin's urgent sexual desires, *Taxi zum Klo* (*Taxi to the Public Toilet*) (1981), urban surfaces – pre-eminently those separating public-toilet

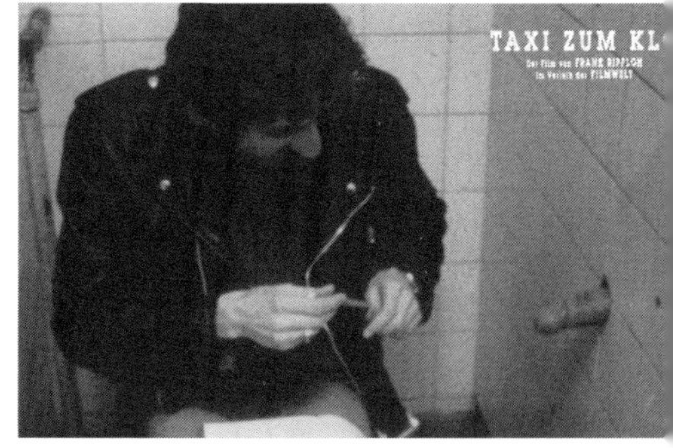

cubicles – carry that desperation to avert lost sexual acts, and can be miraculously holed and literally traversed by a sexual organ, in the form of a penis ready to be consumed by the occupant of the adjacent cubicle. As in the filmic images and novels of Jean Genet, walls mutate into orifices of sexual compulsion through their permeability, forming apertures for the transmission of corporeal traces as well as of vision. However, the open arena of the West Berlin public toilet constitutes a precarious one, that can be infiltrated by violent insurgency as well as sexual desire; in Uli Edel's *Christiane F.: Wir Kinder vom Bahnhof Zoo* (*Christiane F.: We Children of Zoo Station*), from the same year as Ripploh's film, the young drug-addict Christiane has her heroin stash forcibly confiscated, in mid-shot, by another addict who ocularly scans what she possesses, via the holes forged into the cubicles' partition to facilitate sexual contacts, then immediately clambers over that fragile barrier to grab the coveted heroin for himself.

In Ripploh's *Taxi zum Klo*, the entirety of West Berlin forms a set of potential sexual facades, overseen from the interior of cars as Ripploh's autobiographical character relentlessly transits the city in search of encounters, looking out into the neon-illuminated, always-rainsodden night of traffic bottlenecks and garish corporate towers. When he becomes too ill to drive himself around the city, Ripploh hires a taxi to traverse Berlin, from one irresistible sexual axis to another, pre-eminently that of the public toilet behind the Siegessäule war-victory monument, from whose towering summit Wenders' angels also compulsively oversee the city, in *Der Himmel über Berlin*; the urgency of those encounters overrules habitual urban time and space – Ripploh obliviously keeps his taxi-drivers waiting for the duration of his sexual encounters, and the public toilet which initially appears a neglected or marginal site (like the graffiti-strewn entrance of the Schönhausen palace's hotel) mutates into a site of glory that overturns and negates that of the gold-encrusted war-monument beside it. The presence of

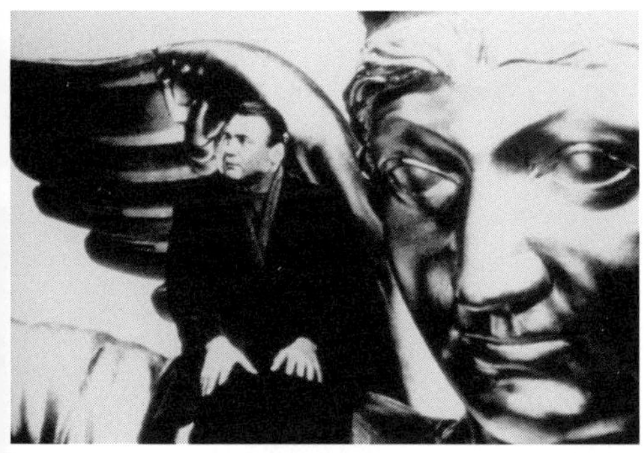

sex is embedded into the city through those transiting movements and urban reinventions, by the conjuring and piercing of apertures and fissures within its surfaces, and via the aberrant imprintation of languages and images over those surfaces.

In the years around the beginning of the First World War, Ernst Ludwig Kirchner painted crowds traversing and amassing within the great squares of Berlin, such as the Potsdamerplatz and the Nollendorfplatz, transmitting their manic sexual energy to those urban spaces; during the same period, he also depicted multiple variants of sexual acts taking place within the city's interiors, as though the enumeration of those acts and their ostensible pathologies – in works with titles such as *Der Sadist* and *Der Masochist* (both 1915) – formed an indissoluble accompaniment to the exterior images of a city gradually unravelling into the convulsions of warfare. Often, Kirchner's sexual acts are illuminated only in shadowy, semi-hidden glimpses, like Berlin's exterior night cityscapes filmed from the interior of Ripploh's car in movement. In Kirchner's paintings and lithographs, Berlin becomes concentrated-down to form a volatile medium that constantly oscillates between its exterior sexual urgencies, and the internal manifestations of those tensions, in the forms of sexual acts or violent beatings, which can only expand and proliferate, rather than resolve themselves. The entrance foyer to the abandoned state-hotel beside the Schönhausen palace, as a perversely peripheral site for the location and concentration of Berlin's sexual obsessions, carries that same desire to endlessly expand its own inscriptions, even when the sexual acts which they enumerate appear debased and effaced.

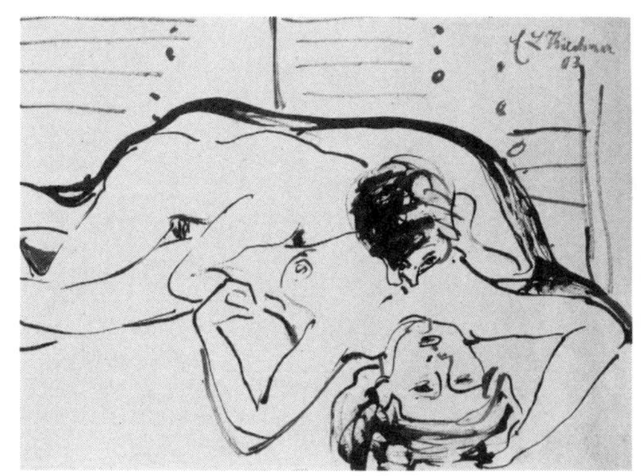

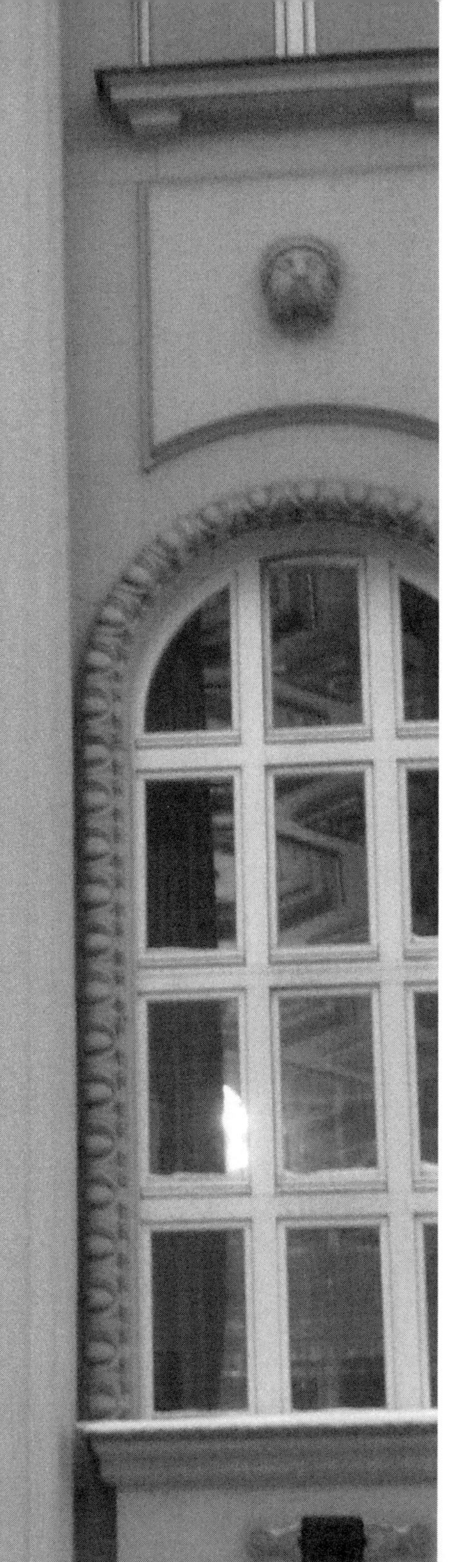

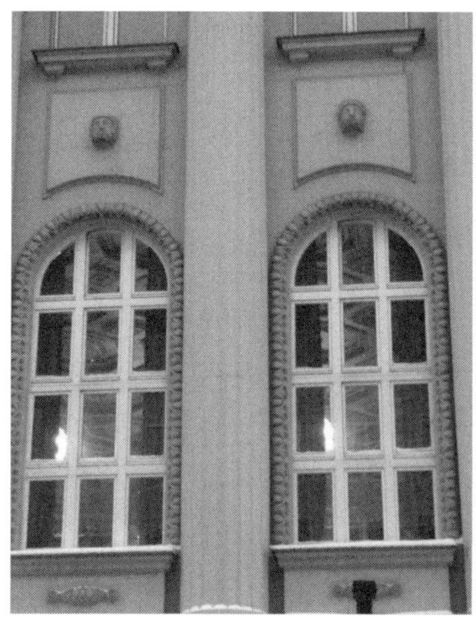

8

The facade of the Hansa recording studio, close to the Potsdamerplatz, forms a colonnaded and luxuriously adorned surface, like that of the Schönhausen palace. Above long, arched windows, disembodied heads of gods look out into the city, and below the roof level, that surface bears one lavish inscription: 'Meistersaal', intimating both the origins of the space inside, constructed as a ballroom in 1910 for ceremonies to accord apprentices the status of master-builders, and also the insurgent power emanating from that chandeliered, high-ceilinged room, as the legendary site of Berlin's sonic eruptions. The multiple golden illumination of the chandeliers inside the room revealed its extravagant wooden ceiling, as intricately carved and corniced as those of the lounges of Hearst's San Simeon castle on the Californian coast; the Meistersaal's facade served as the medium for the expulsion of that sonically charged, burnished interior into the surrounding urban space. At its construction, the Meistersaal was never intended for use as a recording studio, its dimensions profoundly mismatched from those of most purpose-built studios; as a result, the disused Meistersaal's 1960s reinvention as a recording studio constituted an act of obstinate conjuration, like that which had impelled the Skladanowsky Brothers to envision and operate their seminal film projector. The uniquely raw and dense sound of that room, pre-eminently imbued with the fractured urban presence of Berlin through the recordings by David Bowie and Iggy Pop from their 1970s stay in the city, such as *Heroes* and *Lust for Life*, carried a miraculous capacity to materialise the unheard and the unforeseen.

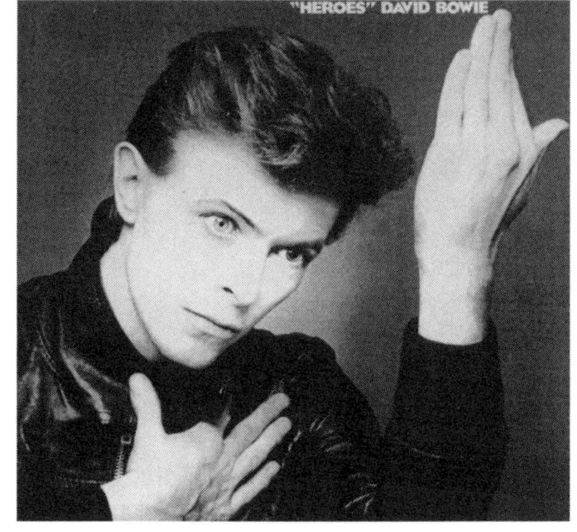

Although originally constructed to resemble an eighteenth-century palatial facade, and thereby accord enhanced prestige to the ceremonies taking place within it, the Meistersaal's exterior formed a fraudulent concoction of architectural elements, retrospectively vaunting its hairsbreadth survival. The pristine contemporary surface of the building, and its location at the edge of the built-up corporate zone around the Potsdamerplatz, appeared to secure it firmly within the urban terrain of Berlin, but that building had veered erratically across space and memory in its century or more of existence, its facade battered and excoriated during the bombing and invasion of Berlin, and then precariously poised alongside the Potsdamerplatz's scorched-earth variant for the decades of Berlin's division. When Bowie improvised the words to his song *Heroes*, in the cocaine-equipped mixing-room and relaxation-lounge adjacent to the Meistersaal, his view through the window faced a manifestation of Berlin as a ripped-apart landscape, in which any trace of a sensorial gesture, such as a kiss, needed to be magnified to obliterating dimensions. After the erasure of the GDR, that landscape around the Hansa studio transformed rapidly, vertically as well as horizontally, with many of its aberrantly surviving elements wiped-out, and the studio's facade,

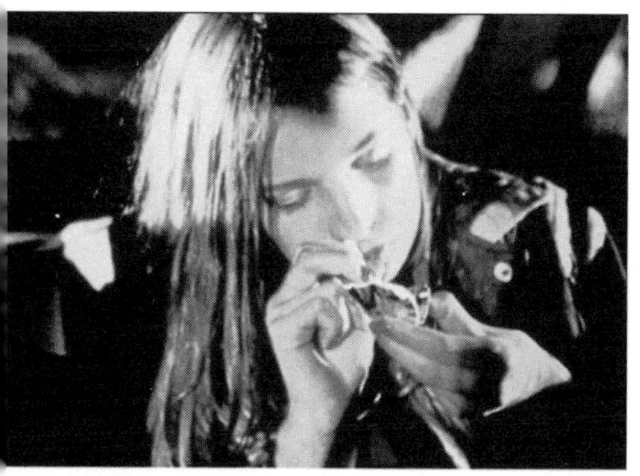

which had appeared marooned beside the voided Potsdamerplatz, was then abruptly engulfed by new constructions, so that the window through which Bowie had gazed opened blankly onto the firewalls and balconies of adjoining apartment complexes. At the same time as Berlin's exterior space seismically manoeuvred around the building, the interior of the Hansa studio itself remained petrified, all renovations directed primarily to returning the Meistersaal to its 1910 moment of conception, in order not to disrupt the fragile mystery of that space's capacity to generate the vital sonic traces of Berlin.

In *Christiane F.: Wir Kinder vom Bahnhof Zoo*, it is Bowie's *Heroes* which initially propels Christiane into her rapturous explorations through the unknown space of Berlin, prior to her drug-misadventures and her incarceration in the public toilet whose cubicle partitions form dangerously porous barriers. Having seen a poster for the 'Sound' nightclub on a wall near her suburban apartment-tower home, with a vivid red mouth emerging outwards from that poster's surface, Christiane determines she will travel to it; it will be a nightclub which solely plays music by David Bowie, and nothing else, like a cinema in which the projection of a single, all-consuming film would suffice. Christiane's journey to the nightclub is undertaken via the elevated subway line through the Kreuzberg district; although the Berlin night cityscape viewed from her train-carriage window is the identical glacial apparition of business towers and rainsoaked avenues which Ripploh surveys in *Taxi zum Klo*, its exhilarated sound-accompaniment is now Bowie's *V-2 Schneider*, recorded in the Hansa studio (in intimate proximity to the overhead subway line's course), as part of *Heroes*, and conducting Christiane towards the nightclub; the train stops at the Möckernbrücke station as the song starts to erupt, and Berlin is filmed from the driver's position at the very end of the platform, with the city ahead appearing as an abyss, both enveloping and irresistible. Just as sex is sieved into the surfaces of Berlin at peripheral sites such as the abandoned palace-hotel and through works such as those of Ripploh and Kirchner, to form a saturated and tangible entity which the city compulsively projects, so sensitised urban eruptions of sound also become embedded within – and are expelled from – Berlin's surfaces, in locations such as the Hansa studio and through the city's film and art images.

Kirchner's painting *Potsdamerplatz* (1914), undertaken shortly before his series of lithographs that enumerate Berlin's range of sexual pathologies, depicts the teeming square at the moment when it effortlessly sucked-in all of the city's sound and noise, as well as its sexual displays and obsessions, and its distinctive movements and prostitutional gestures; every resonance of the city is vertiginously drawn into that space, in a parallel way to that in which the nearby Hansa studio, with its awry architecture, would come to attract and intensify the determining sonic content of Berlin. Kirchner's manifestation of the Potsdamerplatz coincided with the first years of the Meistersaal's existence, and while the urban surfaces of his variant of the Potsdamerplatz would undergo repeated transformations – vanishing without trace in the 1940s, before being reconfigured as a new and near-irreconcilable set of facades and human gestures in the 2000s – the facade of the Meistersaal tolerated its isolations, its immersals in wartime ashes and its bullet-holes, in anticipation of the moment when its windows would release pulses of ecstasy into the city.

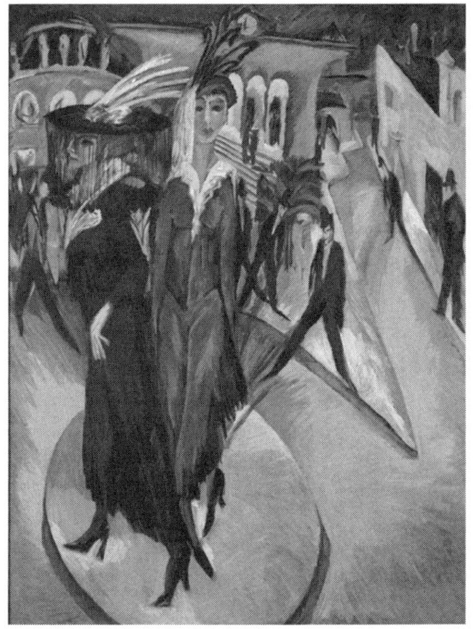

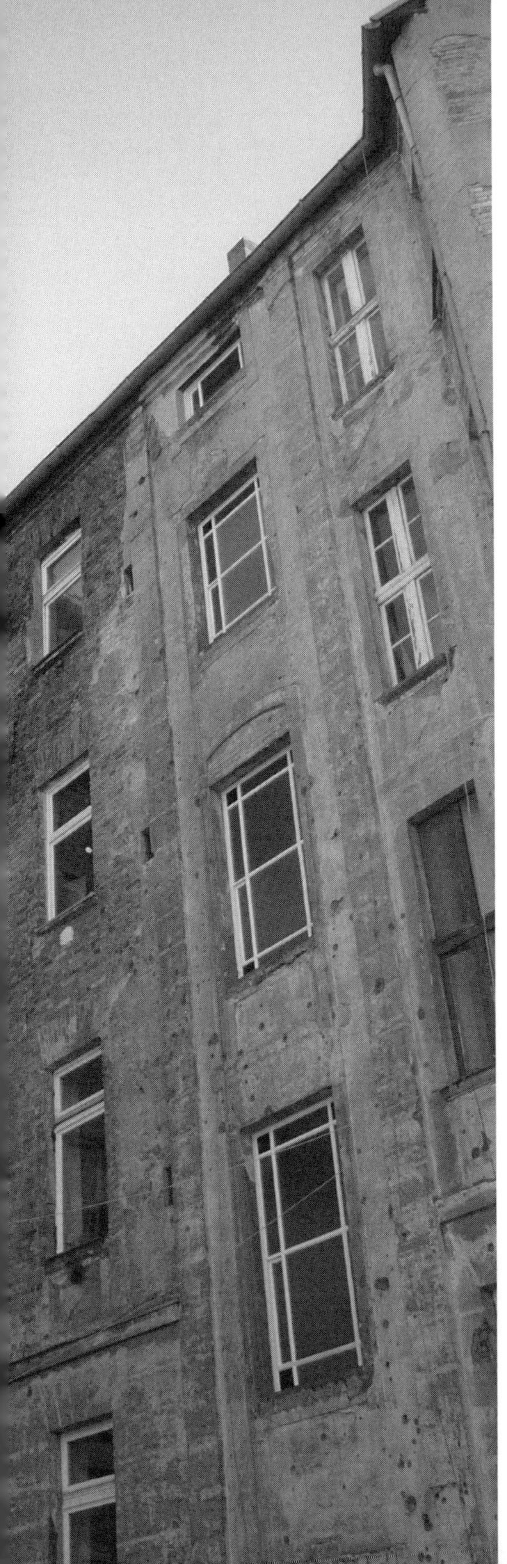

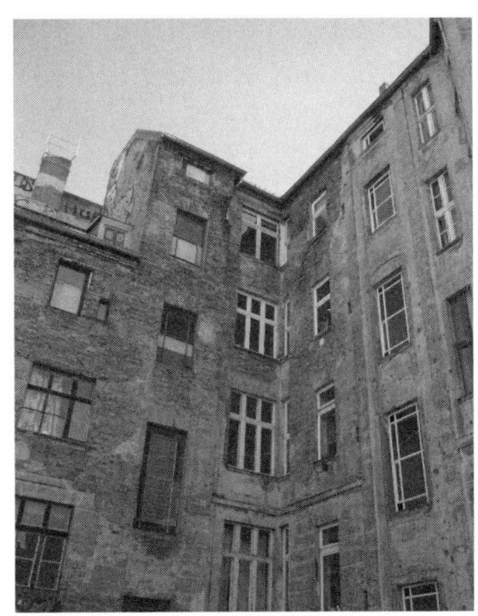

9

In the rear-courtyard of a dilapidated 1890s tenement building, reached through a broken entry-door and a succession of passageways, the final facade formed a terminal screen of oblivion, extending upwards towards the sky. Most of the original plaster had fallen from the walls many decades ago, revealing the ochre brickwork, infused with profoundly accumulated dirt; where the plaster remained, it bore the scars of bullet-tracery around the windows, from the all-out battles of the Soviet army's assault on the city, alongside an intricate language of other indentations, wounds and markings, of indeterminate provenance. At roof-level, a few cursory bursts of already-faded graffiti only intensified the courtyard's aura of silent disintegration. That rear-courtyard was the receptacle of Berlin's most forgotten inhabitants – the neglected, the displaced or exiled, the addicts – who almost never emerged into daylight, consigned to that space located beyond the city, even at the heart of the city. The sudden rise and expansion of Berlin in the final decades of the nineteenth century had generated innumerable tenements in that architectural form, with two or even three back courtyards, to cram-together its factory and menial workers; many of the tenements' exterior street-facades possessed spectacular ornamentation (angels, mythic creatures) and coloration, in defiance of the impoverished human content assigned to them, but once the initial courtyards had been traversed, each becoming smaller and more constricted than the last, and the back-end of the building was reached, such ornamentation had been comprehensively exhausted. The rear-courtyard was invariably light-less, full of garbage cans and a debris of broken implements from the workshops that often formed improvised annexes to those buildings, which constituted Berlin's last-ditch, extreme zones, where all memory and time had lapsed.

That rear-courtyard tenement facade intimated a spatial arrangement which upended all habitual projections and emanations of the city; ocular perspectives requiring distance and focus were abruptly negated in that constricted space. Its narrow dimensions formed the exact inverse of the wide-open rooftop panoramas which had fascinated early photographers and filmmakers of Berlin, such as the Skladanowsky Brothers. That facade appeared on the point of falling out of its alignment, as though no longer forming part of the city, but instead belonging to the subterranea beneath it. The sky above that courtyard seemed so distant that the facade constituted its own precipice, for that fall into the infinite sub-city below its surface layer. In East Berlin, entire swathes of such tenements were demolished in the postwar decades to clear space for the construction, in their place, of immense prefabricated apartment-towers, and the urban fabric of inner-city districts such as Prenzlauerberg decomposed in anticipation of an envisaged mass-flattening that never arrived. When artists of the

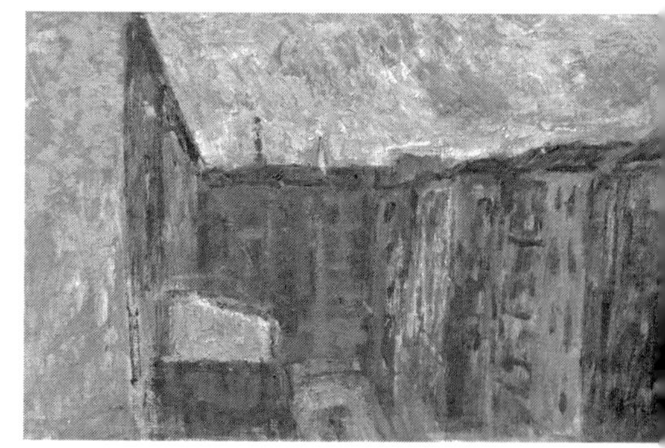

GDR, such as Manfred Böttcher, painted those tenements' rear-courtyards in the 1980s, as in *Berliner Hinterhof* (*Berlin Rear-Courtyard*), the image became one of an unfocused amalgam of cancelled and blurred surfaces, under a deadened sky: an impossible space, so closed-down that it appeared to resist its own perception and its own imagining.

In Werner Herzog's 1977 film *Stroszeck*, the fragile street-musician Bruno S. determinedly enters the spaces of West Berlin's rear-courtyards, to inhabit those peripheral urban end-zones: silenced spaces which initially appear closed-off to the eye and ear, and to any process of being envisioned or heard, but which he is able to transform through his presence within them. In one sequence of the film, Bruno pulls the ramshackle cart containing his instruments along a snow-strewn street and unhesitatingly turns into an apartment-building's entrance; having reached the damp-stained backwall of the farthest courtyard, he announces his performance, and begins to sing and to play his accordion and glockenspiel in that narrow space, commenting on his own performance as it progresses, against a line of black garbage cans and a long-abandoned water-fountain, watched by two children from a doorway; Herzog's camera pans from ground-level around the windows of the courtyard, from which a scattering of isolated figures gaze down at the spectacle, as one which could only take place within that space (Bruno's marginal performance is ineligible in the exposed, 'public' areas of the city) and which has broken-open that space, through an extraordinary vocal and sonic outburst. In the final shot of the sequence, Bruno exits the door of the rear-courtyard, to return to the street outside; once he has departed, the shot remains focused on the figure of a solitary small child with his back to the courtyard, his hat pulled over his entire head, his eyes pressed into the door, as though the insurgent excess of Bruno's performance and momentary inhabitation of that space has rendered it

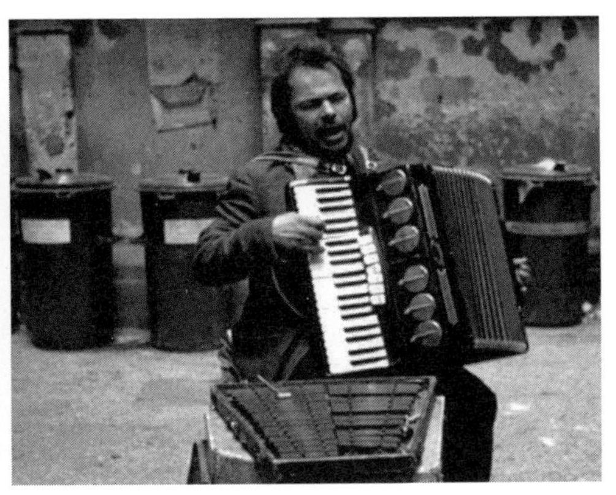

still more unviewable.

Alongside ephemeral shatterings of petrified, silent rear-courtyard spaces such as that exerted by Bruno S.'s performance, those unseen gaps in Berlin's urban fabric allowed disruptions of the surrounding city to develop; many of the covert protest movements which unhinged the GDR intentionally took to East Berlin's most decrepit and overlooked rear-courtyards for their meetings, in order to avoid the prying eyes of the state secret-police, and the sheer neglect of those spaces also allowed squatters, ecologists and punks to seize them, both in East and West Berlin, to turn them into riotous, experimental environments. Rear-courtyards were often the pre-eminent locations of Berlin's murders, unleashed whenever their addicted or desperate inhabitants snapped. After the vanishing of the GDR, many rear-courtyards of districts such as Prenzlauerberg became renovated, and closed-off by locked or coded front-doors, though many other rear-courtyards simply sank deeper into their scarred existence, beyond urban space and time; the screening-away of access to such spaces in the 'redeveloped' city also increasingly took place in the former West Berlin, and Herzog's non-actor Bruno Schleinstein, whose role as a rear-courtyard musician in *Stroszeck* was autobiographical, came to remember with nostalgia the 'beautiful town' of Berlin that once existed, 'where you could go anywhere', and whose doorways remained unlocked, even if that openness took the eye of their entrant into a vision-less terrain of minuscule gestures and occasional sonic outbursts.

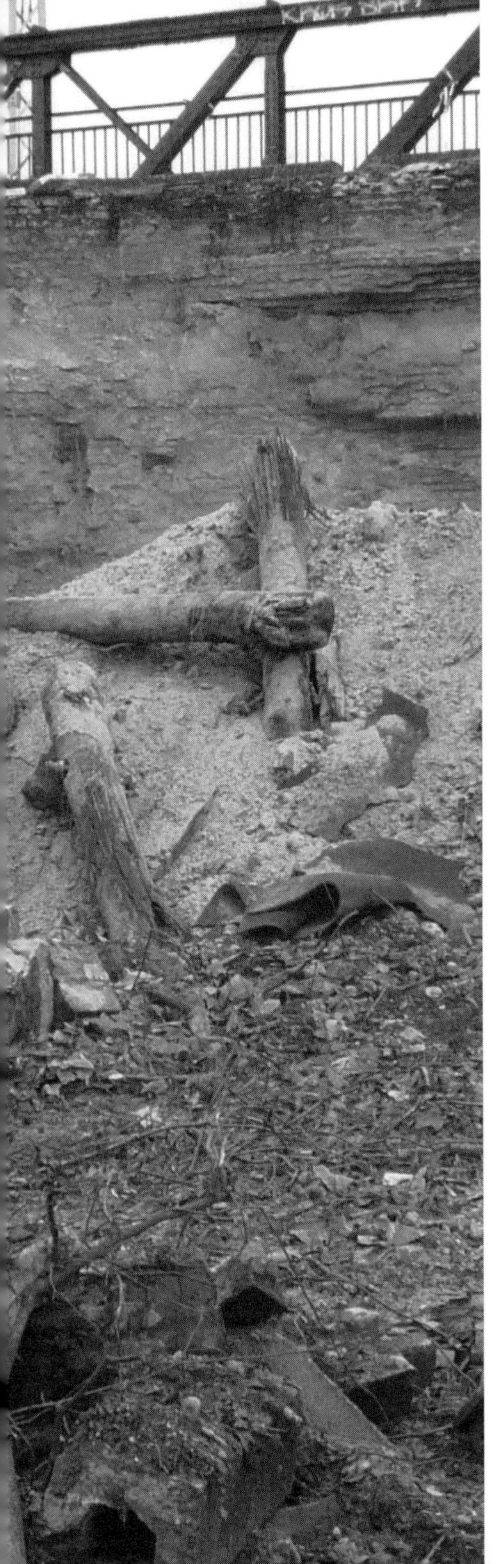

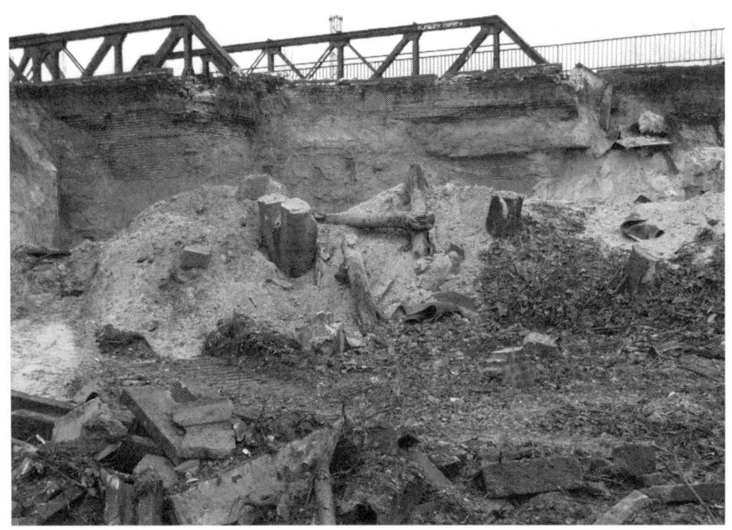

10

In the area to the south of the Ostkreuz station, a vast terrain of ruination appeared out of the destruction of century-old railway bridges and their surrounding water-towers and facades. Berlin was expanded in the final decades of the nineteenth century with the intention of establishing it as Europe's pre-eminent railway city, optimally designed for the transportation of human and material consignments between western and eastern Europe, and from the Baltic sea ports down to the capital cities of central Europe, and back; a near-indestructible network of railway buildings and facades was created around the city, its forms still monumentally present after the postwar skinning-alive and partitions of Europe sent that railway configuration askew, or rendered it redundant. To erase those constructions and facades involved an immense operation, and the Ostkreuz bridges appeared to resist their demolition for months on end, their surviving elements stubbornly poised across void space, their innards half-autopsied but still alive. Finally, as though Berlin's entire urban resources had been harnessed to the accomplishment of that act of self-autopsy, the railway terrain was levelled into ruins, in an expansive multi-layered debris of ochre brickwork, shards of metal, unidentifiably ground-down and ashen objects that had once formed an essential infrastructure, and uprooted and sliced-apart trees that had previously stood alongside those constructions, their now-decapitated trunks marked with mysterious red and yellow spheres, and jutting out of the strata of ashes like the Alexanderplatz's Television Tower in its mid-construction archival film-footage. That amassed terrain of ruination constituted an urban surface of intricately compacted elements, as though the entire history and memory of Berlin had been unearthed and exposed. But it was a momentary landscape, about to disappear, and seizable at its maximal interstice of decomposed ruination only for an instant. A day or two later, all of those ruins had been scooped-up and strategically dispatched to an unknown destination, and the land levelled, for the construction of an inner-city highway or shopping-mall complex. In Berlin, even ruins and ashes disappear without trace.

At moments of conflict or crisis, Berlin has always been a city in which the film and art images of its urban surfaces have themselves been subject to destruction, ruination and vanishing. During its wartime bombing, its museums and archives, depositories and storage warehouses for film and art works (including materials by the Skladanowsky Brothers) became incinerated; in the 1960s, during the era when experimental art and film works were conceived as being vital only for the moment of their conception and realization, with the 'finished' work forming a moribund detritus, those imageries were often intentionally destroyed; subversive works confiscated by the GDR secret-police frequently vanished permanently from view, even when the archiving of data about the works themselves, as art-crimes or film-crimes, accumulated; and art works and films of urban surfaces disappeared too when their media appeared to have become obsolete and anachronistic, or when their digital formats allowed them to be effortlessly deleted. Each of those interstitial moments is one in which the past and future collide, and urban time itself becomes infinitely volatile and fluidic, for a split-second. Whether by accident or intention, Berlin constitutes a privileged arena for the erasure of urban images alongside those that survive, through aberration or obstinacy, with those dual populations of images (the lost and phantasmatic, and the resonantly enduring) forming mutantly conjoined presences, so that erased images of urban surfaces remain indelibly incised into the city's contemporary apparitions.

In the years immediately following the wartime destruction of Berlin, and as part of his obsession with a mysteriously sea-flooded inland megalopolis, the artist Werner Heldt drew images of the city's ruination as one in which the disembodied heads of its inhabitants were now being propelled through those ruins by the irresistible force of its inundation: vertiginously drowning within dissolved urban space. In his ink-drawing *Köpfe in Ruinenmeer* (*Heads in the Sea of Ruins*) (1946), the traumatised inhabitants of Berlin swirl uncontrollably, hemmed-in by urban surfaces that are now unrecognisably displaced and re-arranged. Previously, in the years following Hitler's seizure of power, Heldt had drawn caustic images of Berlin's squares densely 'flooded' with banner-carrying crowds amassed for political demonstrations, such as *Aufmarsch der Nullen* (*March of the Zeros*) (1934-35); but once the city has achieved the ruination which those demonstrations ecstatically prefigure, a decade or so further on in time, that population has passed beyond any rationale for its movement through the streets: no longer a human flood, but subject to an exterior medium of inundation, which carries away the living as well

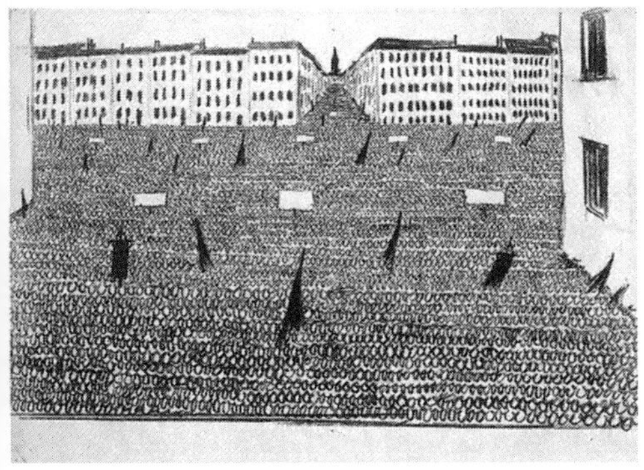

as the dead. In many films from that postwar period, such as *Roman einer Jungen Ehe* and *Berlin Express*, the act of arrival in Berlin by train, from Dresden or Paris, abruptly pitches the traveller into an urban landscape whose orientation has been scrambled beyond repair (all signs are now lost, and the determining status of ruination supplants any residual status of the ex-city), so that those figures move through the nameless avenues as a corporeal flotsam.

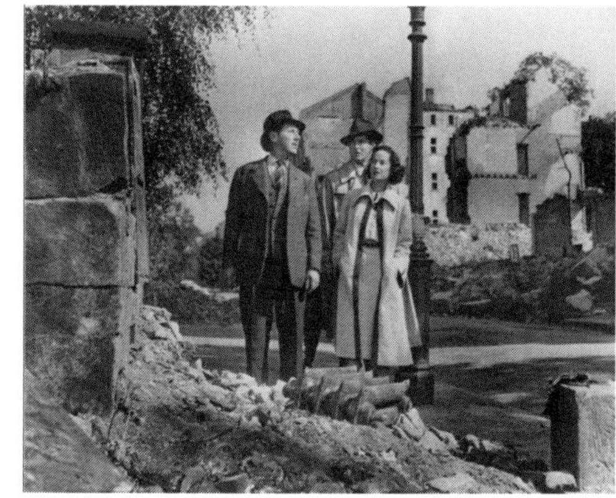

The urban ruin of the Ostkreuz railway terrain, existing only for a moment between redundant monumentality and an engulfing into disappearance, intimated that, in the act of scanning Berlin's surfaces, the invisible always has to be traced and delineated alongside the imprinted. Ruination projects itself like a film image about to combust, or an art image ready to be shredded or deleted, with its incipient invisibility forming an integral element within the intricate manifestation of the city's surfaces. The mass of railway ruins accumulated through the act of demolition inescapably evoked human traces: uncountable mounds of bodies, in the forms of multiple populations of Berlin sifted by time into an identical medium of memory, negated and reduced to ashes. The segments of trees lodged within those ruins appeared to have had their trunks shredded and sharpened by a serrated machine which, while uprooting and obliviously disposing of them, had simultaneously transformed them into weapons of incision, for a future or past urban conflict.

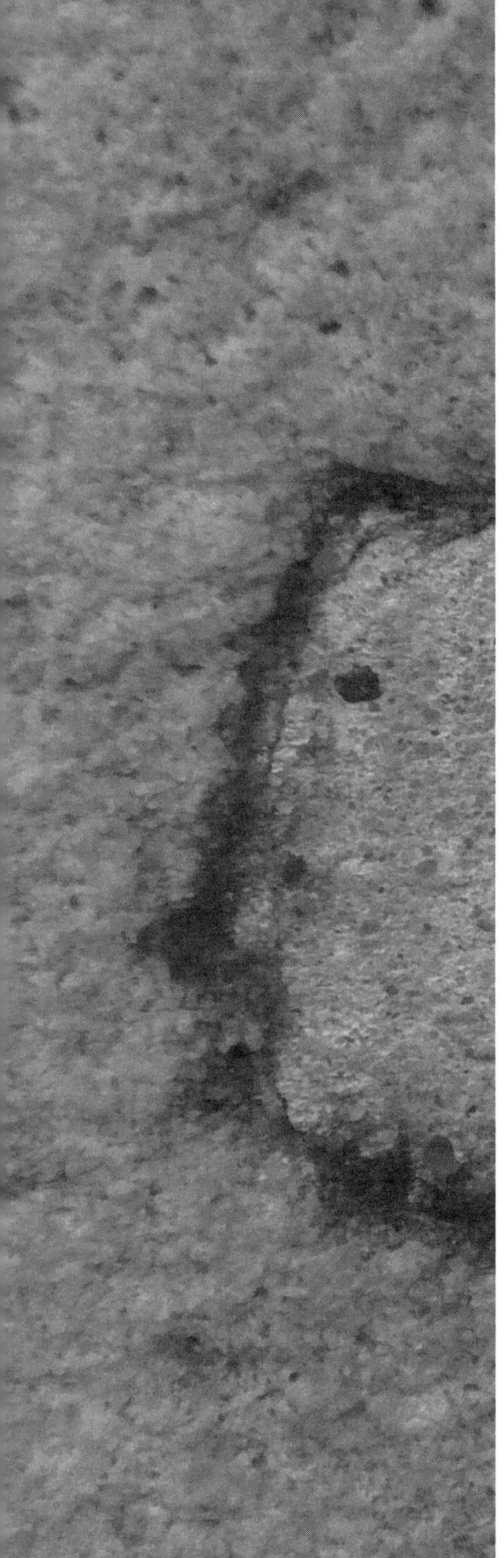

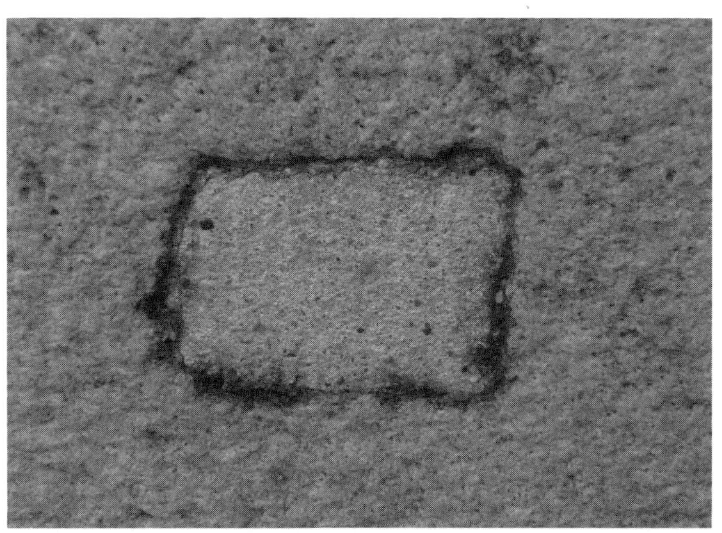

II

Berlin is a city of screens: not only screens which project and reveal, but also screens which exist to envelop its surfaces, to avert the eye, and to conjure memory away through a medium of urban disappearance. But those screens, too, reveal, through their minuscule flaws and monumental misconception. On a portal facade of the Reichstag building, which suffered severe damage during the Soviet assault on Berlin, the embedded trace of a shrapnel- or bullet-strike had been wrapped within a screen of stone that appeared almost identical in texture and colour to the original stone: a rectangular and slightly irregular patch, seemingly floating on air, and flecked with blemishes, as though it were a cinema screen whose surface displayed the impacts of bottles or missiles thrown by restive late-night audiences. And outlined around that rectangle, its essential mismatch with the original stone manifested itself in the slight gap between the two surfaces, and through the darker, adhesive substance that had fixed it to the wounded facade. Rather than suturing that facade, the minuscule Reichstag screen had reinforced both the evidence of its gouged and irreparable history, and also the intention to screen-away that vitally flawed carapace. And in the intended diverting of the viewer's eye, it appeared as though that minuscule stone screen had been created not to wipe away a scar, but instead to guide that eye towards the oscillations between Berlin's minuscule urban screens – those of digital devices and artefacts, essential to all transits through the city – and its all-enveloping and monumental large-scale screens, affixed to its buildings and towers in order to project captivating animations and essential corporate data to its inhabitants. In that oscillation between vast and reduced urban surfaces, the minuscule Reichstag screen would simply constitute one more manifestation of a mysterious content, to be probed, scanned or discarded by the eye, among an infinity of others, wrapped around the city's surfaces.

In the summer of 1995, the artist Christo Vladimirov Javacheff and his collaborator Jeanne-Claude Denat de Guillebon fulfilled their long-term project to wrap the entirety of the Reichstag building in silver polypropylene fabric, with the sole intention, as they said in television interviews at the time, of making it momentarily disappear; from that sleight-of-hand imposition of invisibility, conceived almost like those of cinema's disreputable originators, the atrocious historical weight of the building's interior and surfaces would be cancelled, thereby generating a void that emanated a new origin, for history or for Europe's cities or for the human eye. At that time, the meticulous resurfacing of the facade which included its minuscule stone screen had not yet been undertaken, and its scarring remained still-tangible. During the hot nights of the Reichstag's wrapping, young crowds gathered on the field directly in front of its portal, gazing at its surface as though it were an immense film-screen, that sooner or later would

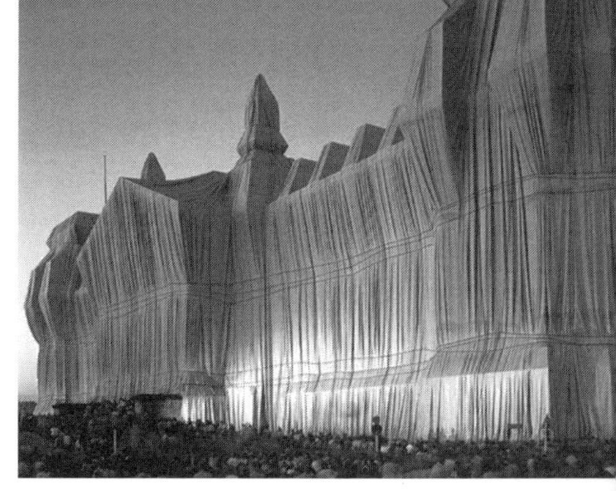

project a definitive, aberrant image, or one which needed to be hallucinated into existence by that transfixed audience. But on the final night of the Reichstag's wrapping, cranes had already gathered alongside the building and had pre-emptively ripped apart some of the seams of the fabric, in preparation for the following day's dismantling, as though the German governmental powers that had resolutely opposed the art-spectacle had become so anxious to erase it that they had prematurely ordered the building's re-exposure; a night's interval had been created in which the building was simultaneously screened, still projecting its hallucinations of new origins, and at the same time raggedly un-screened, its edges undone and flawed. At that moment, the building's surface was held at a precarious, pivoting boundary between oblivion and revelation, like all urban screens of Berlin.

The Reichstag had been the destination-point for the Soviet Army's journey across the face of Europe, that extended from its reversal of the siege of Moscow in January 1942 until its decimating incursion through the avenues of Berlin in April 1945. Although the building had been largely disused and emptied since Hitler's agents set fire to it in February 1933, it still constituted the ultimate, extreme target for that massive human movement. While Hitler had adopted a subterranean presence in the city, for his final moments, in his bunker to the south of the Reichstag, the seizure of Berlin was signalled high above the city, on the building's roof, where the Soviet flag was raised. Alongside the sexual violence inflicted on Berlin's already-battered population, the elation generated by that journey's end forms one of the city's seminal sensorial eruptions, with wild mass-celebrations staged directly outside the Reichstag's portal (at the site where, forty years later, Christo's spectators would amass), the uproar documented or re-staged through the medium of film for Tarkovsky's *Ivan's Childhood* (1962) and *The Fall of Berlin*, among other films. Alongside intensive strata of damage – much of it the result of exhilarated

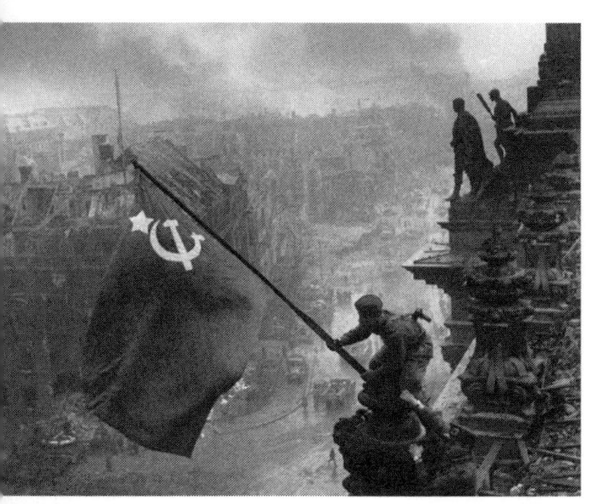

machine-gun fire after the conflict had ended – the Soviet troops also used implements to inscribe dense, filmic constellations of graffiti exclamations on the Reichstag's surface, many of them messages to the dead, or of loss, beginning at the portal and then spreading out across much of its exterior and interior, as though the entire building had become transformed into a terminal screen for that expansive, phantasmatic inscription.

If unpeeled, like skin from a human body, the minuscule stone screen wrapped over a shrapnel blast or machine-gun impact, on the Reichstag's facade, would demonstrate how urban screens always alternate between projecting memories, sensations and images, and obscuring or averting them. Such screens form mirrors for the human eye, their resolution invariably sharpened through their appearances in film and art works. And those screens, finally, comprise urban eyes in their own right, so that Berlin's all-consuming obsessions, ecstasies and scars gaze out multiply from the apertures and flaws of its own surfaces, in the same instant that its inhabitants are compelled to gaze into and through those surfaces.

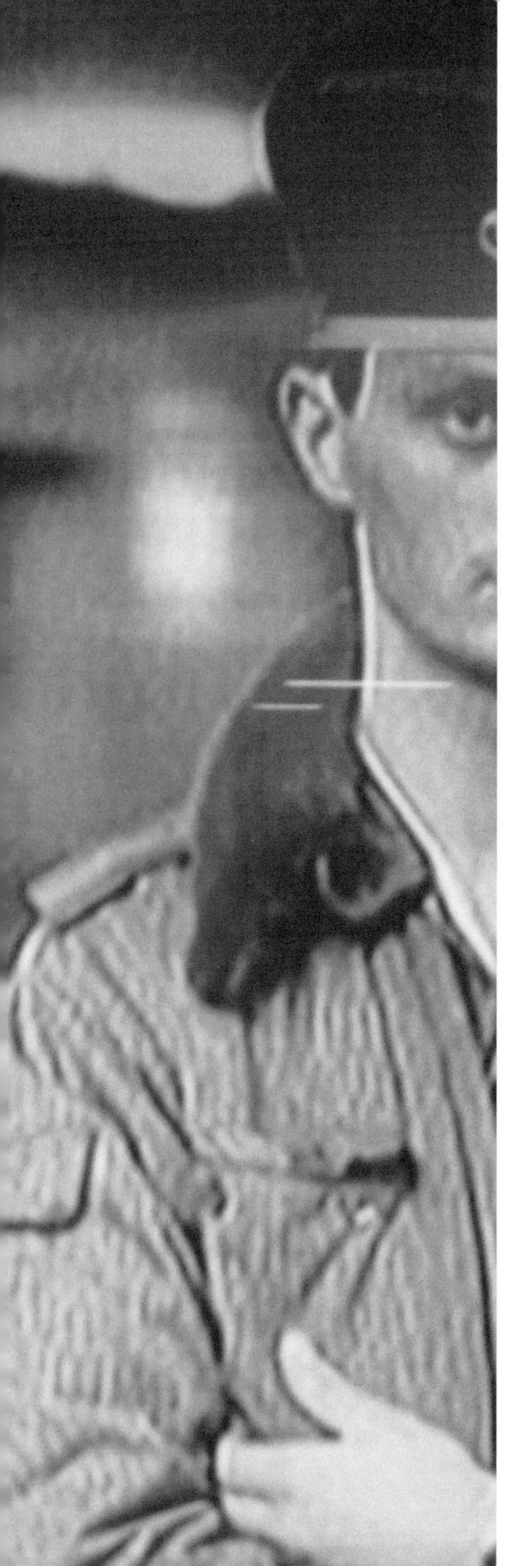

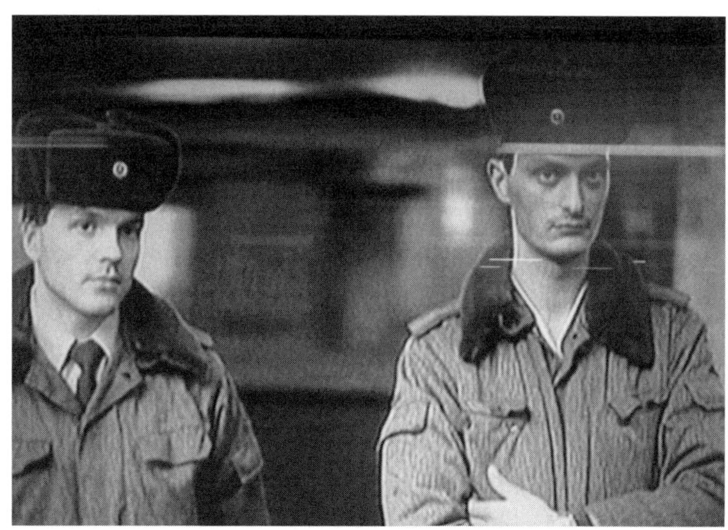

12

Berlin's urban eyes can take the form of film itself, whenever the medium of film irrepressibly projects itself directly through the surfaces of the city, piercing and annulling those surfaces so that its spectator's vision is engulfed directly, without intermediation, into the city's core, as though it were being sluiced into Berlin's infinite layers of askew histories and propelled bodies. A small rectangular screen had been cut into the green-tiled surface of one of the intermediate levels of the decrepit Nordbahnhof underground station, whose platforms and kiosks remained unchanged since their construction in the mid-1930s, sealed in a carapace of dirt and soot that appeared untouched both by the decades of the GDR state and the subsequent period. From that screen, a three-minute loop was projected incessantly, without titles, of an amateur film shot on colour 8mm stock by an anonymous GDR guard in 1989, shortly after the onset of the events which would erase the GDR in the following year. In his film, the guard undertook a journey from street-level, at a station four stops down the same S-bahn line from the Nordbahnhof: that of Potsdamerplatz, which at that time was still closed to passengers, so that trains passed without stopping as they transited from East to West Berlin and back. Shooting his film as he walked, the guard descended the flights of stairs into the closed-down, protected station, eventually meeting his colleagues at the barricaded door which led to the platforms. Those colleagues, disinterested or wryly smiling, unbolted the door for him, and he then filmed the surfaces of the station's platforms, which had been abandoned for almost thirty years, their hoardings still legible within blackened frames, along with the trains traversing the station at speed, observed through concrete observation-slits by his colleagues. Finally, against the background of a passing train, he shot a sequence showing two of his colleagues, in fur hats bearing the GDR insignia, as they stood still, with apparent nervous reluctance, their facial expressions impassive, as though those two figures were either oblivious to the transformations about to upend their lives and bodies, or else so aware of those transformations that they now existed solely as sensitised presences to transmit them, into the medium of film, then out into the space of the city.

Through that pivotal aperture in Berlin's urban surfaces, incised into the Nordbahnhof's Hitler-era green tiles, film formed an archaic medium able to access those surfaces' profound depths, and to project images from that immense and ashen subterranea. Although it emitted only one film, as though locked in an intractable obsession with the tumultuous moment of 1989, that urban aperture appeared eminently capable – if the caprice ever impelled it – to transmit instead every last seminal image ever created of Berlin's surfaces, or of the ocular journeys undertaken across those surfaces; the wilfulness of only projecting one film, in endless repetition, intimated the essential

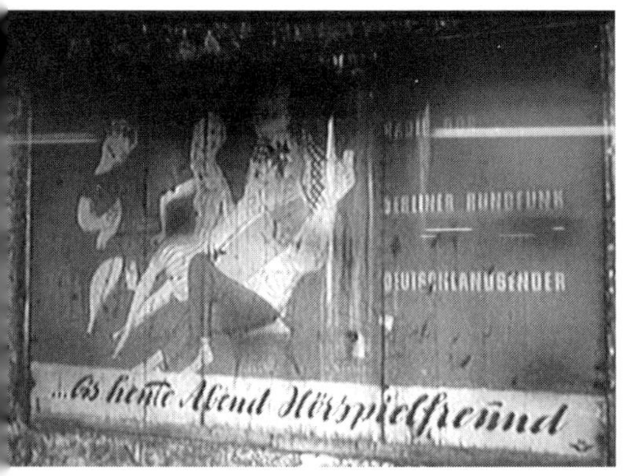

perversity of the filmic medium. But once an opening has been pierced into Berlin's surfaces, and film or art images begin to pour through it, that revelatory urban inundation may appear unstoppable. The texture of the images emitted through the Nordbahnhof's wall-surface also held a confrontation between an archaic medium of memory, in the form of the defunct 8mm stock with which those images had been shot, and the digital screen through which the film now emerged. In the process of digitising the original material, a technical flaw had somehow been generated, so that horizontal green flashes impaired the images; in the sequence showing the two impassive guards standing in front of a passing train, the flashes traversed their foreheads or eyes, as though forming phantasmatic emanations from those guards' perception, as those figures entered a zone of historical and corporeal transmutation.

The anonymous guard's filmic descent into the raw concrete environment of the closed-down Potsdamersplatz station had allowed him to momentarily enter lost time, in the form of the station's surfaces, hoardings and insignia, all frozen nearly thirty years earlier, and to seize those surfaces, at the moment before they evanesced. His camera had focused on damp-warped posters for long-gone GDR radio programmes that displayed a jaunty depiction of a family gathered for the evening's transmission, their now-eroded figures, poised against a lurid orange background, deformed and eroded into monstrosity both by the hoarding's dilapidation and by digital image-damage. In other sequences, the glass-enclosed photographic portraits of the GDR's leaders, such as Wilhelm Pieck, secured to the station's upper walls as a public emanation of their power, had fallen to the platform below and shattered. The guard's exploratory journey downwards, through near-darkness, from street-level into the city's ruination-inflected subterranea, formed an involuntary un-screening of Berlin's amassed memory, with the traces of that act then projected into the immediate moment, through the filmic aperture. But, at a certain point, after carefully scrutinising his two colleagues' disabused faces, the filmmaker-guard is unable to go further with his journey; his film (with its format's fixed, three-minute duration) expires, and the image ends, before compulsively re-starting from zero, three minutes back in time, as though afflicted with long-term memory-loss.

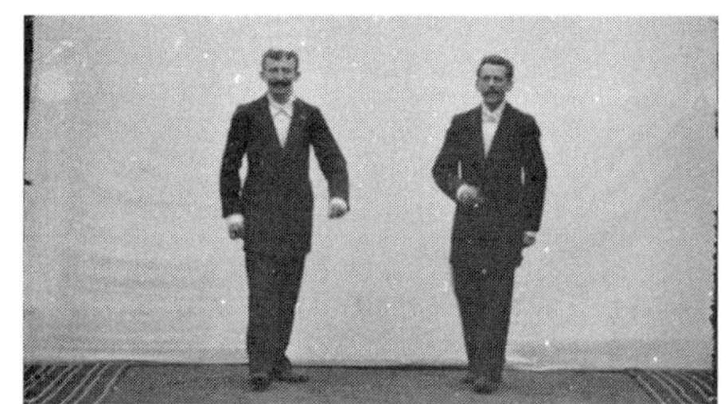

The anonymity of the filmmaker-guard and the opaque purpose of his journey into Berlin's depths serve to connect that film with all of the amateur filmmaking that has ever scanned the surfaces of the city, from the medium's origins. Even the Skladanowsksy Brothers, in some senses, are hapless 'amateurs', gratuitously stripped by the Berlin authorities of their professional license in 1896, despite their having initiated the financial regime of film spectatorship by staging the first-ever screening for a paying audience in the previous year; their films are as finally mysterious in intention as that of the anonymous guard who descended into the Potsdamerplatz's subterranea in 1989. Each of the infinite number of 'amateur' films concerned with tracing the surfaces of Berlin – from the Skladanowsky Brothers' film of 1894 with its roof-top urban panorama, through the intervening decades to the innumerable cellphone-shot image-sequences of present-day Berlin – forms an integral component of the city's visual detritus, and of its inexhaustible archaeological underpinning, even when such films are lost or destroyed. Occasionally, as with the film incessantly projected from the green-tiled station wall, that archaeological detritus can aberrantly work its way back upwards, into Berlin's eyes, in order to become an element of the seminal visions of the contemporary city, impacting upon and illuminating its surfaces.

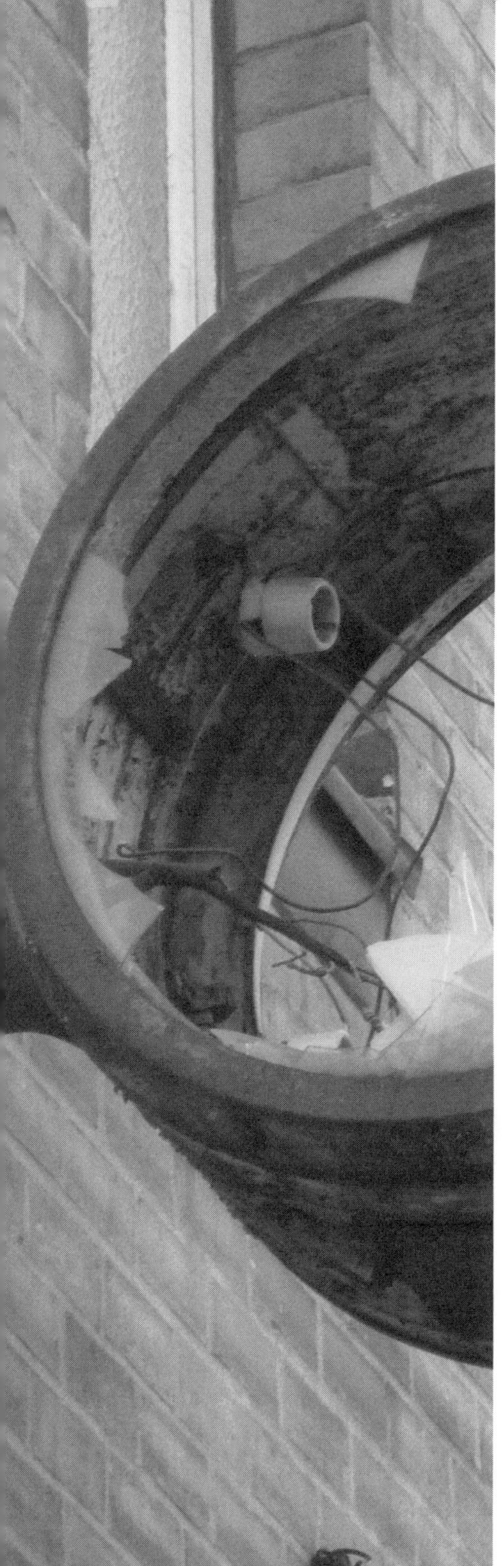

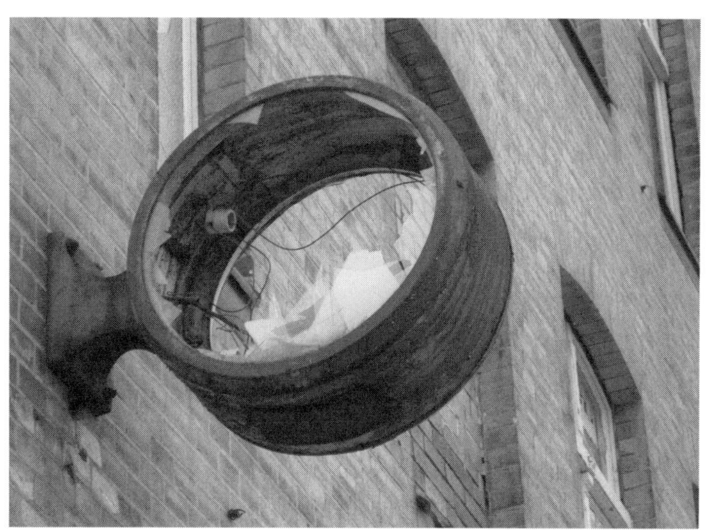

13

The simultaneity of images from irreconcilable moments and memories, densely pinioned together on the city's surfaces, often causes time itself to explode in Berlin, so that all linear time vanishes, and every historical moment may manifest itself from within one compacted amalgam of time, or else time's elements may abruptly veer in wild oscillation, backwards and forwards, in a sensory blur. As in a cybertext depicting a future megalopolis undergoing the fallout from a terminal digital crash, in which time has lapsed but vision endures, oblivion can constitute a far stronger and more consoling medium of survival than memory, but oblivion may itself mutate, into ecstasy or horror, in Berlin's timeless zones. On the Stralau peninsula, alongside the river Spree, a broken and voided clock remained immovably hinged to the exterior surface of an abandoned glass factory. The rusted metal infrastructure of the clock had the rounded contours of a gun-barrel section, as though time itself could be fired through that aperture. Shards from the clock's broken-glass covering – presumably manufactured within the building to which the clock itself had been bolted, and assaulted by delinquent hands, like those which shatter a streetlight's glass with stones in the film *Berlin Ecke Schönhauser* – remained affixed to the barrel's interior edge, into which a light-socket had also once been installed, now empty but still trailing wires, so that night-shift workers heading into the factory under conditions of darkness could have viewed time illuminated. No trace at all remained of the clock-face itself, or of its hands, which had been entirely displaced; the thrown stones which had shattered its glass covering would not have been sufficient to dislodge the clock itself, and it must have been forcibly gouged out, either for the scavenging and melting-down of its metal components, or else through the compulsive desire to erase time itself, and thereby render that clock's remaining infrastructure into the form of a mysterious urban eye: not an eye transmitting film, like that of the Nordbahnhof wall-surface, nor one screening and revealing history, as with the Reichstag stone screen, but a transparent eye, inhabited by the loss of time itself.

In many paintings of Berlin's time, its potential loss is a matter of imminent calamity. In Hugo Krayn's *Grossstadt: Berlin* (*The Great City: Berlin*) of 1914, all time has become urgent and dense, in order to avert its own loss – under the cover of darkness, like that illuminated by the long-gone clock of the Stralau glass-factory, workers in an industrial night cityscape are racing against time to deliver whatever the lit-up factories demand; a horse is being whipped, a hand-cart is being pulled, and the bodies of the workers, sacks on their backs, strain to reach their destination. An extreme corporeal exertion is insistently demanded for the activation and sustaining of the city in overdrive. Even the transport system has to contribute to that concertinaed time, with a train being propelled rapidly across a bridge, between the

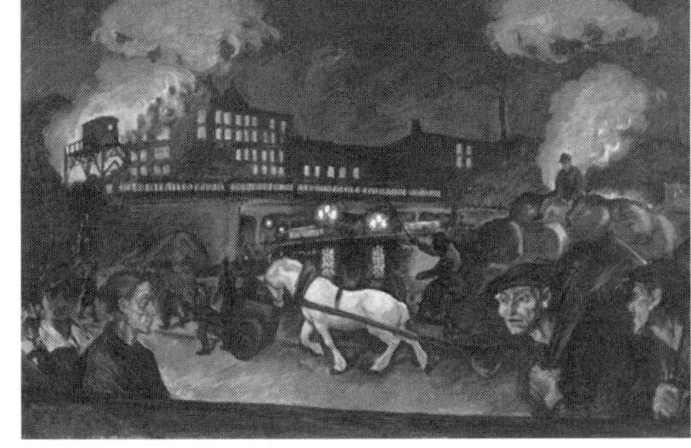

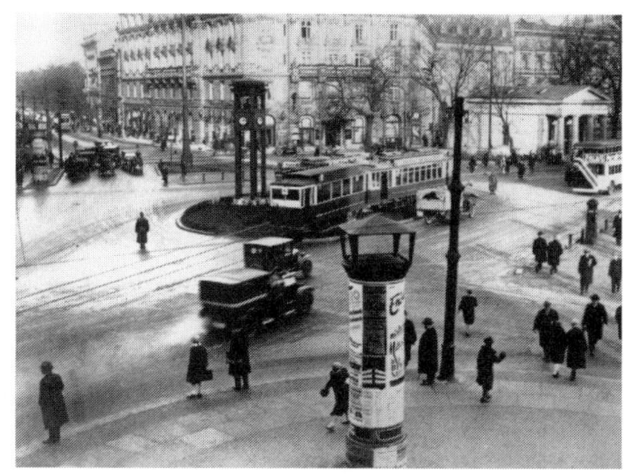

factories and the river. Everywhere, clouds of smoke or steam are being expelled from hidden sources, as though the exertion required to animate the city has caused its inhabitants' bodies to combust. As with the paintings from the same year, by Erich Heckel and Ernst Ludwig Kirchner, of Berlin's relentless subway-train system and its overpacked, prostitution-saturated squares and plazas, time appears pressurised into an awry urgency ready to ignite, whether pitched at the moment before revolutionary turmoil, a sexual act, or all-engulfing warfare.

In the title of Ruttmann's film *Berlin: Die Sinfonie der Grossstadt*, from 1927, the intervening thirteen years since Krayn's depiction of the city's maddened industrial time have not subtracted Berlin's expansive metropolitan 'greatness': a delirious psychosis of time instils infinite grandeur and volume, into Berlin's urban surfaces, so that their time is one inhabited both by magnificence, and by its imminent erasure. Once Ruttmann's suburban trains and trams have emerged from their arc-shaped shed at first light and have been correctly aligned by their turntable, they are immediately integrated within the linear entity of the Berlin day and night, regulated by intervals of work and pleasure. But Ruttmann's urban chronology is one beset by interruptions and incursions, in the form of accidents and malfunctions emerging from the volatile crowds and surfaces of the city, so that Berlin's time forms an unhinged, arrhythmic linearity. The film's night-sequences only accentuate that unhinging of time, in which the city's avenues and nightclub interiors form the site of accelerating sensory excess; the film closes with a sequence of vehicle-transits at speed across the rain-sodden avenues of the Charlottenburg district, before finally focusing on the neon-illuminated facade of the grand Café am Zoo – transformed from magnificence into ruins during bombing-raids in November 1943 – from which the film-image spins in an anti-clockwise revolution (mirroring a previous sequence of a spinning roulette-wheel, four shots earlier in the film), until the only urban time that survives is one of firework detonations.

From the urban surfaces of Berlin, time may often be crushed out, and voided, as with the transparent clock hinged to the Stralau glass-factory, but may then reconstitute itself, as a residue, in the form of the urban images of film and art, which then act back upon Berlin's time, by exploring time's fractures with immediacy, so that urban memory itself may be reactivated, for a moment. But the loss of time may also gather and amass its own durations, across Berlin's lost or neglected facades, so that they can protectively secure themselves, against the psychoses of time that intermittently impel the city into catastrophe or overdrive – and such surfaces then project, instead of the horror of the loss of time, an oblivious sense of bliss, that urban time no longer exists.

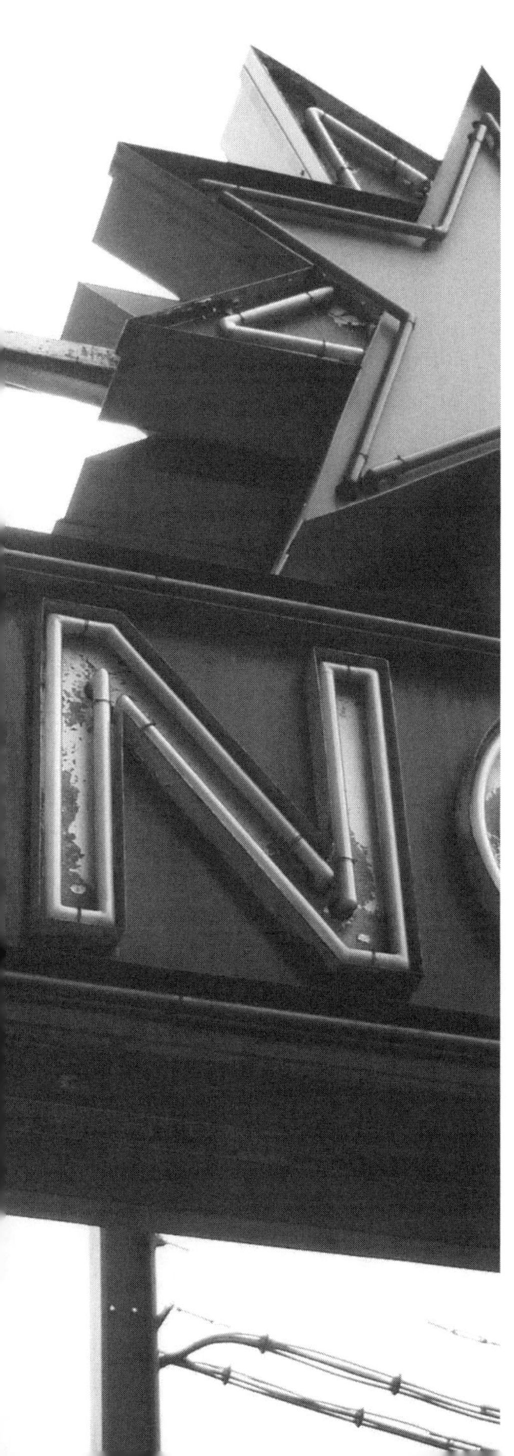

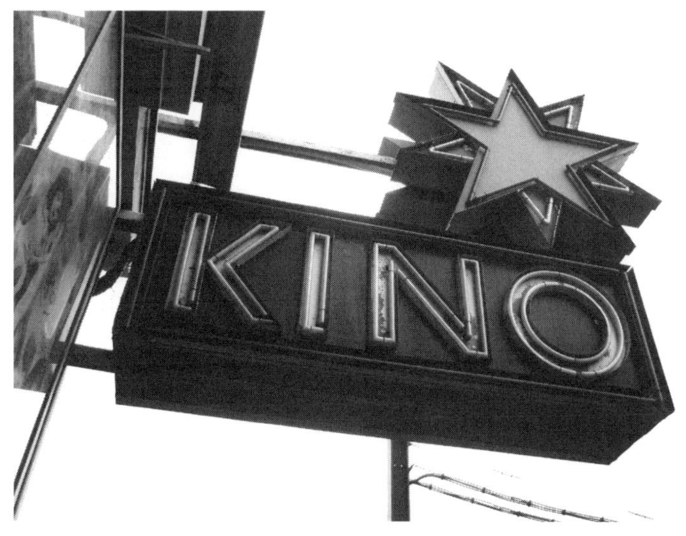

14

A trace of oblivious urban bliss had been hinged to a decrepit apartment building in Berlin's peripheral Pankow district, in the form of a blue star, bolted to that urban surface during the GDR era, and as immovably attached as the voided clock adjoining the Stralau glass-factory. The time of bliss signalled by that blue star, above the entrance to the tiny Blauer Stern Kino, opened in 1917 (then known as the Bismarck-Lichtspiel, and one of Berlin's oldest-surviving cinemas), was that of film, and the experience intimated by that blue star, as it enticed passers-by into the cinema's interior, was that of time miraculously 'regained', sliced-away from the habitual time of the city, and instilled back into the eyes and bodies of its inhabitants, precipitating urban bliss. But the iconic, glacial colour of that star – a world away from the enveloping, hot-hued marquees of such pre-eminently luxurious cinemas as those of Los Angeles' Broadway, and even those of the few enduring grand cinemas of Berlin's Charlottenburg district – intimated too that the time to be experienced, once passers-by had traversed the space beneath it to enter the cinema, as spectators, also possessed an element of 'blue' melancholy, through which memories could be conjured and unleashed within that cinematic space, but would simultaneously be frozen, as though that cinema comprised a no-escape zone of petrified memory, for its unwitting entrants. Within the dense historical strata of Berlin, that blue star also resonated with its visual proximity to the shape of the badges worn by concentration camp inmates of the Nazi era, in which an inverted blue triangle, denoting an immigrant forced labourer, when conjoined with (and overlayering) the yellow triangle worn by Jewish inmates, configured a blue star. As with the time-erased clock bolted to the Stralau factory, that blue star had been electrified, in order to illuminate the Berlin night, but unlike the clock, it had remained haphazardly wired, so that it erratically pulsed out its light after dark, the neon-tubes humming a sonic mantra of malfunction, and signalling the opening of a fissure of vision within the city's surfaces.

Blue stars form a multiple, constellating presence across many of Berlin's urban facades, often in the form of graffitied blue-stars inscribed upon surfaces ready-prepared for their manifestation, usually in the form of silver or golden backdrops which serve to launch them into the city. They recall Patti Smith's visualisation of her companion Robert Mapplethorpe as a 'little blue star', whose unique eruption into the photographic and sexual terrains of 1980s New York City transformed the city, for an immediate and intensive interval, before mutating from the shape of an ascendant star into that of a polished death's-head skull, and vanishing. But in the domain of cinema projected by the insignia of the Blauer Stern Kino, the blue stars of Berlin are often those supernova figures whose seminal presences

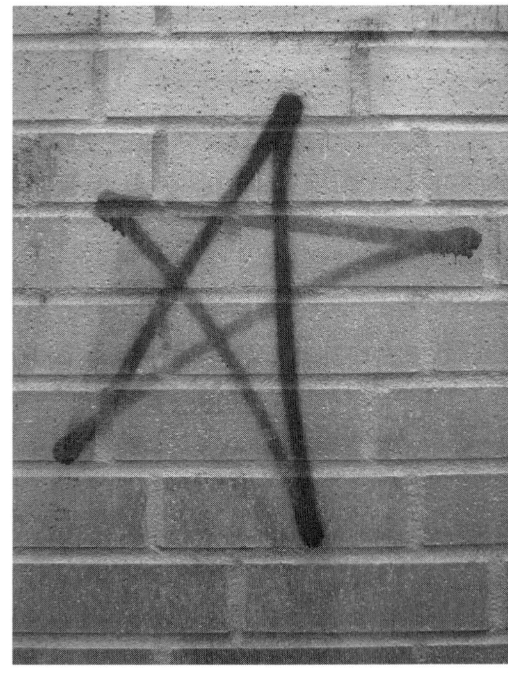

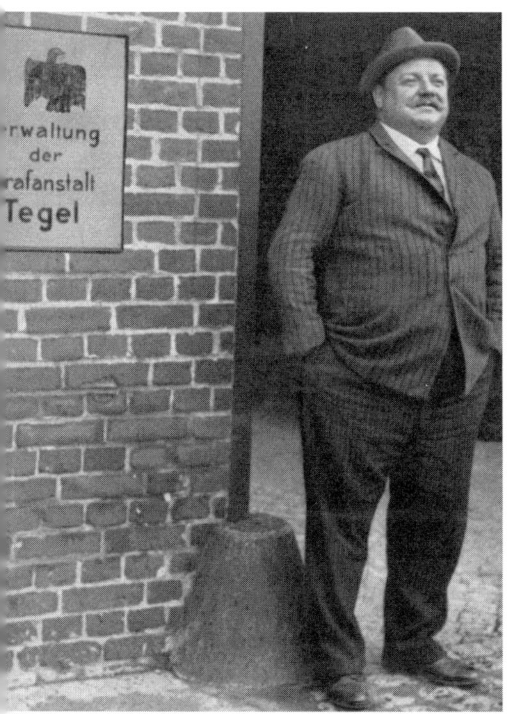

filmically incorporated the city, but whose traversals through it also generated calamities. The actor Heinrich George, who played Franz Biberkopf in the 1931 film of *Berlin Alexanderplatz*, became widely viewed in the 1930s as embodying Berlin with his vocal outbursts and excessive corporeal volume, and allied himself to the Nazi regime during the era when many actors exiled themselves from Berlin. Hitler personally awarded him the title 'state actor' of the Nazi regime in 1937, along with medals and honours for his work in the Nazi film industry, and he was frequently photographed meeting Hitler and Goebbels; on 18 February 1943, as the destruction of Berlin by aerial bombing accelerated, George was filmed among the audience at the Berlin Sportspalast for Goebbels' most infamous speech, on the 'total war' which was now about to be unleashed. After the fall of Berlin to the Soviet Army, George's status abruptly inversed from that of grandeur to ignominy and danger, as the Soviet authorities titled him a 'prominent fascist' and dispatched him to the internment camp of Hohenschönhausen, on the north-eastern edge of Berlin, three months after the war's end; from there, he was eventually jettisoned from Berlin, beyond the city's northern boundary, to the former Nazi concentration camp of Sachsenhausen, whose barracks and execution-grounds had been obliviously requisitioned by the Soviet authorities and simply downgraded from those of a concentration camp to those of a 'special' internment camp, where over 10,000 prisoners, mostly Nazi bureaucrats and police, were kept in harsh conditions. George's health collapsed there, his excessive corporeal presence evanesced, and he died of exhaustion and pneumonia on 25 September 1946, his body initially buried anonymously in a mass-grave before being recovered in 1994 and returned to Berlin.

The most incandescent blue star of Berlin is Marlene Dietrich, born in the Schöneberg district of the city in 1901. During the 1930s, when she was at the zenith of her stardom in Hollywood, Goebbels and

Hitler attempted to entice her back to Berlin to work in the Nazi film industry; while George had been engulfed by the Nazi regime, Dietrich repudiated it, responding to the cinema-obsessed Goebbels' pleas by applying for American citizenship in 1937 and swearing allegiance to the USA. During the final period of the war, she made anti-Nazi propaganda radio broadcasts and performed in uniform for US servicemen, making a long and dangerous journey with them through a succession of warzones, from North Africa to Europe, and finally to Berlin in 1945; after the fall of the city, her fury against Nazi power transferred itself to the power of the Soviet forces who had taken Berlin, and at a meeting of September 1945, with Marshall Zhukov, the Soviet army's principal commander, at his headquarters in the Karlshorst district, she castigated him for his soldiers' frenzy of murder and rape in the aftermath of the city's fall, to Zhukov's own anger. Three years later, she returned to the devastated Berlin to shoot exterior sequences for Billy Wilder's film *A Foreign Affair*, in which her Nazi-aligned cabaret-singer character performs the song 'The Ruins of Berlin'. But Dietrich's wartime broadcasts and her perceived repudiation of Berlin led to new uproar when she eventually returned to the city, twelve years later, on 3 May 1960, to perform her cabaret show at the vast and lavish Titania Palast cinema (architecturally the inverse of the minuscule Blauer Stern cinema, with a spectacular tower of light surmounting the foyer and an auditorium seating nearly two thousand spectators, but perversely lacking the Blauer Stern's endurance, since that palatial cinema's auditorium was abandoned in 1965, gutted, and converted into a supermarket); Dietrich's re-apparition in Berlin provoked intractable opposition, manifesting itself as bomb-threats and picketings of the cinema. And her final, celestial re-entry into the city also generated uproar, with street-protests against her funeral cortege as it entered the Schöneberg cemetery on 16 May 1992.

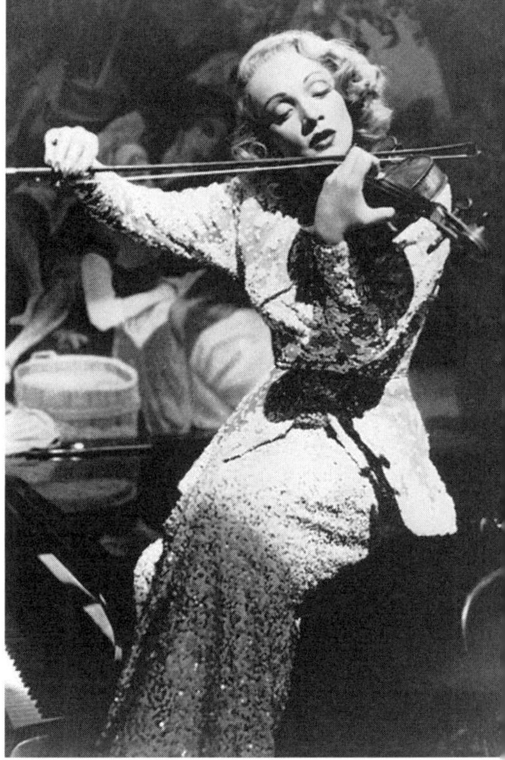

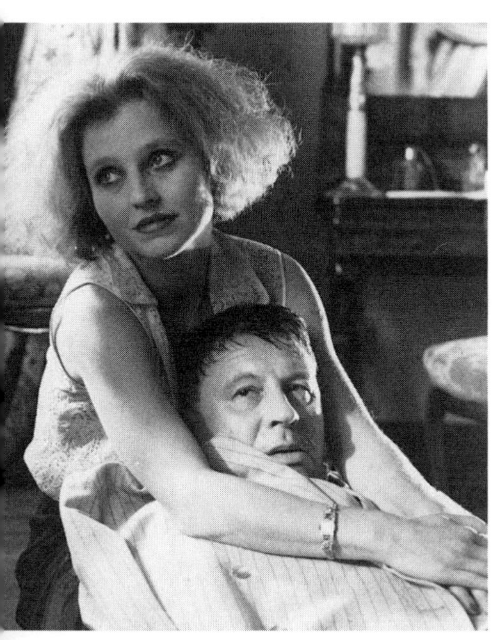

The blue star bolted to the facade of the Pankow-district cinema, projecting its glacial aura of filmic magnificence and calamity, also inflects the adjacent presence of Max Skladanowsky, who initiated the first-ever film screening in 1895, in the centre of Berlin, from his base at his magician's workshop in Pankow, twenty-two years before the opening of the Blauer Stern cinema, and after decades of oblivion, was eventually buried beneath a wreath from Goebbels, in the Pankow cemetery close to that cinema, in 1939. Film possesses an almost maleficent extrusion into the urban surfaces of Berlin, starred with its many legendary figures – above all, those of Heinrich George and Marlene Dietrich – who incorporated the city's sensory excesses but were also at the receiving-end of assaults from its power-formations and caprices. The surfaces of Berlin hold the capacity to be conjured from zero by film, in an infinity of ways – by Max Skladanowsky for the first time, in the 1890s, and also by film-makers such as Rainer Werner Fassbinder, who recreated the teeming avenues of Berlin from scratch, in a Bavarian film studio, for his own thirteen-part version of *Berlin Alexanderplatz* in 1980, with the actor Günter Lamprecht taking on Heinrich George's film-role of 1931. That immense lineage of uproar and mutation can only be momentarily annulled through the experience of film-spectators who, having passed beyond that illuminated blue star, feel the cinema's lights suddenly go down, and fall into entrancement.

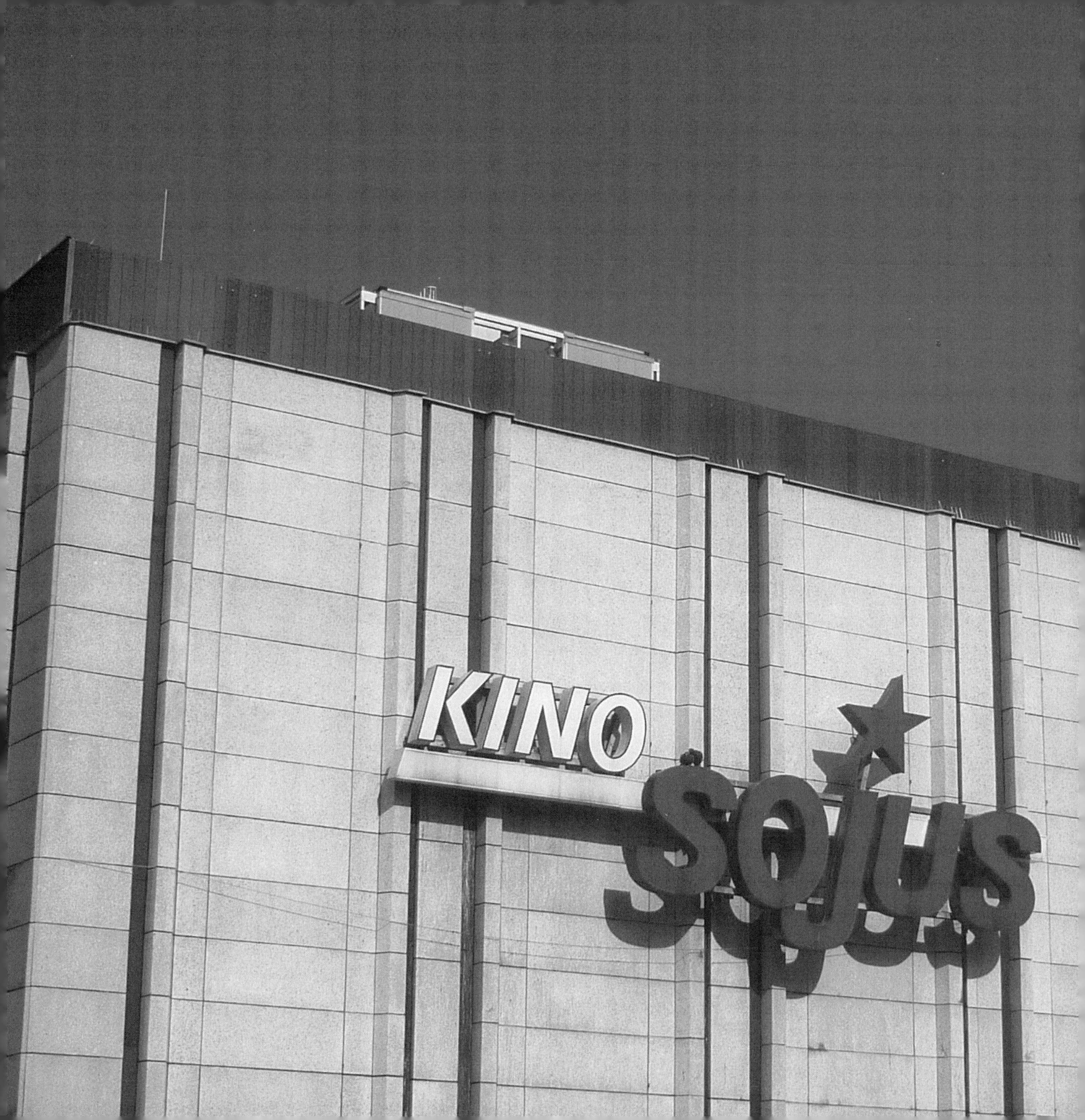

KINO
Sojus

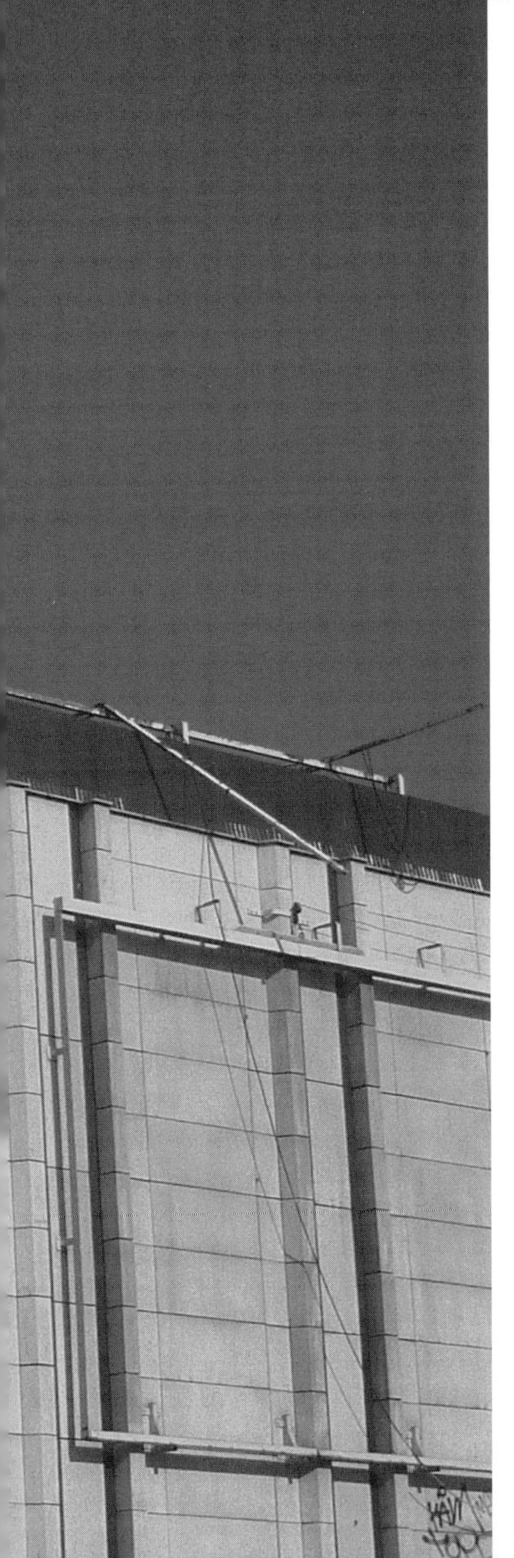

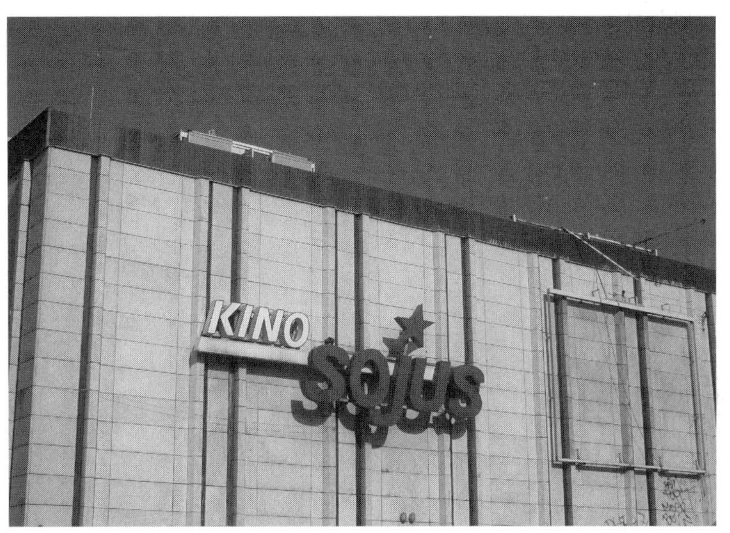

15

Across the eastern face of Berlin, on the edge of the prefabricated apartment-tower zone of Marzahn, the derelict Sojus Kino's insignia held a red star that formed an inverse urban presence to the blue star hinged to the facade of the Blauer Stern Kino. On its opening in 1981, the Sojus cinema had been named in homage to the GDR's only cosmonaut, Sigmund Jähn, who entered outer space on the USSR rocket Soyuz 31 in 1978, and returned in glory to Berlin via a motorcade that drew immense crowds as it descended the Schönhauserallee. For the GDR's constrained inhabitants, Jähn's unique transit from the outlandish, toxic urban landscapes of the GDR (many of them recalling those of Tarkovsky's otherworldly films, *Stalker* and *Solaris*) into outer space must have appeared a journey of near-zero distance, but even after the GDR's vanishing, that journey remained so compelling that, in Wolfgang Becker's 2003 film *Good Bye Lenin!* – in which that country's engulfing hallucination resists being relinquished, except through the loss of vision or death – the narrative's determined GDR-fabricator, who fears his mother will die if she realises the GDR has been erased, appoints Jähn to the position of the moribund ex-country's head of state. The avenue which originated at the cinema's location, before bisecting the volatile terrain of Marzahn's innumerable apartment-towers, had also been named after Jähn and his fellow cosmonauts. But the Sojus Kino's hot red star, originally pinioned as a glorious starburst above the letter 'j' of the cinema's name, on its plastic-faced surface (formed of prefabricated grey panels that replicated those of the adjacent district's shoddy apartment-towers), had now cooled, at the cinema's abandonment and dereliction, to a temperature pitched far below that of the glacial star of the Blauer Stern Kino. The casing for posters of forthcoming attractions, alongside the cinema's red-lettered name, had been voided. Although that cinema's grey-panelled surface presented an optimum target of imprintation for the graffiti that had been Marzahn's pre-eminent visual medium for over twenty years – deployed throughout the early 1990s in competitively overlayered combat, between the district's neo-Nazi and neo-Communist gangs as they conducted their head-splitting warfare – it remained neglected and almost untouched, with only a few territorial claims recorded below the voided hoarding. During its years of operation, the exterior form of the Sojus Kino's windowless container had resonated with the architectural style of the huge, red star-surmounted sarcophagi that commemorated the Russian army's dead from the April 1945 battle for Berlin, located in the Schönholz and Treptow districts, as though those young soldiers (still dreaming, in death, of destroying Berlin) had become transmutated into cinema spectators, within their corporeal containers. Now, emptied of its audiences, the Sojus Kino's abandoned facade appeared as a ruined but still-surviving carapace.

The Sojus Kino projected an aura of being unperceived and untouched by the inhabitants of the surrounding apartment-towers of Marzahn, as though it existed in a parallel universe from those towers,

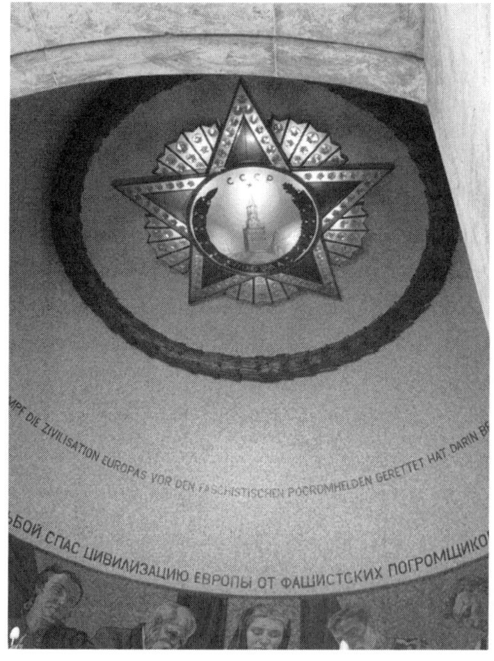

which now held the grandiose corporate insignias of the private companies which had acquired them, in a near-terminal condition of decrepitude; after the erasure of the GDR state, whose authorities had commissioned that entire autonomous sub-city to be built in an intensive burst, from 1977, rising-up from a wasteland on Berlin's north-eastern periphery, the towers had rapidly disintegrated across the early 1990s, along with their alcohol- and Nazism-preoccupied populations. While most of those towers had since been superficially re-surfaced, in lurid colours, the red star of the Sojus Kino's facade emanated a profoundly disparate time, as though an invisible barrier now deflected all habitual perception from that cinema's surfaces, and deterred their use as a graffiti screen. Alongside the cinema building, an additional, free-standing hoarding still stood beside the Allee der Kosmonauten, equipped with a plastic membrane on which large-scale film-posters had once been affixed; unlike the cinema's facade, that membrane had attracted violent assaults, and had been pierced-through, so that it formed another in the multitude of shattered, transparent urban eyes, that now constituted vital apertures for the visions of Berlin. Through both sides of that aperture, the re-surfaced apartment-towers identically appeared, as though transmitting their facades towards one another, and back again, in oscillation, across Marzahn's precariously sliding terrain.

Stefan Hoenerloh's paintings of immense but corporeally-voided cities, with corroded and scarred facades, emanate that same aura of cinema-surfaces protectively carapaced by their abandonment, as well as by the capacity of abandonment to undergo imminent mutations that will engender unprecedented urban formations. Hoenerloh's paintings of intricately disintegrated urban surfaces always resonate with their origin in Berlin, even though the cities in his paintings are cinematically self-projected, imaginary entities, whose multi-lingual titles often indicate an obsession with film, as well as with worldwide urban terrains of dereliction and uproar. In *The Knarz House, Ten Years Later* (2001), Hoenerloh intimates the jolts of time

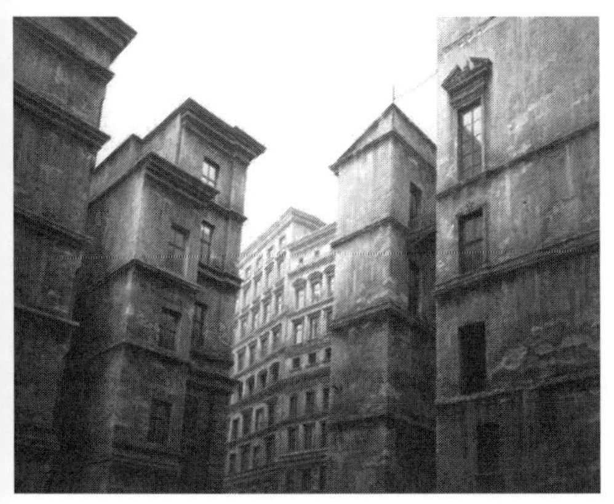

which also unhinge the Sojus Kino from its contemporary moment, and the painting's buildings manifest layerings of urban surfaces; upon one abrasured facade, the glass and frame of a window have somehow disappeared, and all that remains is a rawly open aperture – one that looks directly into darkness, rather than the transparent membrane of the Sojus Kino's pierced hoarding. Hoenerloh's Berlin-infused imaginary cities form near-filmic apparitions, in which abandonment is the determining urban experience.

On a glass partition within the cinema's foyer, its final ticket-seller or usherette had attached a schematic crayon drawing of the Sojus Kino on its day of closure, the cinema itself and its stick-figured staff resiliently outlined against the adjacent Marzahn apartment-towers. For the attention of any covert entrant into that derelict cinematic space, a text accompanying the drawing noted that it had been a wonderful cinema, and that the experience of abandoning it, at the very moment in which that drawing was attached to the glass partition, was one of extreme loss. The foyer was constellated with alcohol bottles and a scattered detritus of indeterminate origin, but the screen inside the auditorium remained intact. It appeared that, for the inhabitants of Marzahn, the red-starred surface of that cinema resisted or negated its own perception, and the distinctive status held by cinemas worldwide – since the moment when the Skladanowsky Brothers first conjured a cinema, at Berlin's Wintergarten Ballroom in 1895 – as sites of urban ecstasy and captivation, had now almost passed from recognition, for many of those inhabitants. Abandonment possesses its own seminal power of urban transformation, and at the imminent moment when that perception of the building as a 'cinema' slipped-away entirely, the Sojus Kino would immediately take on a new entity, as that of an experimental laboratory for the exploration of the future forms of human vision and memory.

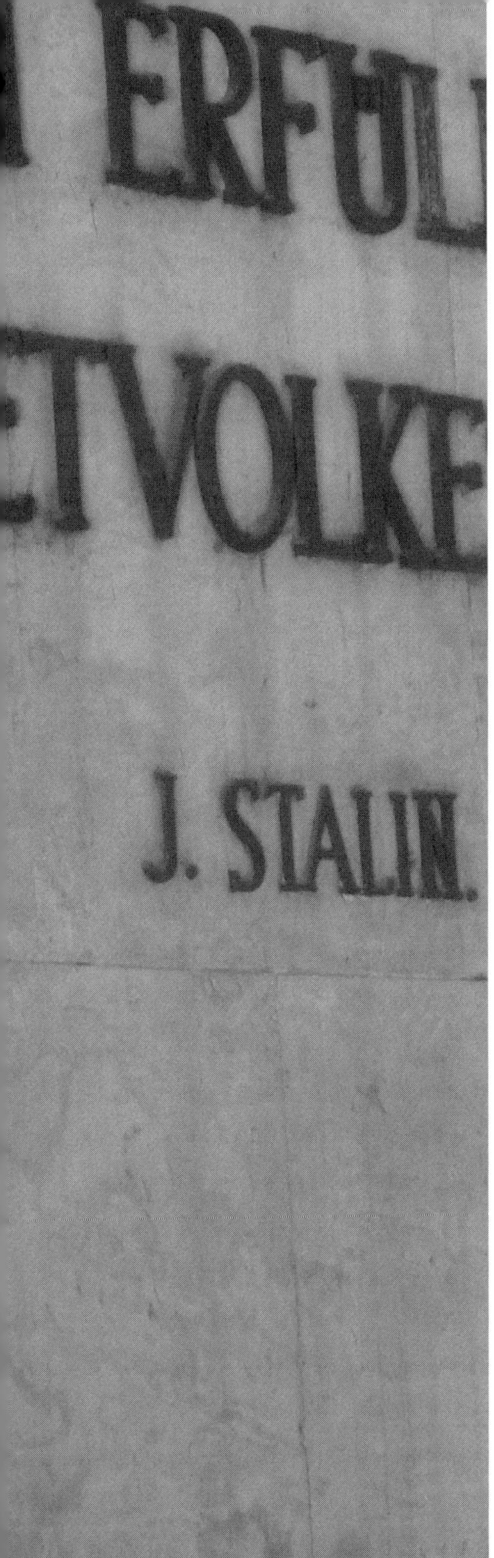

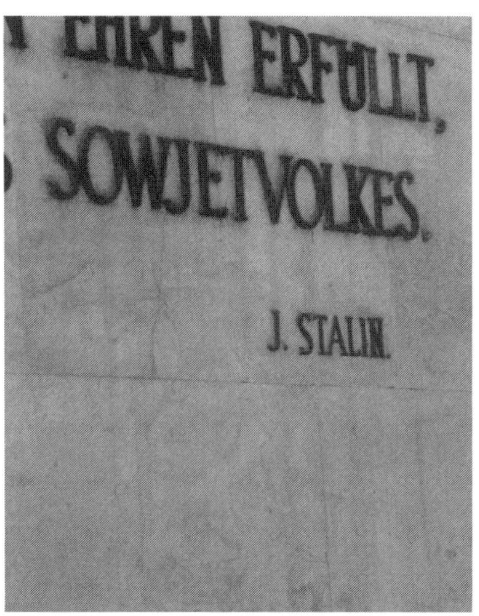

16

At the Schönholz memorial terrain, where many thousands of the Russian soldiers killed during the fall of Berlin were buried in sarcophagi alongside a massive granite stele, further red stars made their apparition from the city's surfaces. As with the Sojus Kino's emptied-out grey sarcophagus of its ex-spectators' cinematic obsessions, those memorial surfaces appeared to constitute another zone now excised from the city, but whose constellations of red stars intimated that the preoccupation with urban decimation which had propelled those tombs' young inhabitants, across the face of Europe, towards Berlin, still possessed an incendiary power, that switched between the overheated and the glacial, beyond death, as between the red and blue stars of those two cinemas, and retained a seminal resonance of volatile historical transformation, for the contemporary city. On either side of the entrance to the memorial-zone, two matching rooms had been constructed, lined with white marble. The ceiling of each room had been surfaced with lead-divided stained-glass segments, depicting an image of the globe with a vast hammer-and-sickle superposed over it, the hammerhead poised above Berlin, and surmounted by a red star. In one of those rooms, the image remained vividly intact, while the other room's image had perversely faded to the point of near-disappearance, as though – as with the Skladanowsky Brothers' dual-lens 'Bioskop' projector – only one image could transmit its vital content, while the other image had to be blocked-out, its content effaced. On the walls of each of the two rooms, texts ascribed to Stalin, from his daily orders to the three marshals who commanded the assault on Berlin, had been traced in lead letters; in one room, the letters of Stalin's own name had vanished, as though they had formed a graffiti inscription whose horror demanded its annulling, while in the room whose glass-ceiling image remained intact, Stalin's name still manifested itself, as though with indelible power. To maintain the fragile equilibrium of historical oblivion, across Berlin's awry urban facades, every act of erasure has to be doubled with its inverse act, so that the glaring aberration of Stalin's name still mediated itself from that surface.

Once Stalin lands in Berlin, in Chiaureli's semi-fictional film *The Fall of Berlin*, mere moments after the capture of the Reichstag and abruptly interrupting the wild, graffiti-signalled celebrations being enacted in front of it, he approaches the lined-up commanders to whom his orders inscribed in the Schönholz rooms were addressed – Zhukov, Konev and Sokolovsky – and nonchalantly thanks them for their 'work', as though that beaming trio were being rewarded for organising the alcohol-fuelled mayhem surrounding the Reichstag's portal, rather than for choreographing the colossal destruction of Berlin and its attendant programmes of mass-reprisals and rape, inflicted on the city's surviving population. Throughout *The Fall of*

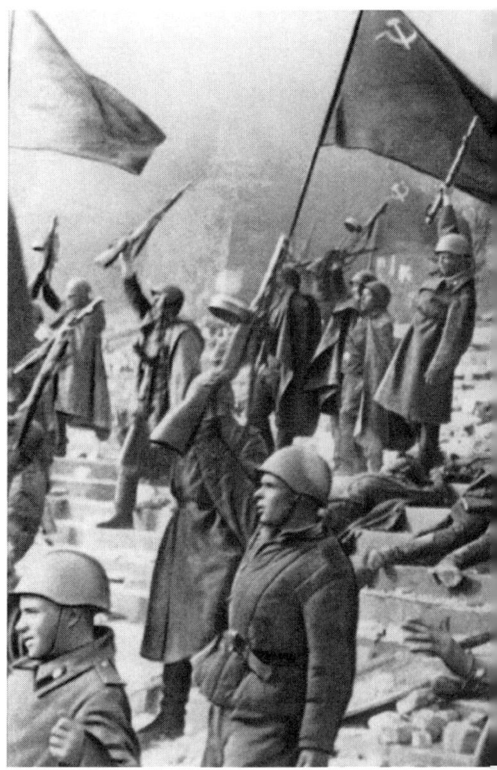

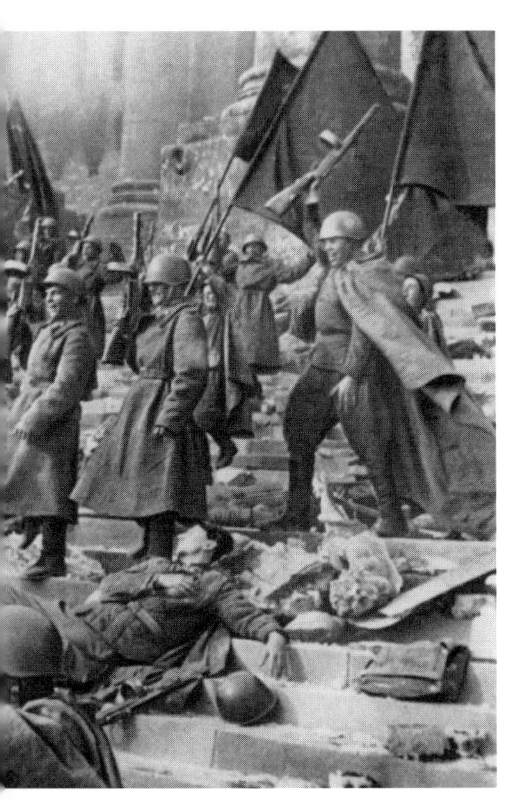

Berlin, Stalin appears detachedly bemused by the ongoing events, as though he were himself watching a film whose narrative constitutes an intractable mystery, that barely merits a solution; when he is informed by telephone of Hitler's suicide in the Chancellery bunker, he calmly asks for Hitler's 'motive'. The filmic fall of Berlin projects itself as an event around which great activity and conflict collects, but which finally appears to be generated internally, as though the capricious surfaces of the city themselves work compulsively to engender their own obliteration and self-wounding, while Stalin's own pre-eminent preoccupation is not focused on that 'event', but with carefully synchronising his white-uniformed figure and facial profile against decorative arrangements of wind-blown, red-starred Soviet flags.

Most of the young soldiers of the Schönholz memorial-zone were buried in collective sarcophagi; archival images show their rough wooden coffins being collected for re-burial from temporary red-earth pits, usually located wherever the soldiers had died, in mid-battle. But directly behind the towering stele which formed that terrain's centrepiece, two or three of the individual lead plaques, commemorating the names and dates of death of those of Stalin's senior commanders who were killed during the assault on Berlin, had been ripped from the stele's side, leaving behind blank facades, that led directly into darkness, like the removed window in Hoenerloh's painting *The Knarz House, Ten Years Later*, through the medium of four deep holes from the nails which had once secured those plaques to the concrete underpinning the stele's granite carapace. At first, it appeared that those plaques had vanished of their own accord, through the caprices of historical oblivion, or else had deteriorated over decades, in that semi-neglected terrain, to the point that their nails had wilfully jettisoned themselves, thereby creating blank but revelatory screens, in the place of those plaques. But it was evident from the traces of crowbar-bucklings, at the corners of adjacent, more obstinate plaques, that thieves of history had, at some point over the past decades, wrenched-out the nails and stolen those plaques (with any intrusive eyes manoeuvred away from that covert act by its location directly behind the stele), along with the lead-lettering of Stalin's name in the room whose global-domination glass-ceiling image had also been lost.

The conjuring-away of what had once appeared ineradicable texts, images and names of power, from the Schönholz memorial-zone, intimated the urban overturnings that are integral to Berlin's surfaces. Whatever appears pivotal can instantly be transformed into the detrital. Just as Stalin, in *The Fall of Berlin*, disregards the all-engulfing urban and corporeal excesses of the city's fall and its attendant, innumerable acts of sexual assault, in order to compose his facial profile for optimum iconic visualisation, the surfaces of Berlin may themselves fluctuate acutely, between their profound historical scarification and the visual ecstasies of the contemporary instant, and then back again. But in the silent and untouched twin of that memorial terrain's dual entry-way rooms, below the glass-imprinted image of a violently subjugated world, Stalin's name enduringly projected itself outwards from its white-marble wall, as though it could still whisper urban commands, in one-word outbursts, even within the sonic furore of Berlin.

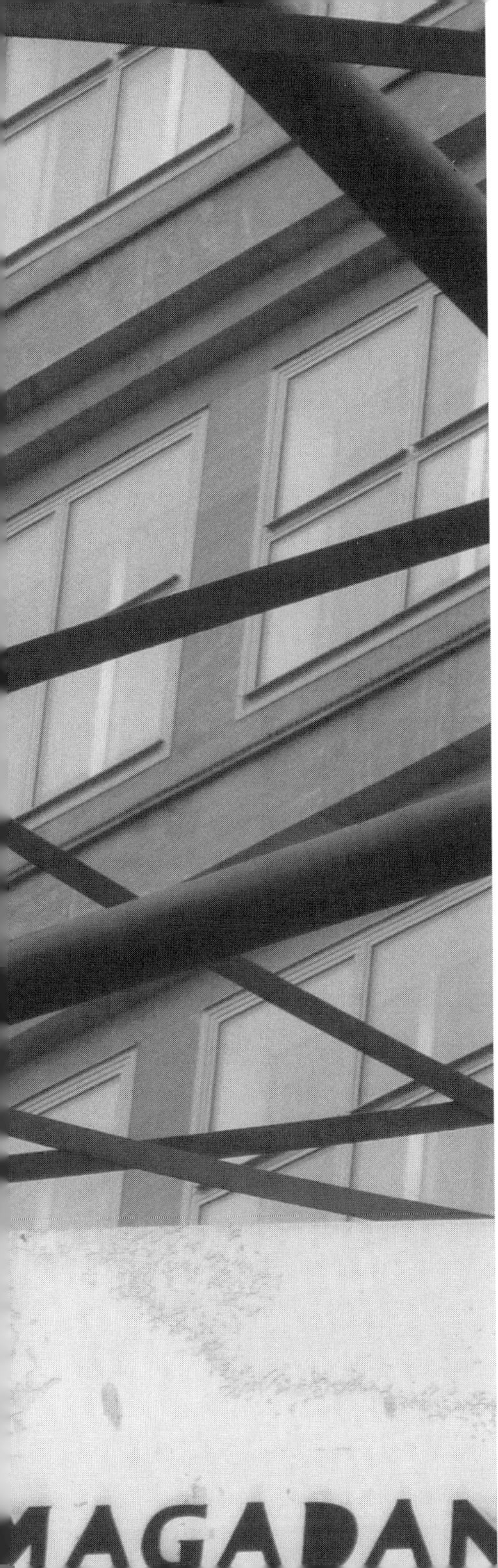

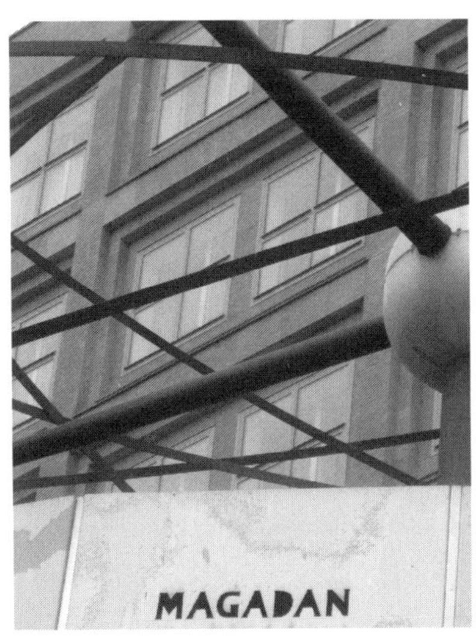

17

On the aluminium-plated surface of the Urania-Clock, which formed one of the pivotal sites of the Alexanderplatz, the name of a city other than Berlin had been inscribed: that of Magadan, the most legendary of Stalin's extermination cities, where millions of prisoners from many countries perished, on the far-eastern coast of Siberia, as though, from its origin in the lead-lettering of his name on the Schönholz memorial-zone's marbled wall, Stalin's tongue had extended outwards across Berlin, like that of a ghost in a Japanese horror-film, encircling the contemporary city in a python-like contortion, traversing the great east-west avenue which had also once held his name and his statue, and been dedicated to his glory, before finally reaching the Alexanderplatz, to exhale one of those whispered, one-word outbursts of power which are inscribed as seminal texts of the city. After the destruction in 1961 of the disgraced Stalin's statue, in the former Stalinallee, by then renamed the Karl-Marx-Allee, the debris had been collected, including a shard of his thick moustache, that was eventually exhibited in an adjacent cafe. But the urban facade of the Urania-Clock demonstrated that it was actually Stalin's tongue which had intractably marked the surfaces of Berlin, with its orders for urban decimation and reactivation, in the period from the fall of Berlin until his death in 1953, but also posthumously, through his phantasmatic and determining presence, as though the architects and reconfigurers of the present-day city, above all those concerned to instil its corporate surfaces with triumphal grandiosity, formed only vacuous mouthpieces, as urban oracles for an enduring inhabitation by Stalin's tongue. Many of the surfaces of those new corporate buildings, with their elevated digital screens, appeared only to be awaiting the enunciation of orders for their effortless amendment into technology-powered totalitarian configurations. In *The Fall of Berlin*, the actor Mikhail Gelovani, so closely identified with Stalin by playing him in numerous films that his appearance eventually superseded and supplanted Stalin's own hunched, pockmarked appearance, speaks with a playful, humorous Georgian accent, as he thanks his uniformed trio of stooges for their work; but that playful tongue is also one whose succinct power precipitates violent human and urban transformations and annullings, on an all-engulfing scale.

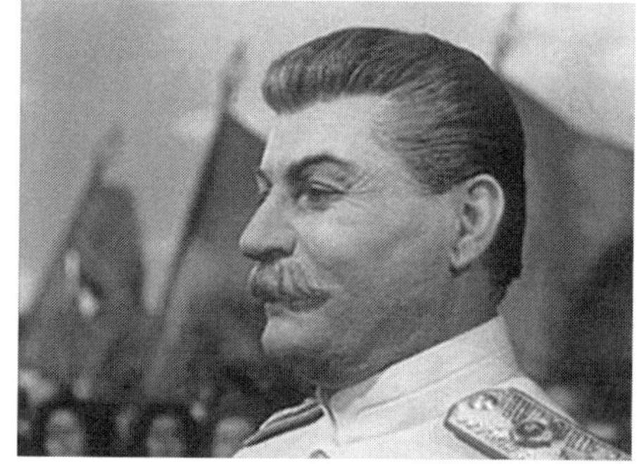

The Alexanderplatz's Urania-Clock, like that of the derelict Stralau glass-factory, possessed no face and no hands; it had been activated during one of the intermittent mutations of that vast plaza, in 1969, at the same moment as the adjacent Television Tower, in order to project the time of Berlin in circular revolutions, with its aluminium-panelled facade, imprinted with the names of cities, gradually spinning to create its own vertiginous urban time, its form surmounted by an interconnected astrological constellation of planets and stars which intimated that, in Berlin's infinite oscillations between glacial blue stars and overheated red stars, an architecture of celestial dissection constituted an essential urban requirement. As well as forming a one-word death-exclamation voiced from Stalin's tongue – as indicative of global butchery as Brando's tongue, terminally whispering of horror, and again, of horror, in Coppola's film *Apocalypse Now!* – the name of Magadan appeared also to have been inscribed upon that surface as a civic endeavour, at that site of optimum visibility on the Alexanderplatz, in order to announce to the eyes of its inhabitants a 'twin-city' initiative, by which Berlin had been coupled with Magadan, to recognise their key role as two extreme urban destination-points, for the movement and the erasure of history and memory.

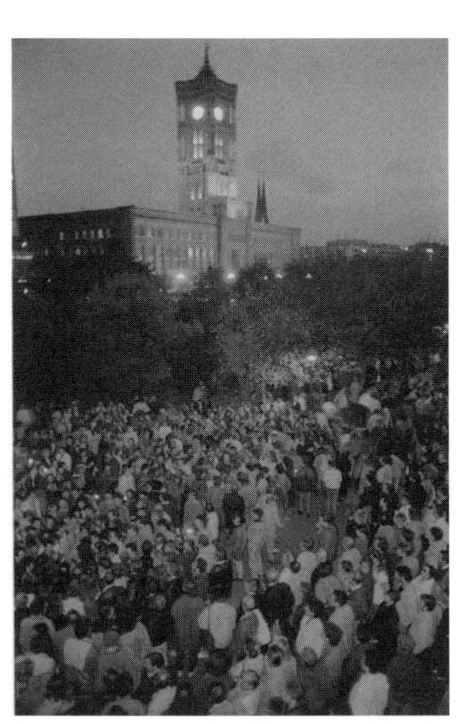

The Alexanderplatz had always been an axis manifesting Berlin's innumerable knife-edged shifts, between urban opulence and its wartime incineration; between the vocal and the visual; between immense gatherings of human figures (such as that amassed there on the morning of 4 November 1989, to repudiate the GDR's political petrifaction) and vastly windswept, unfillable emptiness; and between all-consuming architectural ambition and its obsolescence or overlayering. Film, including amateur footage, has often been the medium used to trace the ways in which the Alexanderplatz may constitute an aberrant fissure, that cracks-apart ambitions for homogeneity in Berlin's urban surfaces, seeping unrest or vocal eruptions. Amateur video-footage shot on the Alexanderplatz on the night of 2-3 October 1990, that of Germany's reunification, recorded chaotic riots on the Alexanderplatz, staged against that historical event then being triumphantly celebrated across the rest of the city, especially in the ceremonies around the Brandenburg Gate; the rioters appeared to form non-cohered splinters of unease (protesters disputing the just-accomplished conjuring-away of the GDR, alongside anarchist, neo-Nazi and neo-Communist factions), until water-cannons unceremoniously swept away all of that fractured urban detritus, to the plaza's far perimeters, in an undifferentiated flood, like that propelling away Berlin's inundated population in Heldt's drawing *Köpfe in Ruinenmeer*. The Alexanderplatz collects and disgorges the filmic and visual traces of vital urban incoherence.

Immediately behind the Magadan-inscribed revolving clock, the streamlined concrete form of the 'Alexanderhaus' building – constructed at the end of the 1920s as an office-block, and redeployed as an austere GDR department-store after surviving wartime bomb-damage – had originated at the moment of spatial mutation which forms the urban core of Piel Jutzi's 1931 film *Berlin Alexanderplatz*. At several points, the film's narrative is suspended, and in lengthy sequences, Jutzi simply films the Alexanderplatz itself, then undergoing its vast rebuilding work, with both subterranean subway-excavations and the assembly of its new towers, alongside the ongoing human flux and gestures of its in-transit inhabitants. The German film industry's sound technology was then still at a formative stage, and Jutzi's maladroit recording of Berlin's intricate sonic textures – traffic noise, drilling and hammering, voices, all oscillating between loud and low volumes – together with his askew editing of that soundscape against the film's shots of urban reconstruction, produced another of the great incoherent manifestations of the Alexanderplatz. The figure at the heart of the Alexanderplatz's flux is Heinrich George as his character Biberkopf, who, contrary to every other figure in that teeming space, stands his ground, for his sales-pitch in front of a construction-site's wooden facade that bears pasted hoardings both for luxuriously chandeliered nightclubs and USSR-supporting political demonstrations. Forming the inverse presence to the one-word, whispered exclamation of the murderous city-name of Magadan which imprints Stalin's indelible presence upon Berlin's contemporary time-machine surfaces, the top-hatted George – after carefully adjusting his tie – unleashes an unstoppable, endlessly voluble vocal exclamation.

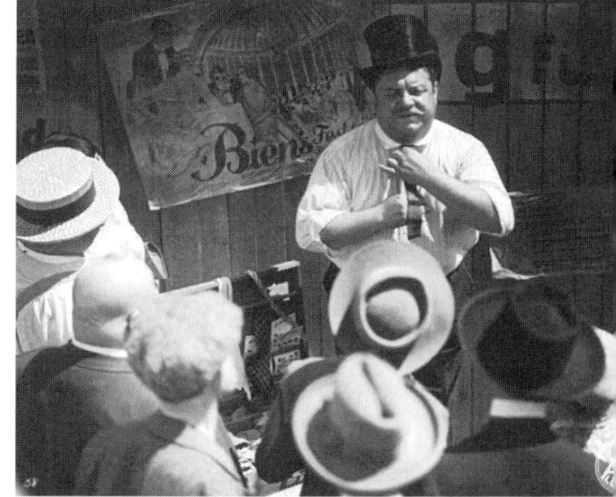

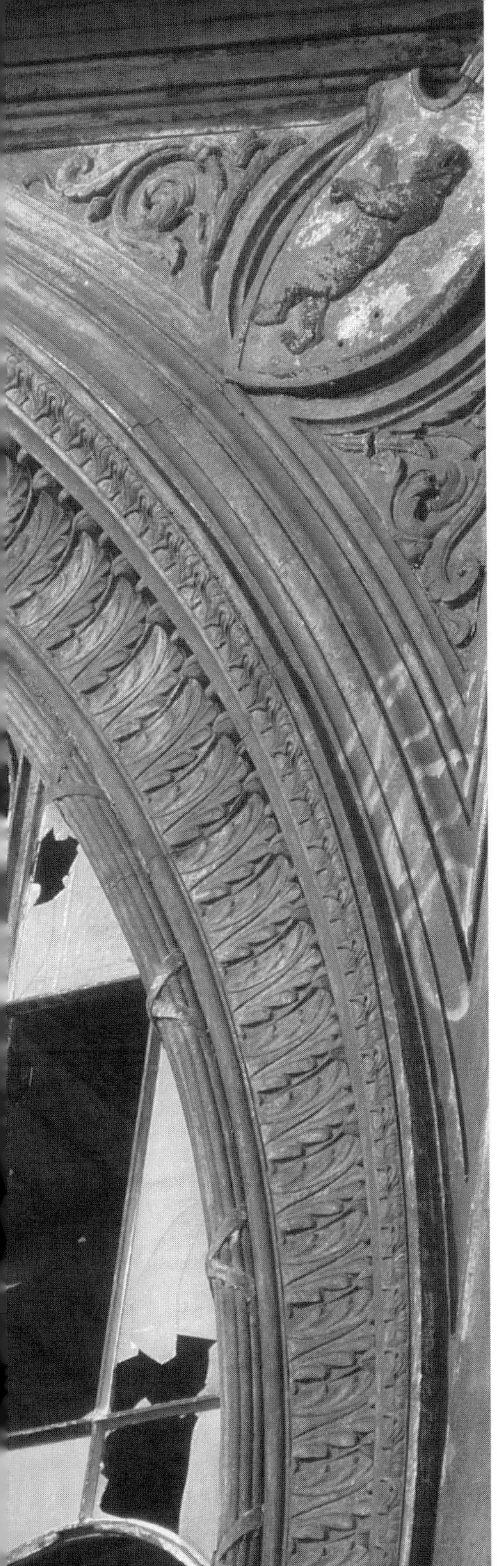

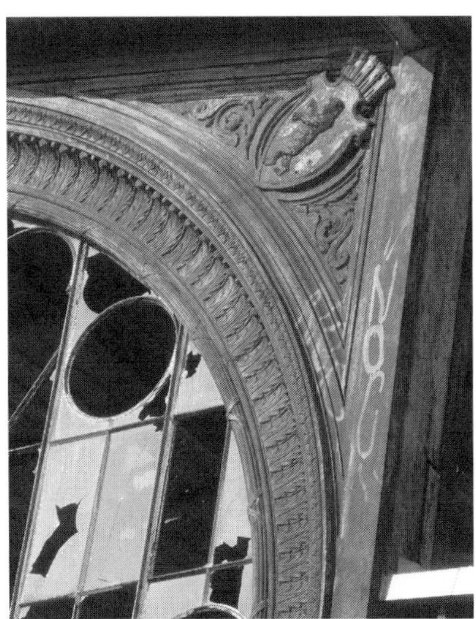

18

The final traces of an immense slaughterhouse sub-city within Berlin lay between the district of Friedrichshain and the railway tracks that looped around the city, with the ornate, rusted portal of the cattle-market pavilion holding the official urban insignia of Berlin, with its stunned-looking bear standing on its back legs, as though it had just received a bolt of electricity in the skull, and were now about to join the infinite number of animals slaughtered on that terrain, across more than a century. Berlin's slaughterhouse sub-city, the most vast and integrated of all of Europe's abattoir landscapes when it opened in 1881, appeared as another receptive candidate for 'twinning' with Stalin's Magadan, since both had now been near-erased (in Magadan's case, uniquely through that frozen site's coruscating climate, rather than any intention to cover-up the evidence of the untold millions of prisoners who died there); since its demolition had begun in 1991, the

Berlin slaughterhouse sub-city had been transformed into large tracts of churned ground, waterlogged and abandoned, and interspersed with shoddy new housing-blocks and the few surviving slaughterhouse pavilions, whose near-indestructible construction in red and yellow brick appeared to resist their final expunging from that terrain. The name of the slaughterhouse sub-city's architect, Hermann Blankenstein, had been attached to a road that skirted the site's periphery, as though that vast complex, otherwise textually voided, now possessed the name of its conceiver, just as the architect who had envisioned the great sub-city for Berlin's mad, Ludwig Hoffmann, in the northern suburb of Buch, two decades or so after the construction of Blankenstein's slaughterhouse sub-city, had his name enduringly attached to one of the asylum-buildings, in which Hitler's charred body, after its discovery following his suicide, was autopsied by Russian doctors who used the buildings as pathology laboratories. Those two seminal urban satellites – the sub-city of slaughter and the sub-city of the mad – incorporated within Berlin as sensitised but powerfully eruptive presences, had been erased or else consigned to neglect, within the contemporary city's configuration; but those sub-cities' surviving traces and surfaces intimated that, in an oscillating variant of the contemporary city (like that of the closed lens of the Skladanowsky Brothers' projector, which permitted the other lens to open, but which could just as well have itself been open), they had possessed the irrepressible capacity to expand and finally engulf the remainder of Berlin's space, rendering it entirely a city of slaughter and madness, renamed 'Blankenstein-Hoffmann City', and rivalling Stalin's Magadan as an embodiment of Europe's urban history and memory.

High up on the portal of Blankenstein's emptied-out cattle-market pavilion, the rusted figure of Berlin's emblematic bear had been positioned at an askew angle, in order to fit into the ornate corner between the portal's glass facade and its roof, so that the bear appeared, in its stunned state, to be already falling backwards, into dreaming unconsciousness. Below that bear's insignia, two shreds of now-faded graffiti had been traced, as evidence that, at some point in the past, through a mysterious act of urban compulsion, it had been necessary for a human figure to climb precariously to the summit of that slaughterhouse-portal, and inscribe the text 'NOC' twice upon it, vertically along the portal's exterior metal strut, and then again, in densely concertinaed letters, around the curved boundary of the glass facade, as though, for that place of horror, as in Brando's whispered exhalation, a text demanded to be inscribed twice over. The delicate metal frame of the glass-faced portal had, along with other shapes, held two circular panes, each of them now shattered and voided of all traces of glass, like two apertures which needed to be rendered equivalently transparent, through repeated throwings of stones, in order for the total horror of their content to be emitted. Alternatively, the inscriber of the graffiti on that facade might well have taken on the additional urban mission of removing the entirety of the glass from that slaughterhouse surface's dual lens, so that the two circular frames now served to resonate, in a visual match, with the letter 'O' in the adjacent graffiti inscriptions.

The rusted carapace of the slaughterhouse's cattle-market was all that remained of the building, which had been comprehensively gutted, like the bodies of animals first bartered there and then assigned the locations for their subsequent killings. In Döblin's 1929 novel *Berlin Alexanderplatz*, from which both Jutzi and Fassbinder drew their films, the scale of the slaughter undertaken in Blankenstein's Berlin sub-city is carefully enumerated in statistical data (the costs of the complex's construction, the numbers of the animals consumed by that avaricious sub-city, and the details of its spatial expanse), alongside sequences that explore the corporeal parallels between those animals' ephemeral transit through the

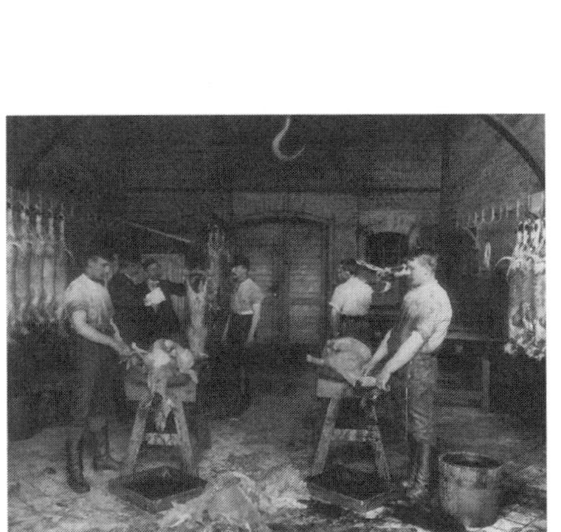

buildings, in a fog of blood, and Biberkopf's own progressive 'slaughter' within Berlin, after his release from the Tegel prison, along with that suffered by his lover, Mieze, who is battered to death (for Döblin, like a rope-led calf tenderly slaughtered in Blankenstein's sub-city) by Biberkopf's associate, Reinhold, in the forests at the edge of Berlin; the human and the animal are intractably meshed together, although Biberkopf retains enough non-animal traits to finally be expelled northwards, in Döblin's novel, to the sub-city of the mad, in Buch, as though he were inhabiting that aberrant variant of Berlin in which only urban traversals from zones of slaughter into madness were viable ones. Jutzi's 1931 film elides that final journey (although Jutzi's Biberkopf, the actor Heinrich George, made his own northwards journey of expulsion from Berlin, fourteen years later, to the Sachsenhausen 'special' internment-camp), but in the epilogue to Fassbinder's 1980 thirteen-part film, *Berlin Alexanderplatz*, Biberkopf's experience of catatonic trauma in the Buch asylum is one still pivotally inhabited by slaughterhouse imageries, in which his body is meat-hooked and heaped-up with others, for dismemberment (and, in other sequences, heaped-up for collective sexual encounters, as though Berlin's sexual acts were invariably conducted under slaughterhouse regimes), overseen by the figure of Fassbinder himself, who presents the epilogue's title as his 'dream' of Biberkopf's own Berlin 'dream', of an upended urban journey that oscillates from slaughterhouse to asylum, and back again.

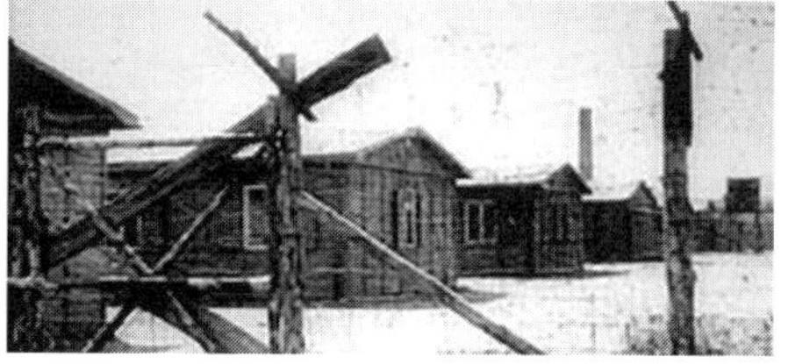

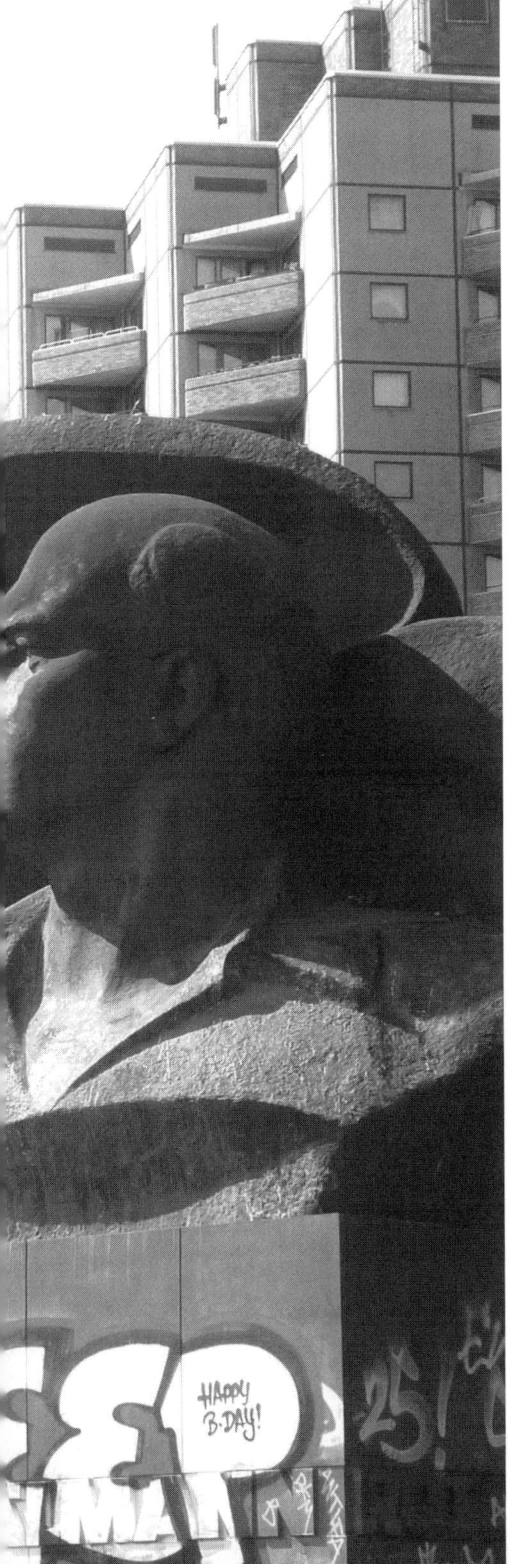

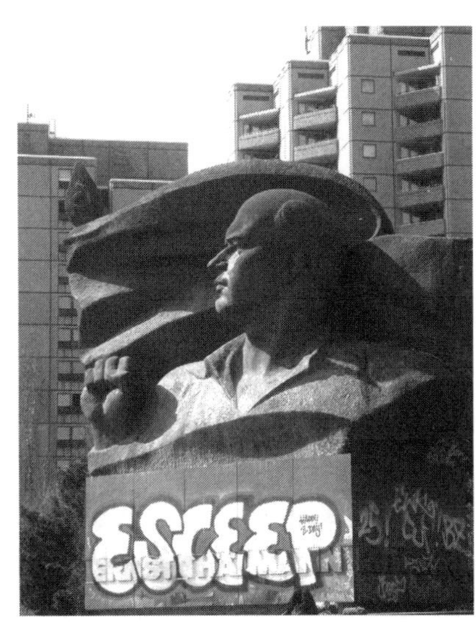

19

Against the urban surfaces of Berlin, other enduring figures of slaughter made their apparitions, often performing gestures of power or anger, as though the hallucinatory interzones positioned between Berlin's sub-cities of the slaughtered and the mad formed aberrant sites for the instigation of urban transmutations and impacts. In front of a constellation of prefabricated highrise apartment-towers, alongside the railway tracks extending from Blankenstein's slaughterhouse remnants, an immense statue of Berlin's 1920s Communist leader, Ernst Thälmann, had been installed by the GDR authorities in 1986, shortly before that country's abrupt vanishing, as with the metal plinths on the Karl-Marx-Forum plaza that held the image of Berlin's hardhatted generator of urban obsessions, as though those statues and plinths had been constructed exclusively to serve as mysterious steles of oblivion, in the event that they miraculously survived the oncoming disappearance of the city around them. Thälmann had been arrested by Hitler's police almost immediately after the Nazis' rise to power in 1933, but had remained poised in solitary confinement, in prisons and concentration-camps, as a living figure of imminent but stalled slaughter, until Hitler finally gave the order for his offhanded execution in 1944. The statue of Thälmann as a figure of glorious resistance, his facial profile cinematically backed by a windblown Soviet flag like those framing Stalin in *The Fall of Berlin*, had itself pivoted between imminent obliteration and neglect throughout the decades since the GDR's own erasure, its colossal form preserved in part due to the excessive costs which its detonation would entail for the present-day city, and also through its graffitied base's optimum role as a horizontal resting-place for schnapps-incapacitated dwellers of the site. In the time before the statue's construction, the site had been that of an equally monumental gasworks complex whose razing, through a sequence of detonations, in 1984, had engendered one of the city's great sonic outbursts, like Biberkopf's Alexanderplatz vocal glossolalia, immersing the adjoining districts in a swirling layer of debris and toxic dust, as though to smokescreen the city's surface in advance of the conjuring-trick that would generate the figure of Thälmann.

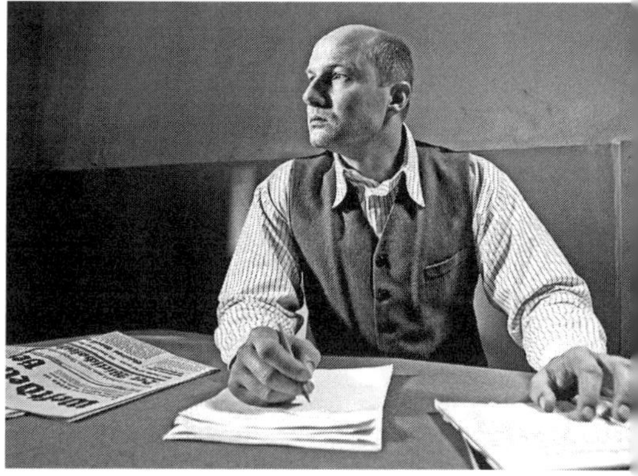

Thälmann's fist, in its gesture of power, appeared to emerge directly from his statue's shoulder, as the result of a perverse anatomical reconfiguration which had excised his arm altogether, and thereby inflected that fist-gesture with an awry dimension, performed at too low an altitude to successfully project a spectacular momentum able to dominate the political dynamics of the city, and resonant, instead, of a fist about to be deployed in a sexual scenario. That fist also possessed a cinematic inflection extending beyond that of the visual choreographing of power which it shared with *The Fall of Berlin*, as though it had abruptly burst-through Thälmann's own body, like a horror-film alien whose irrepressible manifestation into urban space is designed to open-wide all spectating eyes in terror. A graffiti inscription in huge white spray-can letters, 'ESCEEP', had supplanted the name of Thälmann on the statue's base, which served as a pre-eminent screen for the transmission of urgent texts into the surrounding urban space, able even to penetrate the schnapps-induced comas of the base's occupants; the colour of the statue-base matched that of Blankenstein's now-rusted slaughterhouse-pavilion metalwork facade, and the white-lettered text it held constituted the latest in an almost infinite lineage of inscriptions that had been positioned below Thälmann's fist, commencing, in the early 1990s, as intricate narrations of conflicts between neo-Nazi and neo-Communist factions, and then serving either as commentaries on that statue's intended aura of power, or else as acts of oblivion towards it.

From the vantage-point of the plaza created in front of it, conceived for rallies and ceremonies, Thälmann's statue had been positioned directly against the groupings of shoddy apartment-towers, which dated from the moment of its own construction. In that juxtaposition of the corporeal with the urban, the low-strung trajectory of Thälmann's ineffectual fist-gesture intimated a constrained, short-range impact of fury, necessarily exerted against those apartment-tower facades, as though the collective status shared by that corporeal figure and the cracked-panelled buildings behind it – forming equivalently surpassed and memory-voided urban entities – did not serve to protect those towers' surfaces from a final, drained projection of anger. Even with all emanations of power squeezed-out from that fist, it still demanded an oppositional conjoining with those friable surfaces, in order to perform its afterlife gesture of urban subjugation.

Once all of the great conflictual pairings that generated the dynamic political charge originally assigned to Thälmann's statue become levelled, and made equivalent, that figure is incapacitated, in anticipation of its own eventual razing from the face of the city, like that of the gasworks complex which preceded it on that site, and also, in its denudation, is rendered open to being phantasmatically inhabited by all images from art or film which foreground a corporeal figure poised in tension against a backdrop of Berlin's urban surfaces. In George Grosz's painting *Der Mädchenhändler* (*The Dealer in Girls*), from 1918, the fraudulently elegant pimp, operating in Berlin in the chaos of the war's end, is shown against a compacted cityscape of exploded and apocalyptic building-facades, into which components of prostitutional flesh are deeply embedded. Seated below the maleficent red sun of Berlin, Grosz's pimp has no need to demonstrate or enact his power, other than through the elegance of his suit; his fists rest in immobility on the cafe-table in front of him, although the back of one fist bears the wound of a traversal slicing, indicating that, at some past moment, his enmeshing within Berlin's strata of power took on a different form, and while that pimp's figure appears static, his eyes wildly veer, as though they were engulfed in the detonating and disintegrating city behind him, which serves uniquely as a medium for his sexual visions and urban scars, just as the brittle apartment-tower landscape located directly behind Thälmann's statue now exists solely to form a potential impact-zone, for that figure's raised but displaced fist.

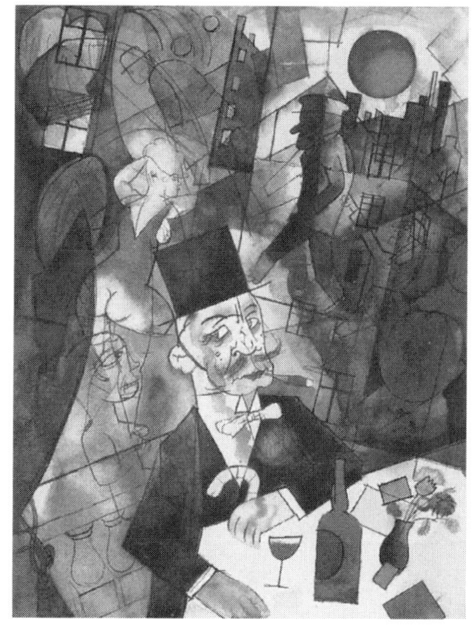

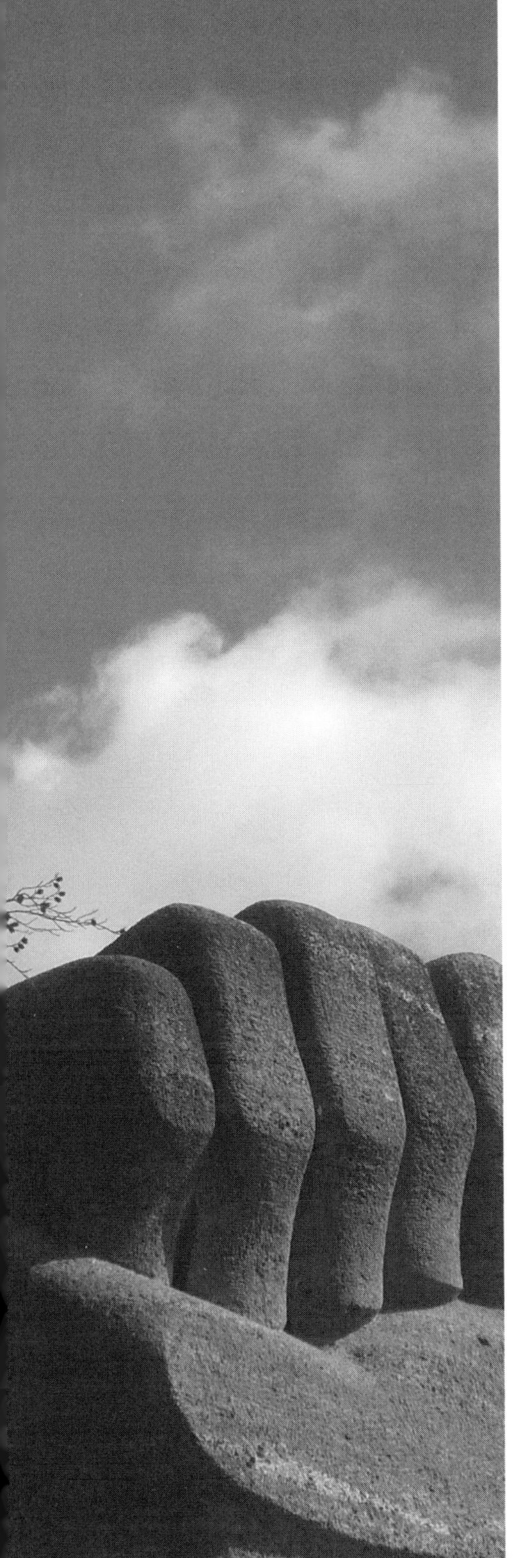

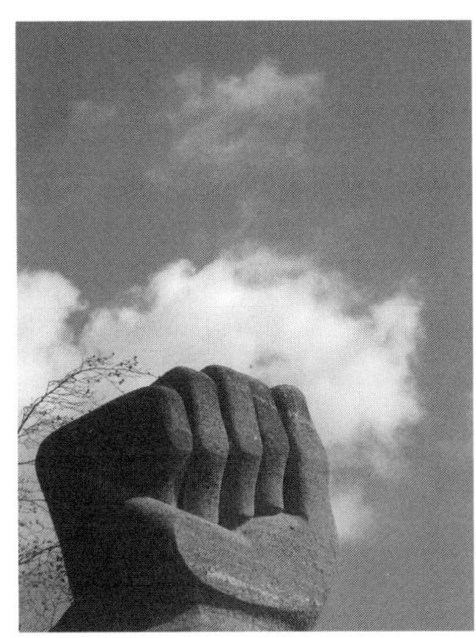

20

Rising from the river's edge in the district of Köpenick, another fist had been launched from Berlin's slaughter-terrain, but while Thälmann's clenched fist, uprooted in the contemporary city, still possessed an ostensible target for its askew gesture, in the fissured facades of the adjacent apartment-towers, the anonymous fist of Köpenick ascended vertically out of the ground, from a concrete pedestal, and appeared to be directed towards Berlin's skies, or at the celestial red and blue stars that watched over the city's erased memories, as though all potential urban or human targets for gestures of fury or subjugation had been exhausted, but the compulsion still to deliver those gestures of power perversely endured, even when projected into a void. That concrete fist had originally arisen from the memory of another of Berlin's infinite acts of slaughter, during the 'Blood-Week' of June 1933, in which the Nazi paramilitary forces, exhilarated by their recent seizure of power, had terrorised that district, torturing and killing all those of its inhabitants who might potentially prove incompatible with the future Nazi regime. The fist had been erected in 1969, by the GDR authorities, at a moment when its skyward movement could still be understood as intimating the ascent into divine glory of the GDR's self-serving regime. But in its site's subsequent abandonment, and the erosion or jettisoning of any texts that had once accompanied it, that fist had fallen through all strata of history and memory, to take on its status as a memorial to oblivion, equivalently glorifying both the power of the Nazi paramilitaries who elatedly slaughtered the inhabitants of Köpenick, in their role as seminal urban-exterminators prefiguring the coming years' Europe-wide mass-eradications of cities' populations, and also the power of the GDR authorities who had propelled that fist skyward, as though presciently envisioning the momentum of the Soyuz 31 rocket which would carry Sigmund Jähn into outer-space, almost a decade later. The nameless fist, its concrete fingers still honed and streamlined despite its decades of dereliction, now launched itself vertically from Berlin's urban surfaces as a decapitated but still virulent organ of power, negating without exception all of the city's 'official' memorials and monuments; that fist was no longer constrained to weld itself to any specific history, category or human experience, and instead now possessed the infinite capacity to vacuum all manifestations of power into itself, and incorporate them into its vertical momentum, in order to project its status as a monument to the future of slaughter.

On Berlin's urban surfaces, emanations of power often appear conjoined in haywire juxtapositions and entanglements, veering across time and visually activated by resonances of slaughter, their contents alternately oscillating between the excessive and the bleached-out, so that the only coherent direction for the trajectory of human vision may be a vertical one, like that followed by the Köpenick concrete-fist. The act of looking upwards in Berlin, from street-level, enables the pinpointing and collection of detached images that permit moments of an ocular lull: the ornately sculpted faces of indifferent deities at the summits of nineteenth-century facades; piratical or anarchistic black-flags still flying from the roofs of buildings, in tatters, decades after the expulsion by the police of the squatters who once occupied those buildings; indelibly tea-painted hoardings for enterprises which ceased to exist, untold years ago; and upside-down graffiti inscriptions painted by hands precariously hovering over the precipices of forty-storey apartment-towers. Even though each rooftop image may still carry its own distinctive visual resonance, of power or subjugation, that ocular act – of a vertical ascent from the city's ground-level surfaces – allows the overcharged power-dynamics, so deeply engrained into Berlin's walls, to momentarily seep away.

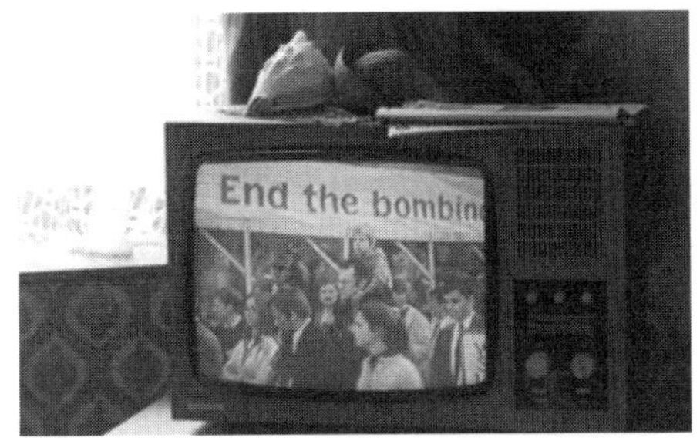

In Matti Geschonneck's film *Boxhagener Platz* (2010), set around the crumbling apartment-buildings of the Friedrichshain district of East Berlin in 1968, a policeman's restless wife covertly watches television images of the street-riots and protests against the Vietnam war that are ongoing at that moment in West Berlin; but almost all of the film's other characters appear equally indifferent both to those worlds-away images of West Berlin, and also to those that acclaim the GDR's leaders, Ulbricht and Stoph, as those characters' preoccupations remain locked in vitriolic feuds that propel them backwards to time, towards the political chaos of the period immediately following the First World War – the moment of Grosz's urban-hallucinating 'dealer of girls' – and the scrambled origins of Berlin's Nazi and Communist factions. Those irresoluble feuds eventually lead to the killing of an ex-Nazi shopkeeper and to the incarceration and death of a former member of the left-wing Spartacist movement, which had generated its own Berlin street-riots, in 1919.

The manifestations of those conflictual variants of power are observed with bewilderment by the policeman's twelve-year-old son, Holger, whose schoolteachers approvingly project to their pupils photographic slides showing Russian tanks crushing that same year's protests in the avenues of Prague. Finally, all of that swirling and maleficent history evanesces in the perception of Holger, as he locates a zone of momentary respite in the silence of the district's cemetery, above which the almost-completed Television Tower – rising from the Alexanderplatz and still so new (not yet inaugurated by the GDR regime) that it carries no apparent trace of the excesses of history that submerge Berlin's ground-level surfaces – forms a medium of vision into the future.

The ascendant digital image-screens and hoardings, poised high above Berlin's contemporary plazas, such as the Potsdamerplatz, and designed to laud corporate insignia or to project animation-sequences extolling new products, also carry their own powerful captivations and ecstasies, for the eyes that scan and absorb them, from the city's ground-level. The installation of media of power in the sky above Berlin immediately places such digital hoardings within the intricate lineage that encompasses such gestures as that of the abandoned fist, emerging from the slaughter-imprinted terrain of Köpenick. Once that fist's accompanying texts are entirely effaced, and its specific history has become undifferentiated or lost, it constitutes a medium of pure visual spectacle, closely allied to that of the city's corporate digital-screens, but possessing the aberrant capacity to infiltrate, into the images projected from those screens, its own enduring aura of slaughter and power.

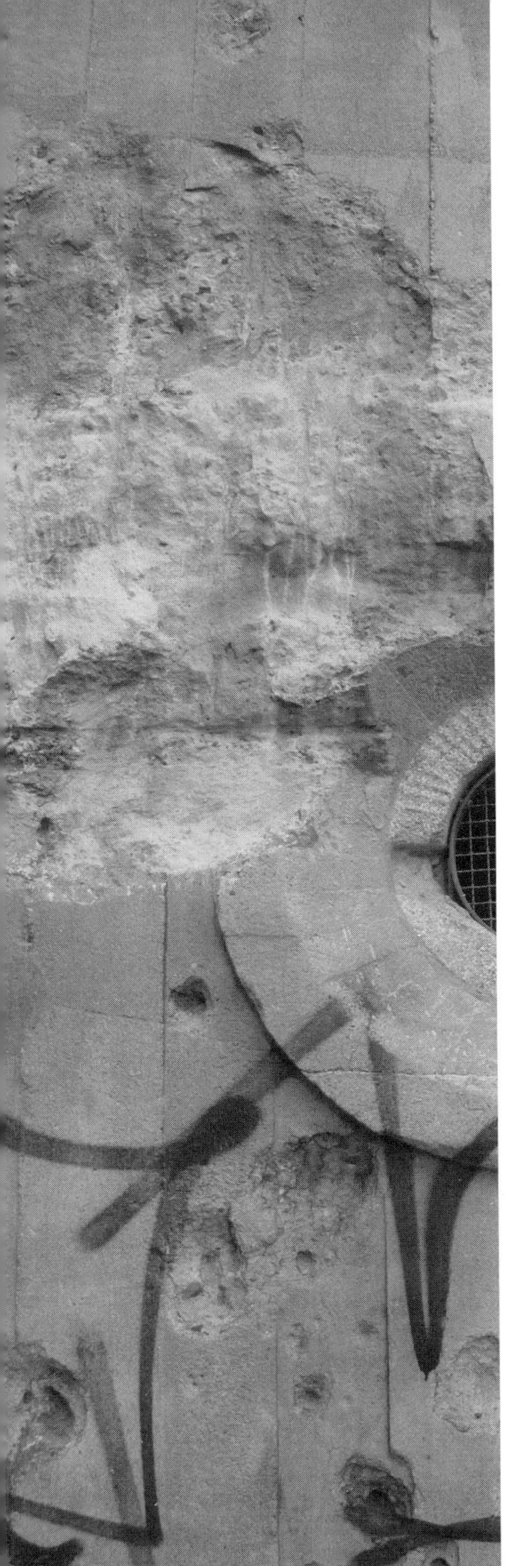

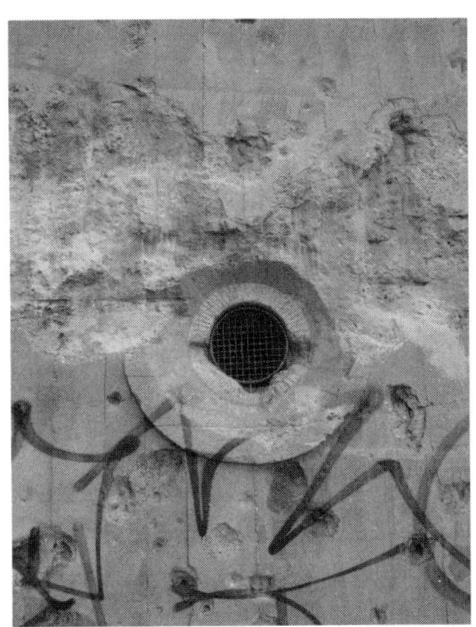

21

The abrasured eye traversing the city demands intervals of respite among Berlin's dense urban surfaces, as Holger discovers in the film *Boxhagener Platz*; a vertical ocular movement, directed towards the summit of the Alexanderplatz's Television Tower or a history-stripped concrete fist, may engender that respite, and even propel the eye further, through the neck-tilting manoeuvre that enables that ascent, into a blood-drained elation which contrasts with Berlin's ground-level slaughter. But a maximal respite is always generated by the eye's peering into its own urban image. Within the exterior wall of an overground bunker constructed in 1942 near the Friedrichstrasse railway station to shelter its bomb-threatened travellers, an eye-shaped orifice looked out into the city, and into its inhabitants' own eyes. That orifice, profoundly embedded within the bunker's reinforced concrete surface, was covered only by a wire-mesh, as though it could instantly filter-away the maleficent urban visions which any passers-by directed towards it, and then project those visions back out again, sieved of horror. Above and around that orifice, the bunker's surface-layers had been blasted-away by shrapnel damage, while the area below it held graffiti inscriptions, intimating that the surface belonged to two disparate moments: the upper level to an attempted obliteration of that orifice, and the lower level to its rapidly-imprinted embellishment. The spokes of serrated concrete bordering that orifice's arced lower perimeter evoked eye-lashes, although a shrapnel impact had excised those lashes' central section. The phosphorescent interior of the bunker had been transformed, after decades as a fruit and textiles warehouse in the GDR era, into a legendary hardcore sex-club, during whose pre-eminent moment of glory, in the early 1990s, acts of corporeal perforation had been relentlessly performed against extreme sonic cacophonies, unheard outside the bunker's reinforced walls, but still intimated by its surface's eye-penetrable aperture. Later, after police shut-downs of the club's black-tarred interior-walls and sweat-and-semen drenched floors, its raw sexual aura (which, during that evanescent era, also occupied several of the district's other derelict buildings, among them an abandoned margarine factory in the nearby Auguststrasse) had been voided; the space eventually accommodated itself to the presence of art-works, installed by a wealthy collector. Throughout those mutations, the bunker's meshed orifice looked out imperturbably, allowing incoming, scarred eyes momentarily to cocoon themselves within that opening.

The bunker's two-way eye indicated the pivotal status of such sensitised apertures, incised within Berlin's contemporary urban surfaces, as transit-points for conflictual historical journeys. The abrupt urban oscillation in Berlin between the Nazi and Communist eras, signalled by the text-denuded Köpenick fist, attained its optimum manifestation via such openings as the bunker-eye, through its ability to blissfully elide all jarring moments of passage between the divergent terrains of subjugation-intent political regimes, so that one side of the bunker-wall could hold the power of Nazism, and the other side, the power of Communism, with any orifice-traversing eye able to successively inhabit and absorb each of those irreconcilable zones of power. Whatever was once contrary, is visually sieved and levelled, in the contemporary city. The bunker-eye took the form of an 'impossible' aperture – as impossible as the projection of film-images had appeared, prior to the first deployment of the Skladanowsky Brothers' projector at the Wintergarten Ballroom, on the opposite side of the Friedrichstrasse station to the concrete bunker – with the capacity to transmit vision through, and between, historical zones that would otherwise stop the eye dead.

An essential element of that bunker-aperture's status, as an impossible, history-mutating medium of vision and perception, lay in its ability to transmit extreme shifts in urban sensations, alongside irreconcilable shifts in political power. Like the blue and red stars of the Blauer Stern and Sojus cinemas, that orifice could intimate a sudden switch between freezing cold and consuming heat, between the glacial temperature of its use as a storage-facility and the incandescent cooking-up of its sex-club pandemonium, and back again. Those interfaces between seemingly-opposed sensorial conditions, their contents effortlessly switched and reversed through the transforming channel of the bunker's aperture, formed the projections of vital media, among the infinite ocular revelations of Berlin's urban surfaces.

In Billy Wilder's film *A Foreign Affair*, shot in 1948, partly among the then-ruined Berlin's exteriors and partly in Hollywood studio-interiors' urban re-creations, an American de-nazification officer arrives at a bombed-out building (a building, as he says, with almost no remaining walls, so that interior and exterior are near-interchangeable) to visit his lover, a cabaret singer played by Marlene

Dietrich. He has just attended the arrival at Tempelhof airfield of a governmental delegation dispatched from the USA not to assess the destruction of Berlin, but instead the prevalence of covert sexual activity, between the American occupying forces and Berlin's starving inhabitants, in that ruined, black-market landscape. Dietrich's character, Erika, is in her bathroom, behind a charred wooden door which has been pierced, in the shape of a revealing, circular aperture, by one of the bombing-impacts that have served to externalise the building's interior. At first, glimpsed through that door, it appears that Dietrich's character has a mouthful of semen, but when the camera begins to penetrate further into the door's gaping aperture, it becomes evident that she has been vigorously cleaning her teeth, before turning to confront the American officer, eyes blazing, and spray the contents of her mouth through the opening, and into his face, after haranguing him for obsessively watching her. Like the eye-aperture of the concrete bunker, with its perimeter edged by injury and graffiti, that film image of buccal expulsion is one of a captivating orifice, surrounded by marks both of irreparable damage and of exclamation. In a further sequence, a member of the sexually-preoccupied governmental delegation is investigating Erika's past history, and coolly watches an extract from an archival newsreel-film of the Nazi era, documenting a lavish opera premiere attended by Hitler, with the newsreel-images projected onto an office wall. In that extract, Erika, then the lover of a prominent Nazi figure, puts her lips directly to the eardrum of Hitler, and whispers through it; whatever she says, in that act of sensory perforation, appears to send Hitler into a state of bliss.

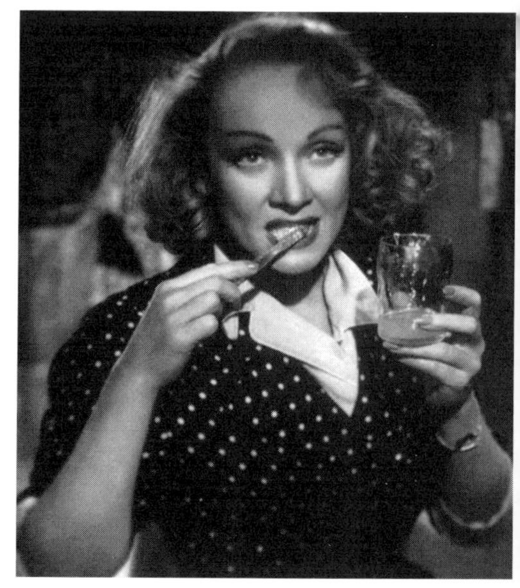

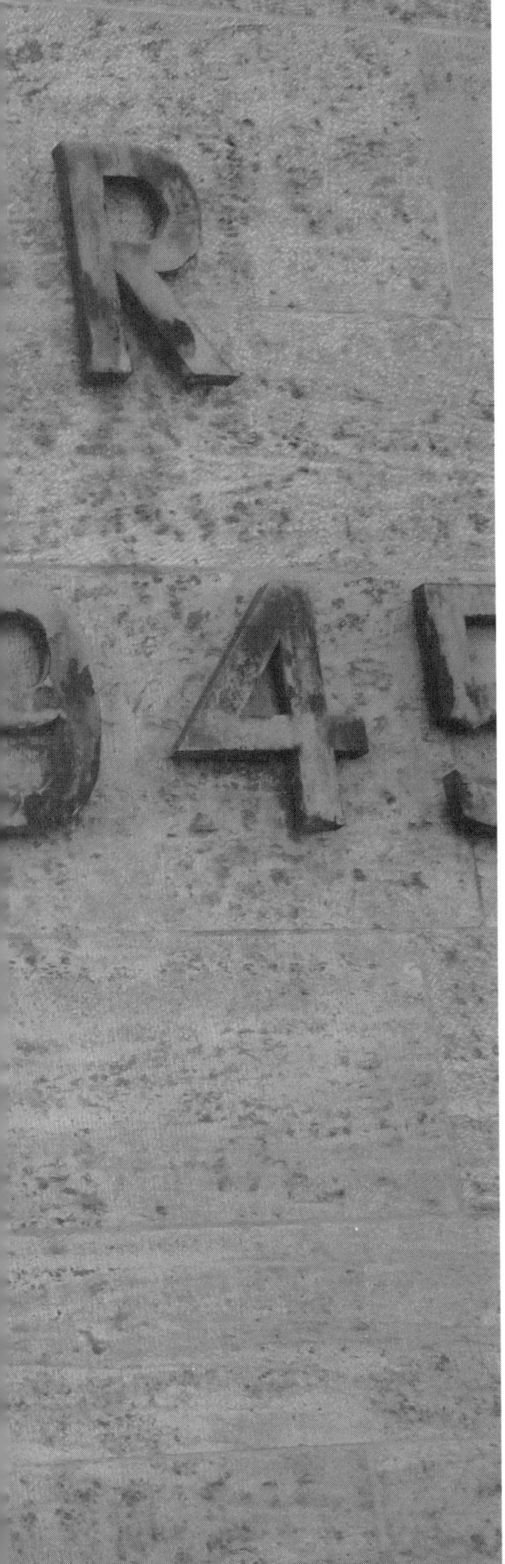

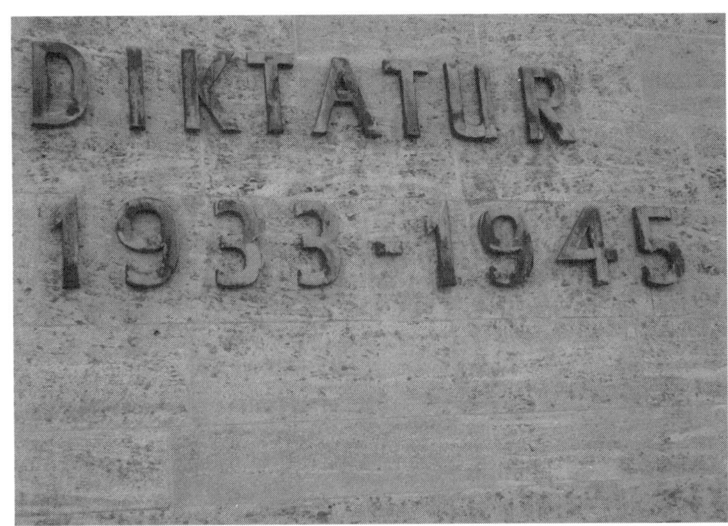

22

On an austere granite wall enclosing the execution shed in which the group of plotters, led by Claus von Stauffenberg, who had attempted in July 1944 to blow Hitler's body apart, at his Wolf's Lair headquarters far to the east of Berlin, were mercilessly hanged with piano wire, an inscription had been made: 'Dictatorship 1933-1945', as though the spraycanned Nazi graffiti lauding that era had become detached from the contemporary surfaces of buildings in the impoverished districts of Marzahn and Lichtenberg, its typography and medium mutating, before aberrantly veering westwards across Berlin's time-scrambled terrain, to that former prison tool-shed close to the Plötzensee lake, and coming to rest on the shed's granite facade, in order to state a negation of that era. The lead letters of that inscription, installed in 1952 when one half of the original execution shed had been razed and the remaining part of the building was sealed with that memorial wall, carried their text of repudiation, although the corroded letters appeared almost identical to those in which Stalin's name had been inscribed, as a text of reverence, during that same era, on the wall of the Schönholz memorial's marble-faced room. A temporal delimiting and definitive closure had been conceived for dictatorship, and written in lead on the execution shed's enclosing wall, but retrospectively, after the vanishing of the GDR state on 3 October 1990, that state's power too had been officially assigned the status of a 'dictatorship', with its own systems and sites of torture, execution and surveillance, so that, as with the concrete bunker-eye beside the Friedrichstrasse station, that inscription of dictatorship was subject to contemporary Berlin's oblivious historical levelling and its equivalences between Nazism and Communism, and to abrupt reversals, as with the exterior and interior of Dietrich's bombed-out building in *A Foreign Affair*. The execution shed's interior had been deployed for the decapitation and hanging of petty chicken-thieves and bomb-site looters as well as forming the pivotal site for the execution of the Nazi regime's political opponents; prominent dissidents, such as the Czech writer Julius Fucik, had been transported from all over Europe to Berlin, as though only an act of execution staged within Berlin's urban parameters could successfully uproot that resistance. But the execution shed became renowned pre-eminently as the site of the hanging of the von Stauffenberg plotters, and of the filming of those executions.

In Hitler's fury at the plotters' bomb, which perforated and deafened the eardrum into which Dietrich whispers enticing obscenities in the faked newsreel sequence in *A Foreign Affair*, as well as shredding his clothes, he notoriously demanded that the remaining plotters (von Stauffenberg himself had already been shot, together with his closest co-conspirators, on the night following the botched assassination) be executed with piano wire, to render their deaths agonisingly protracted, and that the executions be filmed, as though Hitler, displaced from Berlin at his Wolf's Lair headquarters, were to

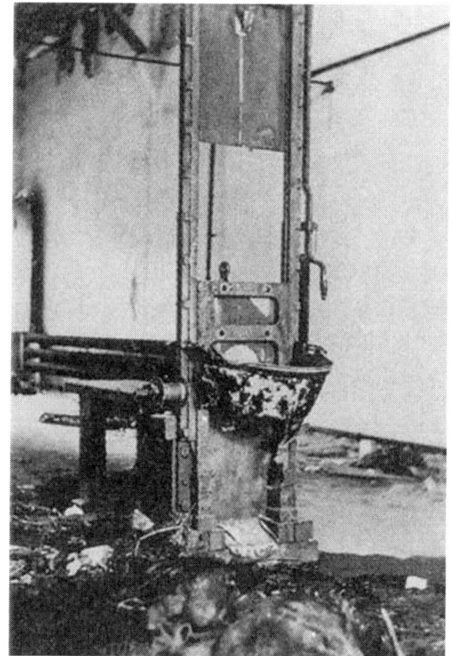

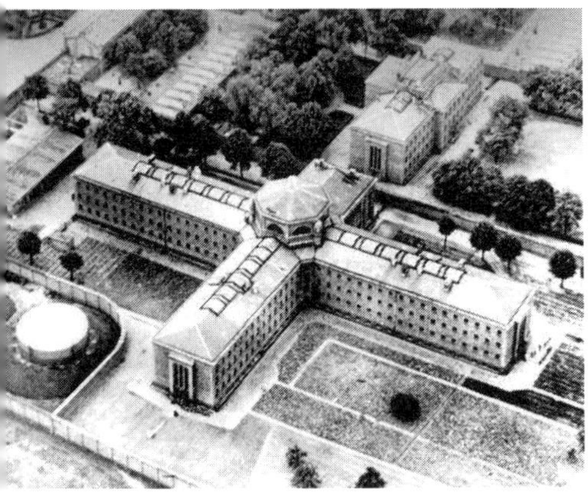

himself be the absentee director of the resulting film, offhandedly subordinating the actual cinematography to his subordinates, under the supervision of Goebbels, and the Plötzensee execution shed (similar in construction and dimensions to one of the very first film-studios, that of Georges Méliès, in the Paris suburb of Montreuil) were to be transformed into a terminal film studio, for that purpose. The resulting film disappeared without trace after the fall of Berlin to the Russian forces, nine months after it was shot, but passed into legend. Myths or imaginary narratives invoking both its horror, and its impact upon its spectators, appeared in second- and third-hand accounts, from Soviet and American military sources: the cinematographers assigned to the task had been so appalled by the plotters' extended agony that they had filmed only the first two of the thousand or more executions, and had then abandoned the film in an abbreviated state; in defiance of that curtailed form, Goebbels had been so proud of his unique film-product that he had screened it to an audience of SS cadets, in an improvised cinema at their barracks in the Berlin district of Lichterfelde, generating such an unbearable act of spectatorship that many of the cadets had exited the cinema, vomiting or weeping; and Hitler himself, despite having commissioned the film and being its absentee 'director', hated all images of blood or death, and had never watched it, preferring instead to view sentimental musicals and the late-1920s films starring Marlene Dietrich and Leni Riefenstahl.

In its disappearance or intentional suppression, the legendary but erased film shot in the Plötzensee execution shed – its granite-clad exterior now marked with the announcement and fixed time of dictatorship, like a cinema-hoarding declaring the title and starting-time for the screening of a film which has unaccountably vanished – takes on a strange spectatorial power, with the sparse and tenuous accounts of its existence compelling visitors to the Plötzensee site unconsciously to conjure up the film as they enter the sombre, glacial execution-room, and to imagine the horror of that film, at the same time as they visually reconstruct the event of the executions from the steel beam that spans the room just below ceiling-level, holding a line of wire nooses. The disappearance of the execution-film necessarily causes it to be relentlessly generated, again and again, and internally self-projected, by those visitors, with that imaginary charge accentuating and even exceeding the horror of the actual film (if it ever existed, outside of its horror's legend), unless the execution-room's own compelling emptiness may supersede, and thereby void, such imagined filmic images of horror.

Immediately after Hitler came to power in 1933, Berlin's urban facades began to be rigorously re-surfaced with the insignia and texts of his regime; alongside the all-engulfing architectural reconfiguration envisaged for the city, intended to re-align its principal avenues and instil it with grandiose governmental and cultural edifices, Berlin became the site of a vast programme of exclamatory imprintations, re-namings and excisions, exacted on its buildings' facades, as well as upon its inhabitants and their corporeal presence within Berlin's urban space. In photographs taken in the Schöneberg district of the then recently closed-down Eldorado nightclub – the city's pre-eminent gay venue, and in many ways the forerunner of the sex-club housed sixty years later within the eye-perforated concrete bunker – every window of the building's facade has been blocked-out, and covered either with swastika-hoardings or with exhortations to vote for Hitler in the federal elections of 5 March 1933; in the previous year, with the last exhalation of the sensory and visual decadence subsisting from 1920s Berlin, the nightclub's facade had held an exactly contrary content, of extravagant, sexually-inflected posters, then jettisoned or overlayered at the onset of the Nazi regime. But even after the building's near-comprehensive re-surfacing, two elongated signs holding the club's suppressed name still extrude into the surrounding space from its facade, as though irresistibly piercing and annulling the new aura of power enveloping it.

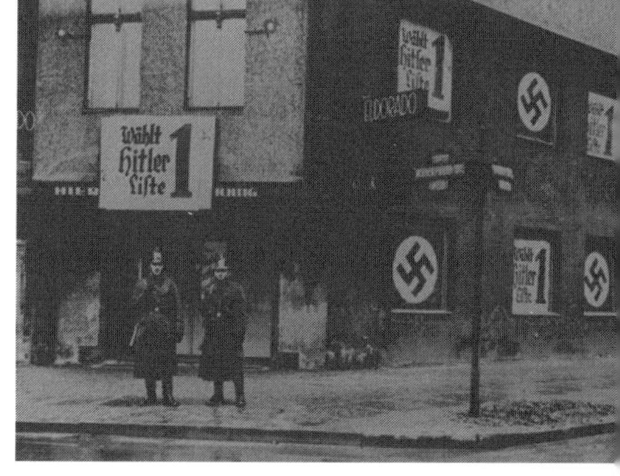

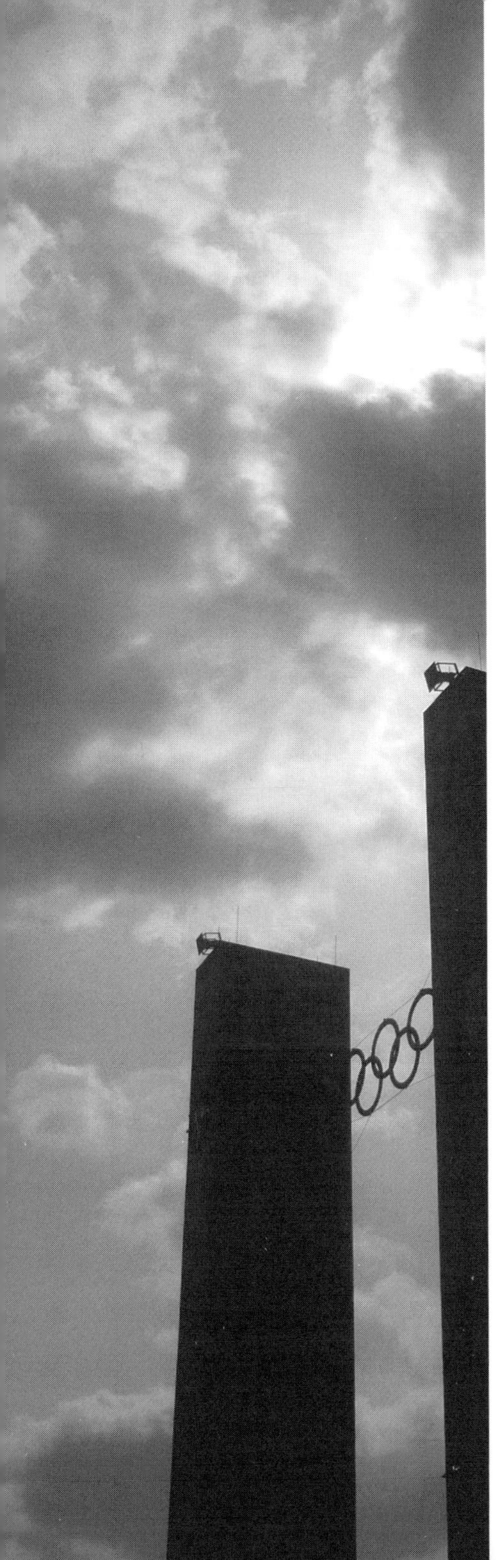

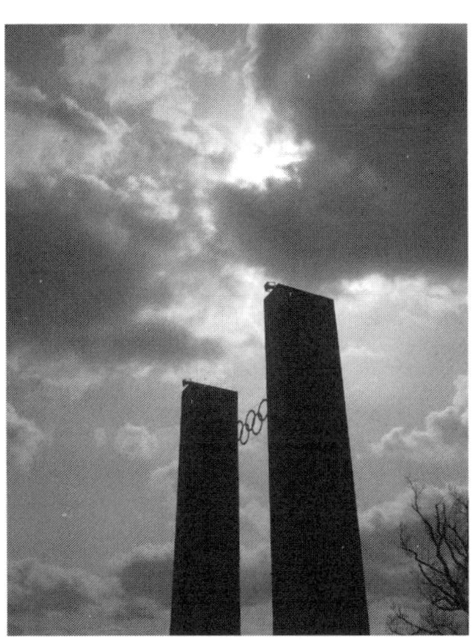

23

Suspended by wire between the twin towers of the Olympic Stadium, constructed for Hitler's 1936 games, the five rings of the Olympic symbol had been drawn tight into mid-air, like the indefinitely-strangled bodies of the von Stauffenberg bomb-plotters. Those stone towers formed the portal leading into Hitler's immense stadium, designed by the architect Werner March and constructed over the two years preceding the games, which were intended to open Berlin to global perception as a city simultaneously of persuasive grandeur (at the games' opening-ceremony, the athletes of France and other nations enthusiastically gave Nazi salutes towards Hitler on his podium) and of forbidding power, notably that of expulsion and eradication; the transparent apertures of the Olympic rings formed the inverse urban presence to the blocked-out windows of the Eldorado nightclub, and between that venue's shutting-down in 1933 and the games' opening in

1936, much of Berlin's gay population had already been jettisoned to concentration camps such as Sachsenhausen, beyond the city's perimeters, as one strand of an ongoing programme of urban disappearances and eradications. The stadium's towers had survived the following decade's conflict almost intact, losing only the swastika insignia that had been attached to the upper surface of the northern tower, its location marked by incised constellations of machine-gun fire; but, in their survival, they had mutated into mysterious steles of urban oblivion. The Olympic rings suspended between those towers now comprised elevated orifices for the transmutation of history and sensation, operating like the two-way eye of the concrete bunker by the Friedrichstrasse station, able to sieve all urban images and texts traversing them in either direction, and remaining infinitely manipulable in their impacts upon human vision and sensation. In the opening sequence of her film-document of Hitler's games, *Olympia* (1938), Leni Riefenstahl appears naked beside a marine landscape, manoeuvring a wooden ring around her own body, before abruptly elevating it against the sky, as though aligning a camera lens, so that the ring's configuration and position exactly match that of the Olympic rings suspended between the stadium's towers. Every malleable aperture forms a unique medium for compulsive urban visions.

In Riefenstahl's film, the act of crossing Europe, from an origin in Greece towards Berlin, undertaken at ground-level by a succession of athletes holding a flaming torch, itself abruptly elevates to become an aerial journey that passes rapidly, in dissolves from city to city, encompassing those to be shortly amalgamated into Hitler's domain, such as Prague and Vienna, as though that film's covert purpose were to omnisciently scan optimum invasion-routes. In all films that seek to anatomise Berlin's distinctive space and time, from *Berlin: Die Sinfonie der Grossstadt* onwards, the moment of visual entry into the city forms a determining event. *Olympia*'s aerial arrival, in the sky above Berlin, emerges from banks of clouds, like that of *A Foreign*

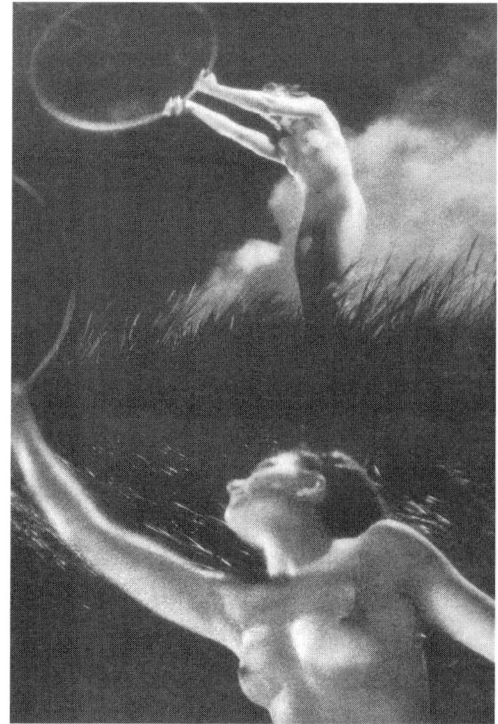

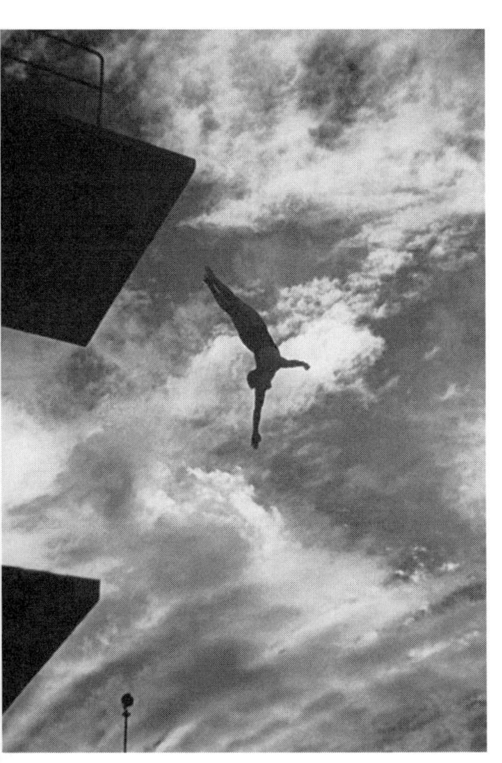

Affair and *The Fall of Berlin*, so that the city is unscreened as a site of seminal revelation; in that sequence, *Olympia* elides the sprawling expanse of Berlin surrounding the stadium, concertinaing the city to the densely-packed stadium's parameters, which themselves constitute an ocular aperture channelling the obsessions of its occupants. Riefenstahl's celestially air-borne camera appears to be indefinitely suspended over that stadium, as though to absorb the full charge of corporeal elation and sonic uproar emitted vertically from its occupants, before finally swooping down into the arena itself.

In *Olympia*'s diving sequence, filmed at the swimming-pool alongside the main stadium, the competitors' bodies transiting vertiginous mid-air are rendered as stretched or contorted arrangements of corporeal momentum, marooned in empty space, with those bodies' impetus occasionally reversed, back in the direction of their launching-boards. Initially, Riefenstahl intercuts shots of the audience's rapt responses; then, those shots lapse, and the focus is entirely on the divers. The final diving figures, filmed against dark clouds, undertake plummetings whose ground-level destination-point has vanished, framed out-of-shot, so that they appear to be executing exploratory journeys from which any guiding sense of cogent spatial resolution has been lost, as with all journeys taken within the erased or illegibly overlayered parameters of Berlin's urban facades and precipices.

Behind the stadium's main arena, at the opposite end to the twin steles that held their five wire-strung apertures, an aberrant trace subsisted of the Nazi-sculpted corporeal art that had otherwise been comprehensively expunged from Berlin's surfaces, in its postwar period. At either side of the entrance to the Waldbühne outdoor concert venue, stone friezes by Adolf Wamper, one of Hitler's preferred artists (an endangering condition of approval that, as with the Hitler-endorsed actor Heinrich George, would lead to Wamper's postwar incarceration) showed male and female bodies, holding torches and lyres, the two sexes separated by the entranceway, but gesturing to one another in sexual invitation while instigating an ocular connection that spanned the distance between them. The figures had been commissioned by Goebbels, and added to the concert venue's entrance in 1938, two years after it had been completed by the same architect who had designed the Olympic complex's main arena; although that concert venue had subsequently been destroyed twice over (once during wartime bombing, and then again, in 1965, by haywire Rolling Stones fans during an out-of-control concert), those figures had remained intact. The immense and undemolishable presence of Hitler's stadium constituted such a fortified urban entity that those sculpted figures, as peripheral annexes to it, appeared to have been able to conjure a precarious medium of survival, in defiance of the deletion of Berlin's Nazi-era facades, by becoming simultaneously visible and invisible, able to vanish into walls and emerge again, like the figures in Jean Cocteau's films who cross-over zones of death and life. Although those figures had been conceived by their sculptor as embodying an ideal corporeal form (epitomised by the works of Hitler's favourite artist, and Cocteau's friend, Arno Breker), the feet of one of the female figures indicated that any downwards-angled gaze, like that directed from the sky above Hitler's stadium in *Olympia*, could reveal profound fissures as well as emanations of glory. The splayed feet had suffered an erosion over time that accentuated the original grain of the stone, so that their surface had become a deeply pitted one. During its construction, the sculpture had evidently been separated into segments and then re-assembled on-site, so that the increasingly gaping division between its feet and the legs above them now intimated a botched act of dissection, or the residue of a psycho-killer's assault. All sensitised feet that walk on Berlin's urban surfaces traverse seismic terrain that may captivate and illuminate them, or else calamitously engulf them into itself.

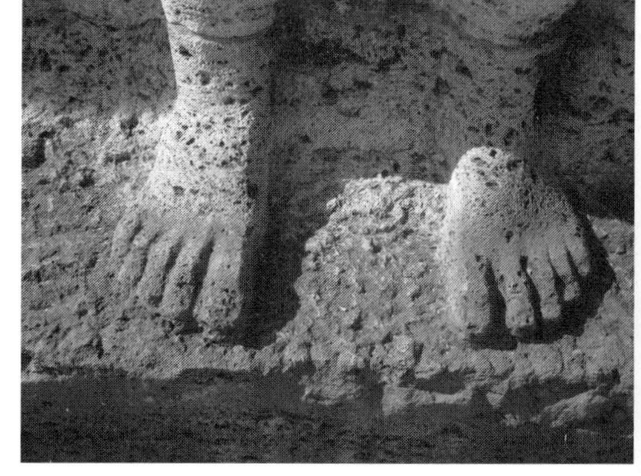

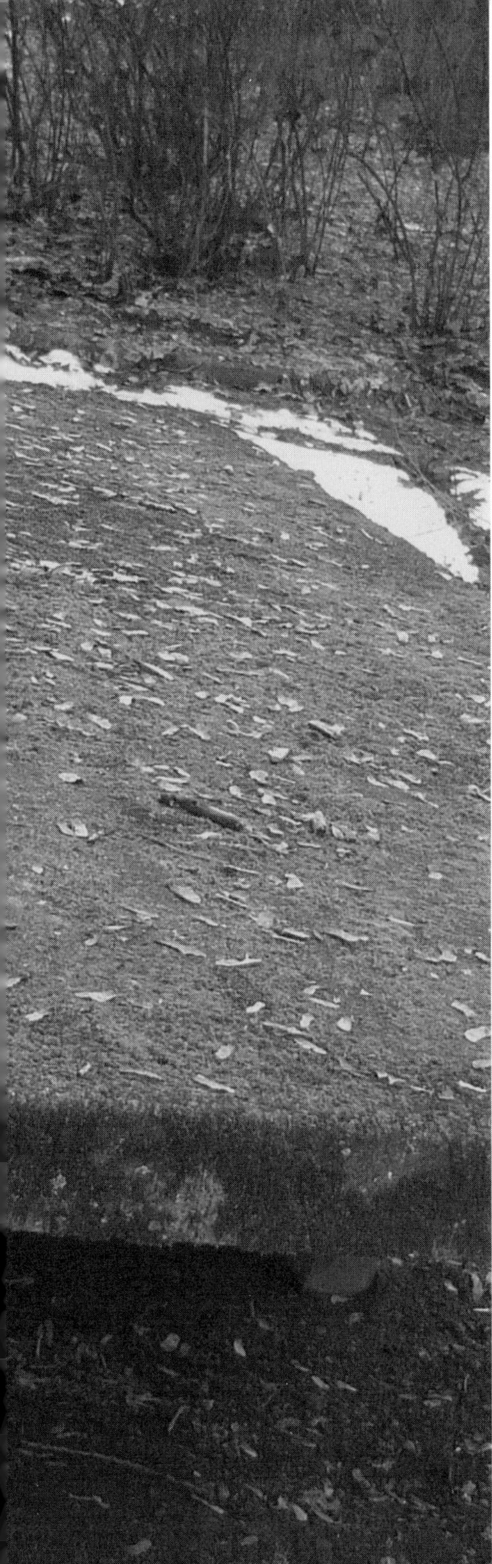

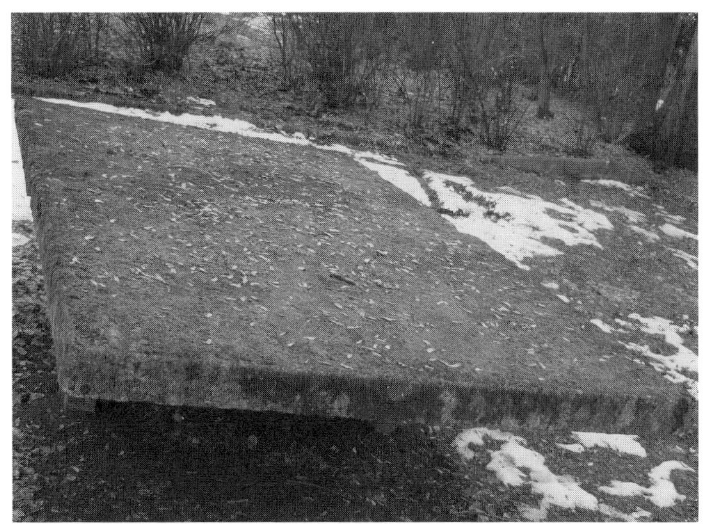

24

Across the face of Berlin, in a silent backstreet interzone between plastic-facaded apartment towers, in the district of Pankow, a moss-coated concrete table-tennis slab had been forgotten, many years ago, so that its intricately void surface, of ruination and urban negation, projected itself vertically, transmitting an inverse content to that of the Olympic stadium's arena as it directs its corporeal and sonic uproar upwards towards Riefenstahl's film-camera, and to all other vertically-directed projections of Berlin's elations and obsessions. Like the pitted stone feet of Wamper's Nazism-imbued sculpted figure at the periphery of that stadium, poised for survival by inhabiting the knife-edge between visibility and vanishing, that slab formed an overlooked surface, activated only by a downwards-directed ocular movement. The concrete slab's surface had been assembled in two parts, but the hinges pinioning the segments had rusted and broken-away, allowing a deep fissure to form along the mid-point of that surface, like that separating the feet and legs of Wamper's statue; that fissure aligned between the two segments of the slab intimated that, once its surface had reached a status of terminal unreadability, it could be mercifully folded closed, and withdrawn from all exposure to the city, as vitally illegible as one of Kiefer's lead books. The concrete slab formed an obscure display-surface whose content – a decades-long transmission of corrosion and neglect – had been unseen, even from its origins; the serrated texture of the slab had evidently rendered its assigned sports-use impossible, and that table must have been produced and installed on its site solely to fulfil GDR quotas, or as an attempt to lessen the emptiness of that urban interzone. The surrounding apartment-towers appeared entirely depopulated, their friable facades and virtual inhabitants pitched at the point of deliquescence. Whereas the Olympic stadium's twin towers formed still-upright steles of oblivion, that slab appeared as an upended, never-righted memorial to the overlooked presences of the city.

In defiance of its excision from all domains of urban power, the table-tennis surface carried a voluble charge mediating the temporal dynamics of abandonment. Like all permanently discarded surfaces, it had amassed a distinctive residue, its moss-coating densely coagulated as a living organism around the fissure separating its segments, and sparse at its edges, where the raw concrete remained intermittently visible. Traces of rust from the long-gone hinges that had once held it together still stained the crack at the slab's centre, and an unfathomable strata of minuscule debris-traces (insect-bodies, oxidised nails) had arranged itself across that facade. Never-cleared, desiccated leaves scattered the expanse of the slab, like the massacred bodies of battle-fields, filmed from above. Lost from sight and optimally overlooked, that slab constituted a cinematically-resonant screen that channelled all of Berlin's averted presences, from its subterraneas and interstitial zones, into an infinite medium for urban abandonment's manifestations, before they were projected vertically from that surface.

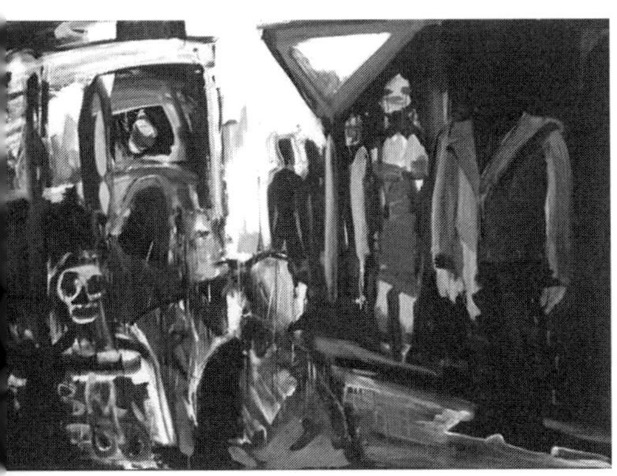

Berlin's urban cracks and overlooked surfaces have always formed a compulsion for its visual artists. While Manfred Böttcher and Gustav Wunderwald painted the unseen, silence-enveloped rear-courtyards that also drew Herzog to film Bruno S.'s marginal performance, his figure poised against a tenement's far back-wall, in *Stroszeck*, other artists explored the cancelled-out presences at the very heart of the city, under its ocular glare. In Karl Horst Hödicke's painting *Bahnhof Zoo (Zoo Station)*, from 1981, West Berlin's pre-eminent zone of destitution, prostitution and drug-dealing, in the subterranea below that station and its ground-level, ill-lit halls, is presented as an abyss obscured from visibility within the surrounding furore of the city. Like the teenaged addicts who haunt Edel's film *Christiane F.: Wir Kinder vom Bahnhof Zoo*, filmed at that same moment, the anonymised figures in Hödicke's painting are irreparably detached from the city: one carries a skull incised within his face, another has entirely misplaced his own face, and stands still, erased but monolithic (his splayed feet planted like those of Wamper's statue), invisible to the gazes of passers-by. Other figures have transmutated into shadows who cannot cohere with the city, and all of those figures are enmeshed within a darkness that hides them still further from sight. The only discernible urban landmark, visible in the distance from the Zoo station's benighted terrain, is the Kaiser Wilhelm Gedächtniskirche, a vast church which, around the end of the 1920s, had been surrounded by grand cafes and formed a particular axis for the exploratory urban transits collected in Kracauer's book *Strassen in Berlin und anderswo (Streets in Berlin and elsewhere)*; in Hödicke's painting, that wounded building – its steeple hit during a wartime bombing-raid and subsequently preserved in its sliced-apart state – exists only to accentuate the effacement of the figures hovering below it. The inhabitation by those peripheral figures of the area which, in 1981, formed both the corporate centre of West Berlin as well as its infernal core, serves to exacerbate their expunging from the city's infrastructures of power and visibility.

In Berlin's invisible zones of neglect, where its urban surfaces and corporeal figures have irreversibly fallen through the cracks, the only power apparent is that of an inversion and withdrawal from power, and of power's consequent denudation, engendered by imperatives which conceive of urban time in a contrary form from that of the city's power-instilled agencies – as one in which abandonment's intricate traces require decades or more to amass before they can be fully projected into the sky over Berlin, even unseen, from the corroded surface of the Pankow table-tennis slab, or else as one of urgently repetitive intervals between the accomplishment of addiction-fixes or sex-acts, as in Hödicke's *Bahnhof Zoo* or Ripploh's *Taxi zum Klo*. The dynamics of time, in those urban zones, may accumulate with infinite slowness, or accelerate into adrenalised bursts, but will always fail to connect with the city's sanctioned time. Those volatile temporal dynamics demand a corresponding sense of alteration in the ocular movements which scan them, so that Berlin's urban surfaces may appear unseizably stalled, or blurred, until the eye is able to intimate itself into that aberrant time.

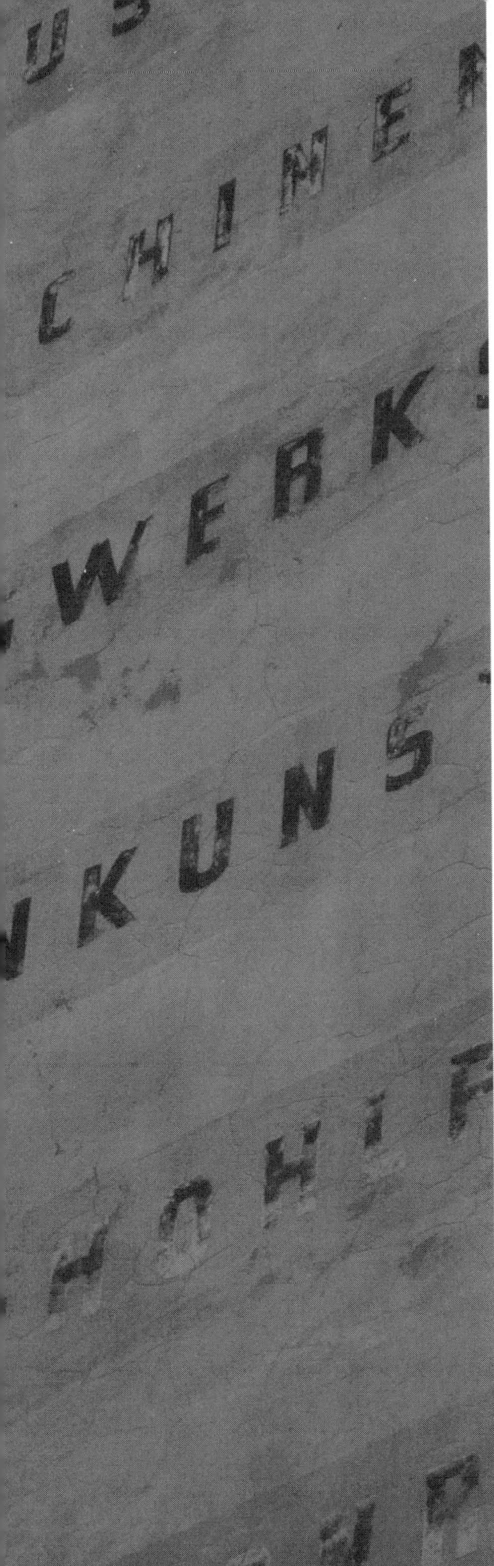

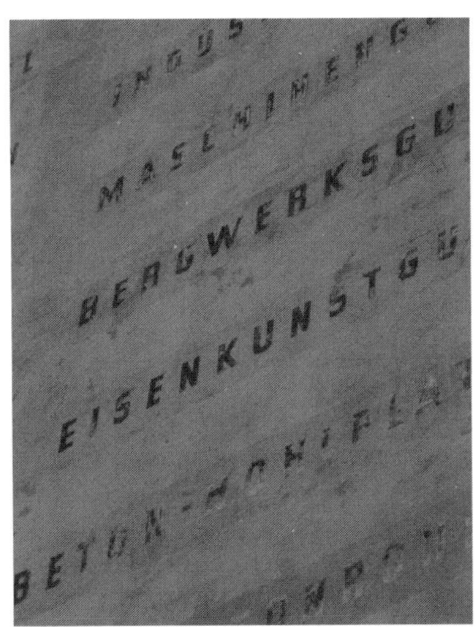

25

On a firewall facade close to the reverberating site of the Hansa studios, on the edge of the Kreuzberg district, a vast and resilient hoarding had once been inscribed in white and black tea-paint, enumerating the range of products of an industrial company. While most hoardings installed on Berlin's surfaces in the early decades of the twentieth century had been rendered in vivid colours and incorporated the insignia and location in Berlin of the corporation that had commissioned it, that austere hoarding appeared strangely reticent, stripped even of the exclamation of its originating company and subjected, over the decades since its installation, both to processes of erosion and to the intentional erasing, as an act of urban sabotage, of every second product-name inscribed upon it, the names' letters inexplicably concealed beneath white paint, as though that hoarding had been subject to an urban ordinance which decreed that half of its ocular impact must capriciously be subtracted, in order not to excessively encumber the eyes of Berlin's passers-by. Even the remaining product-names appeared to have been arbitrarily assaulted with gestures of cancellation, that had deleted occasional letters at random, so that those names had to be reconstructed through a near-forensic ocular process. Although the hoarding's immense, half-annulled expanse matched that of the digital image-screens attached to the glass-faced summits of corporate headquarters in the adjacent Potsdamerplatz, its content had become an enigmatic and misfired one, rivalling those corporate image-screens only at the moments when they entered a condition of partial malfunction, or meltdown, which scrambled half of their digital code. The hoarding's lines of product-names formed an urban incantation that originated at the firewall's pinnacle, but extinguished itself far from the wall's base, tailing-off with the stranded inscription 'ZEMENT', as though that urban text had become exhausted with the exhalation of its last word, or else its inscriber (already determined not to incorporate images into their urban mission) had been seized by a paroxysm of terminal concision, leaving the lower expanse of the hoarding as a blank, text-less space, still meticulously striated by the oscillating lines of cancellation which had retrospectively been applied to that hoarding.

The product-inscribed firewall facade appeared as the emanation both of Berlin's excoriating impacts on its own surfaces, that worked to bleach-out and scour that eroded facade, but simultaneously leave it exposed in its skinned-alive state, together with the revelatory trace, on that surface, of a rogue element of urban maleficence, which had judged that the hoarding's enumeration of industrial products had to be coupled with an equivalent effacing. But the reduction of those inscribed names had perversely created an urban text with its own distinctive visual emanation: while the original hoarding had been comprised solely of textual elements, it had then been transformed into an urban image-surface through the process of semi-cancellation which had ousted every second product-name. That oscillation between visibility and erasure, projection and negation, resonated with the seminal impetus determining all of Berlin's urban transmissions, from their point of origin in the Skladanowsky Brothers' 'Bioskop' film-projector and its alternately revealing and concealing dual-lens. The hoarding's surviving elements had amassed into a resurgent visual residue that demanded to be reconstructed as a new urban language of Berlin, pitched between perfect clarity and utter illegibility, and scanned by adept ocular manoeuvres that veered between blurs and 20/20 vision.

The painter Gustav Wunderwald, often immersed in depicting Berlin's rear-courtyard dead-ends, also alternately focused on the city's street-front urban hoardings, which projected outwards to impact upon and attract the vision of Berlin's inhabitants. In *U-Bahn-Station Schönhauser Tor*, from 1927, he paints a dual firewall facade located on one of Berlin's main arterial avenues, just south of the building-roof from which the Skladanowsky Brothers had shot the city's first filmic urban-panorama. That facade, against a virulent yellow background matched by that of a truck in the street below, bears the name of another pair of brothers, the Gebrüder Manes, with the doubly inscribed letter 'M' magnified to excessive proportions, and mirroring the firewall's dual surfaces; in the late 1920s, the Manes Brothers' textile company owned men's clothing-stores in several German cities, and their Berlin store, in the Rosenthalerstrasse, was situated close to that hoarding, so that the gaze of passers-by, irresistibly directed upwards towards that projecting surface, would then be deflected in the direction faced by the hoarding, towards the store's adjacent location. The projections emitted by that firewall surface appear oblivious to the red-facaded cinema which stands immediately below it, with its own exclaimed name incorporated into

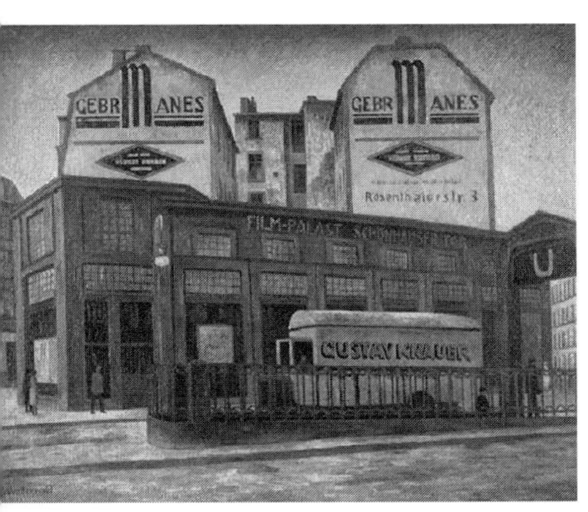

Wunderwald's painting, in a uniquely intersecting amalgam of visual art, the urban, and the filmic. That cinema, the Film-Palast Schönhauser Tor, also known as the 'Ton-eck Lichtspiele', seating between 500 and 600 spectators, had only recently been completed at the moment when it became enmeshed within Wunderwald's painting; it remained on that site for sixteen years, until 1943, when it was destroyed without trace in wartime bombing, while the name of the underground station in front of it mutated flexibly across the coming decades, from 'Schönhauser Tor', to 'Horst-Wessel-Platz' in the Nazi era, to 'Rosa-Luxemburg-Platz' in the GDR era (retaining that name in the contemporary city, as though the process of relentless renaming had itself reached exhaustion-point, while the firewall facade bearing the 'Gebrüder Manes' insignia survived the incendiary-bombing that erased the cinema below it, to become subsequently layered-over with successive inscriptions, until whitewash covered that momentarily voided facade in Berlin's current variant).

Berlin's urban surfaces and hoardings intimate intricate, volatile projections, embedded with mysterious amendments, erasures and resurgences, often caught in film and art works, and entailing an ocular archaeological excavation that may be undertaken upon vertical rather than horizontal surfaces, but which demands an identical, rigorous unearthing of profoundly conjoined and intersecting strata, to that of ground-level archaeological work. The more vanished, hidden and eroded the elements of Berlin's surfaces have become, in their interlayering within those dense or manipulated facades, the more vital those traces appear, in the ocular reconstruction of urban projections, sensations and memories.

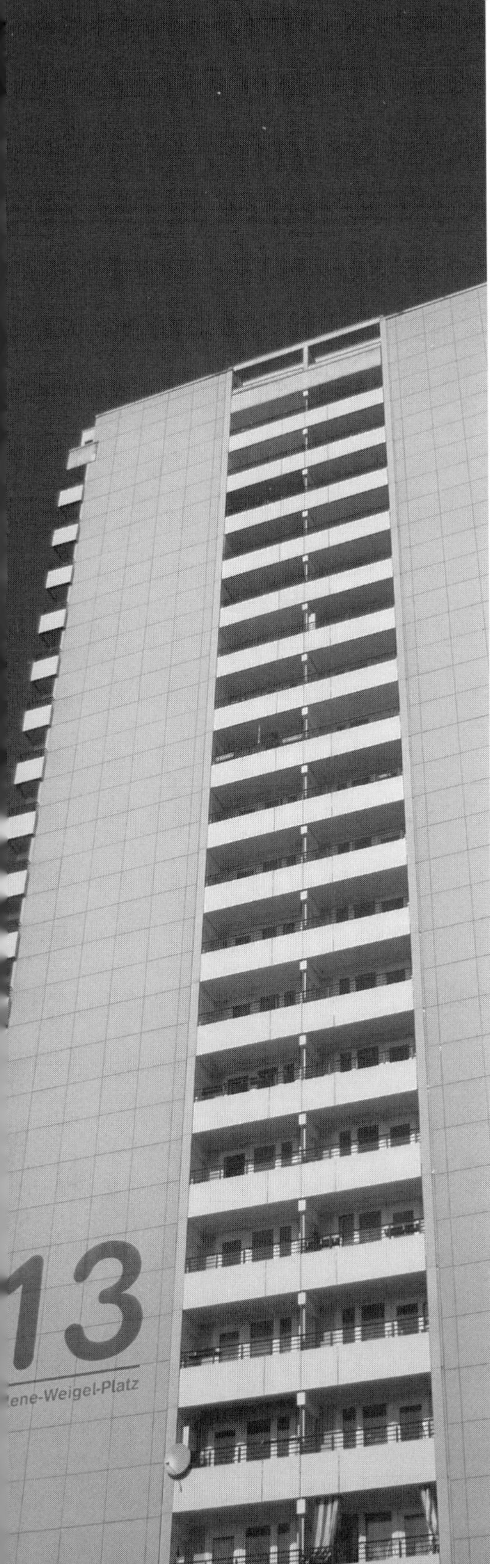

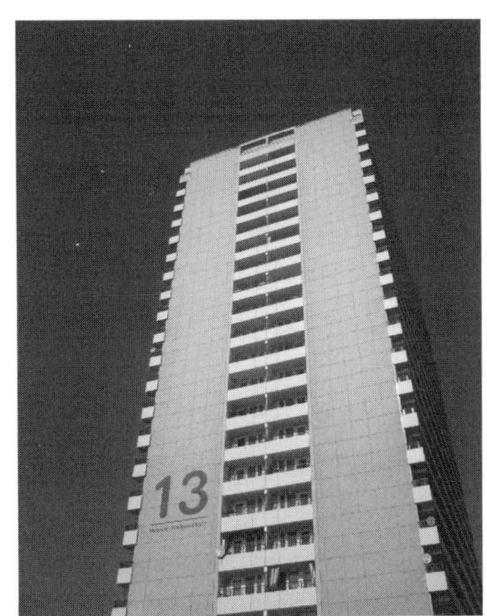

26

In the volatile urban zone of Marzahn, on Berlin's eastern periphery, an immense apartment-tower, its facade once terminally excoriated and consigned to ruination, like that of the adjacent Sojus cinema, had been entirely re-surfaced with a vivid set of yellow and blue panels, replacing the colour-voided plastic panels that had formed its permeable carapace during the GDR era, so that it appeared abruptly displaced to a Mediterranean ocean-side location, in the form of an aberrant 'Berlin-by-the-Sea' that, instead of a marine landscape, looked out onto a scorched-earth wasteland, once occupied by forced-labour camps and transit-buildings for Auschwitz deportations, and now constellated by innumerable near-identical towers, their ground-level doorways still inscribed with the fading remnants from decades of graffiti affrontments between neo-Nazi and neo-Communist factions, finally reconciled in alcoholic nihilism. In an inverse process to the underground station of Wunderwald's 1927 painting, repeatedly re-named across its future decades and sensitised to Berlin's upheavals, the contemporary Marzahn apartment-tower irresistibly mediated its past surfaces, from its current oblivious facade back to the engrained, conflictual neglect of the 1990s, and finally to the urban visions of its original plastic-panelled facade, at the moment when Marzahn had been conceived by its planners as an edenic sub-city annex to Berlin. Many of the surrounding apartment-towers bore the diverse insignia of the corporations which had acquired those buildings, the companies' names and slogan-texts (exclaiming the paradisiacal existence to be had by the towers' incoming occupants, in a perverse restatement of the heated urban ideals driving Marzahn's original planners) often inscribed vertically and covering almost the entire surface-area of the towers, as though only a textual envelopment could constrain those facades' movement backwards in time. By contrast, the facade of the twenty-storey apartment-tower alongside the Sojus cinema appeared as reticent as the firewall-hoarding close to the Hansa studios, inscribed solely with a vast number and its street-name, at its mid-point, and with all of its balconies mysteriously emptied of eyes, so that the apartment-tower appeared transmutated into a colossal commemorative stele, like that emerging out of the Schönholz terrain of death, marked number '13' as though by some omniscient hand compiling an infinite enumeration of the facades that projected Berlin's erased urban memories.

Berlin forms a maximally re-surfaced city, repeatedly enduring the consequences of all-engulfing imperatives for its comprehensive visual transformation. Those imperatives take diverse forms: from the political compulsions that overhauled the surfaces of the Eldorado nightclub with Nazi insignia, and later coated Berlin's GDR-era buildings in banners and hoardings lauding chemical industries and proclaiming the creation of urban paradises; to the imperative for destruction that immersed Berlin's surfaces in an incising layer of impacts during the Soviet army's transit through them; and to the demand for corporate re-surfacing that turned Marzahn's shoddy facades into gleaming carapaces, and also transformed squatters' graffitied hold-outs such as those of Prenzlauerberg into luxuriously restored edifices. Many of those urban re-surfacing projects – such as the contemporary restoration of entire districts of century-old, terminally disintegrated tenements to their original condition – constitute immense spatial reformulations and movements back across time, unearthing and highlighting the buildings' lost visual strata while covering-over or expunging layers of seminal urban decay. At the same time, such wide-scale exterior reformulations of Berlin's districts, as in Prenzlauerberg, extend also to the buildings' interiors and their inhabitants, with cultural and financial consequences able to generate mass-displacements or exchanges of populations (minor variants of those which Stalin capriciously enforced in the USSR), across the face of Berlin.

Urban re-surfacing often entails juxtapositions and re-alignments in which elements of a city become displaced, and abruptly impact against one another in unprecedented, mysterious ways. In the Berlin-based artist Beate Gütschow's work, such as *S2* (2005), the photographic traces of urban components are digitally reconfigured to form new cities, that appear abandoned, now populated only by a few detrital human presences, and simultaneously grandiose, as though immense architectural ambitions have, only a moment ago, gone awry, slipping from the contemporary into a mutable condition in which any of that city's previous variants may manifest themselves, as oscillating apparitions. As with Hoenerloh's eroded, depopulated cities, entirely composed of their stranded facades, those of Gütschow form imaginary, entirely autonomous and self-generated entities, with worldwide urban resonances, but possessing their origin in Berlin.

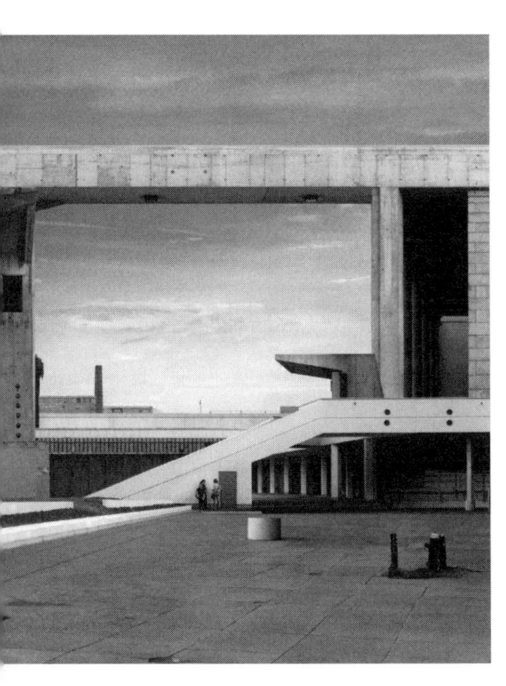

Gütschow's *S2* image initially resonates with the landscape constructed at the end of the 1990s beside Berlin's Reichstag, in which politicians' offices comprise glass-faced blocks spanned by an aerial bridge across the river Spree; but in Gütschow's image, that specific point of origin in Berlin is displaced or erased from the first moment, so that all that remains of Berlin, in its vanishing into the *S2* image, is the experience of an irreconcilable conjoining of disparate urban elements, and of their space and time: the pivotal ocular experience of Berlin.

Gütschow's work intimates the vital re-mappings of urban space that are precipitated by transformations in the forms of facades, and by the realigning or sudden deletion of cities' components, so that an exacting process is demanded of the eye (like that of the experience of an art-work or film), in transit through such reconfigured space. In Berlin, that ocular process reveals a ready propensity for all-consuming shifts and reversals in the appearance of urban facades, often choreographed in intensive moments of transmutation, so that those facades' projections may oscillate from one extreme content to another, and back again, thereby generating a variant of urban time in which juxtaposed, inassimilable images and preoccupations appear concurrently. The eye may become as stranded within those charged emanations of urban time as that inhabiting the displaced terrain of Gütschow's images. As a result, the perpetual ocular re-mapping of urban space demanded by Berlin often renders conventional charts untenable, and requires instead to be reconceived from moment to moment, conjured from out of that space's dynamically alternating surfaces and facades, in the forms both of their distinctive projections and their fissurations.

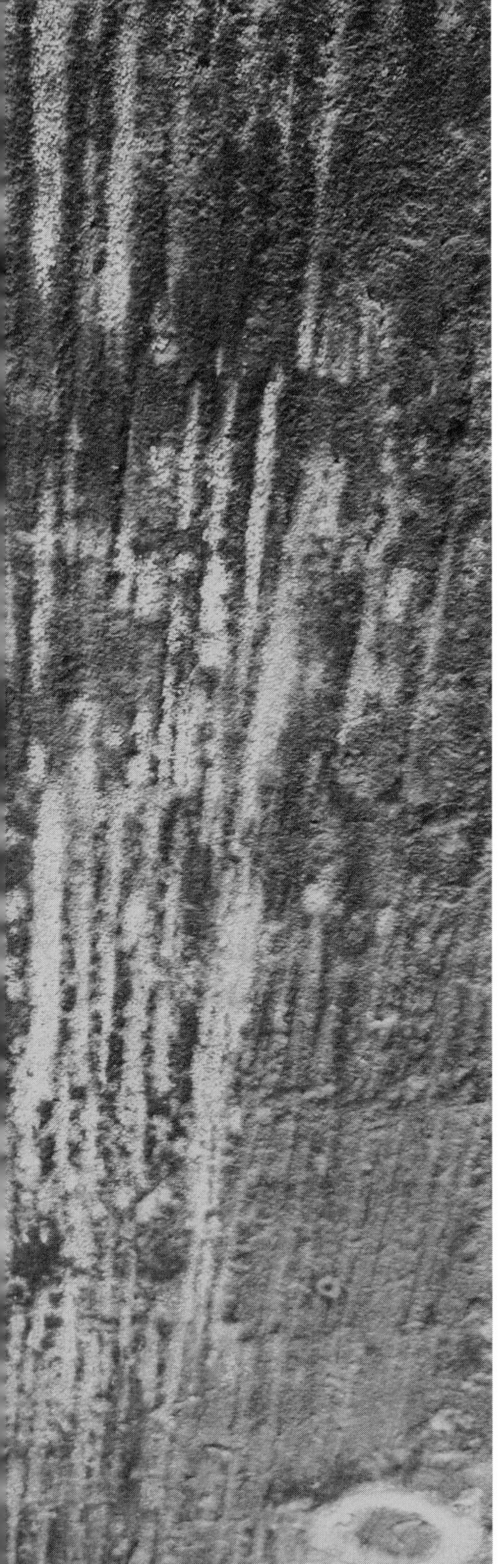

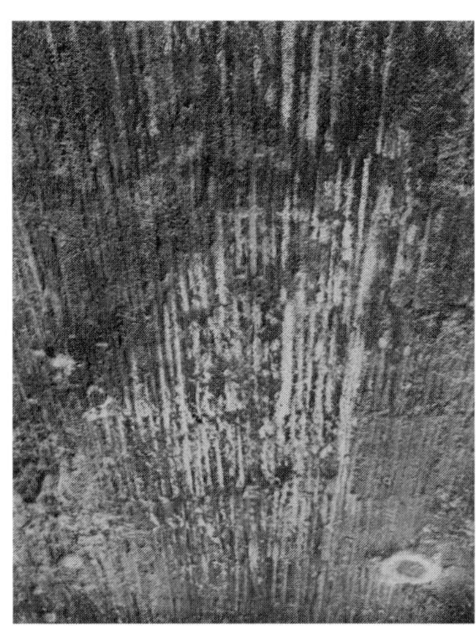

27

Every tenable map of Berlin involves an act of projection, from fire, light or the human eye, and a sensitised screen. On the rear facade of a memorial building in the heart of the city, a Berlin map had been inscribed. The cartography of Berlin's projections always proceeds via the deletion of extraneous or ephemeral elements, so that the streets, districts and transport networks had been annulled from that map as negligible presences, leaving an essential urban imprintation: an image in negative, that burst out from its surface. In many ways, that map resembled the corporeal image-projection held by the Turin shroud, oscillating between a conjuring-trick and a divine mystery: a set of traces barely visible except through the medium of photography, or by some other means of intensive ocular scanning, its form cohered only by the traversing presence of fire (from the symmetrical dripping of molten silver through the folded shroud), the corporeal and facial residues accentuated by trajectories of blood, and bordered by eye-resistant, near-illegible textual markings. Berlin itself forms an urban shroud for the projects of genocide and oppression devised there, and for the innumerable dead it holds, as those projects' result. The map of Berlin, inscribed at the heart of the city, appeared to take the form of a set of vertically directed projections, like those launched at ground-level from such sites as the Olympic Stadium (in Riefenstahl's *Olympia*) or from the Köpenick concrete fist, those striations profoundly embedded in the stone that comprised the map's surface, as though a determining impact or detonation had taken place just beyond the lower boundary of the map, and the sole purpose of that map was then to reveal the resulting imprintation of the dynamic impact upon its surface. The striations fanned-out across almost the entire, fire-blackened expanse of the map, occasionally impeded by gouged-out voids, indicating the map's capacity to register sites of urban oblivion. And at the lower right-hand corner of that map, the presence of an eye had been embedded, with a gazing pupil, as though that map of Berlin possessed the omniscient ability to scrutinise itself and its own incessant mutations, and thereby to determine whether its form was to be that of an adept conjuring-trick (like that executed by the Skladanowsky Brothers, in originating cinematic projection) or else a figure of divine urban elation.

Although that map of Berlin, imprinted over time and via maleficent interventions into its surface, formed a seminal projection of the city, it comprised only one in an infinite archive of potential maps, to be generated through ocular tourings of Berlin's urban space. The city's surfaces irresistibly emit sequences of unforeseen and unique maps as they are scanned in transit, on journeys on foot across the city, and those maps constitute corporeal as well as urban projections, that closely shadow and duplicate such journeys. The ocular touring of Berlin's space unleashes multiply-dimensional, transformational maps,

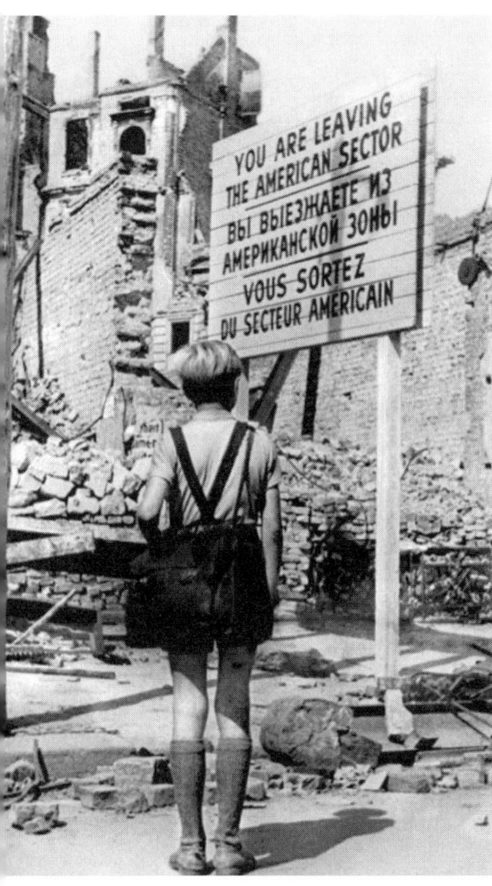

that surround the transiting body like intimations of lost ghosts, or of erased human forms, that demand acts of consolation.

In films depicting tourings of Berlin's urban space, such transits can be sources both of danger and of elation. In Roberto Rossellini's *Germany Year Zero*, from 1948, the twelve-year-old Edmund perpetually tours Berlin's ruins on foot, often moving arbitrarily, but otherwise scanning its surfaces for elements to detach and exchange for food; at one point, he becomes the cheated proprietor of a bogus bar of soap that may be used by more proficient black-marketeers, in the exchange of money for nothing. While Edmund excoriates the city's surfaces with his ocular and on-foot manoeuvres, he is himself the focus of predatory attention during those tours, falling into the hands of his former schoolteacher, whose intentions are both to sexually molest and financially denude him. Edmund looks for solace or bliss, in the form of participation in a football-game among the ruins, or in the company of a girl who lives in a cellar, but he is constantly barred from those sensations. Finally, having poisoned his father, and undertaken a terminal, directionless touring of the city, he climbs broken stairways to the summit of a hollowed-out building, that vertiginous ascent generating a trace of elation, before plummeting into death from that summit, his fall precipitated by an engulfing tram-cacophony from the street below. In Slatan Dudow's 1932 film *Kuhle Wampe (Empty Belly Camp)*, co-scripted by Brecht, another desperate touring of Berlin – by bicycle, undertaken at speed by an unemployed young man searching the city for work – also generates a fatal plummeting, as the man first removes his watch and then jumps from his apartment's window into the rear-courtyard below, in which, as in Herzog's *Stroszeck*, itinerant musicians are playing. In another seminal filmic-touring of Berlin, in Wilder's *A Foreign Affair*, from that same 'year-zero' as Rossellini's film, a disabused American army colonel takes the governmental delegation, which has just arrived in the city by air, on a tour by jeep through Berlin's ruins, maintaining an unending, ironic commentary of wisecracks, as though Berlin's destruction were the ultimate black joke. With the sirens of its accompanying motorcycle-escort blaring, the zigzagging tour passes eastwards through the Brandenburg Gate, the Tiergarten, and a 'typical residential area', of houses whose interiors are hollowed-out by incendiary bombs, leaving standing only their wall-surfaces. A member of the delegation meticulously films the non-linear tour of urban devastation with a handheld camera, but – in one of Berlin's vital misalignments – the figures in the jeep are evidently displaced, in a Hollywood studio, with more darkly-grained archival footage of Berlin's ruins projected behind them. Like the other members of the delegation, the congresswoman Phoebe intently scans the surrounding city and its surfaces, but she is preoccupied solely with her mission of unearthing traces of illicit fraternisation between American soldiers and Berlin's survivors, so that, instead of urban destruction, she perceives and records only the evidence of sexual acts.

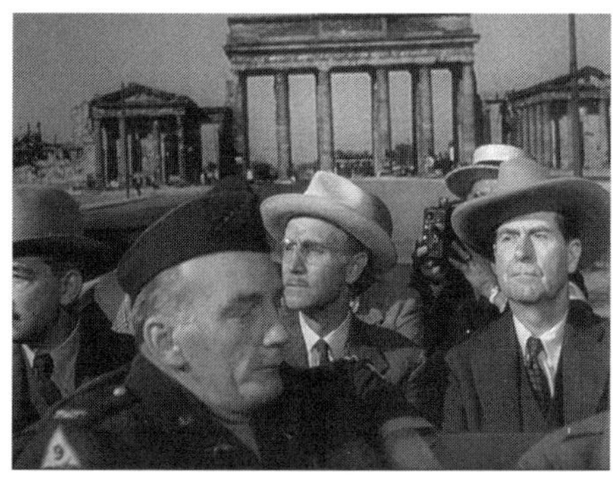

Tourings of Berlin, undertaken both filmically and on foot, within the parameters of its urban surfaces, are always impelled and guided by the mappings and cartographies – including those of its pivotal sub-cities, such as those of slaughter and of the mad – that delineate that space. At every momentary contact with those maps, an aperture into Berlin's surfaces is revealed. Those mutating maps also serve to intimate that, while elements of vertiginous urban elation are often generated by such ocular and sensorial urban-tourings, their momentum will invariably return the eye in movement to the integral fissurations that mark out Berlin's terrain.

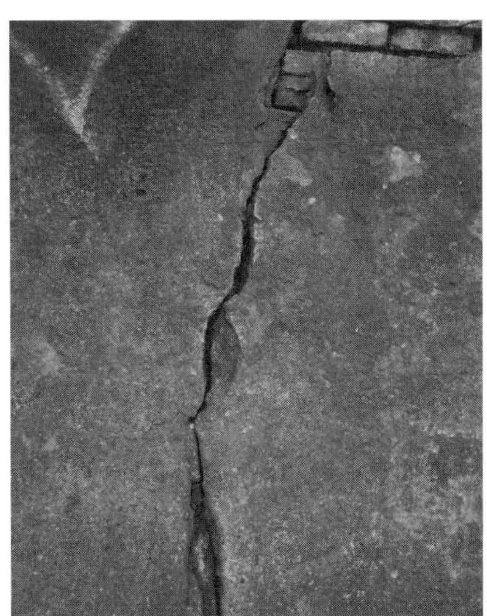

28

In Berlin's great sub-city of the mad, Buch, with its two immense asylums intended to channel urban psychoses from their embedded mappings within the city's heart, propel them northwards, and confine them on Berlin's periphery, a wall had cracked apart, as though impelled by the perpetual re-imprintation of the city's vital fissurations. That fissure, on the asylums' boundary-wall, had evidently been created by the over-accumulation of a mound of debris (its contents now thickly grown-over with moss, and indistinguishable) directly behind it, so that the convex wall-surface had first become distorted by the pressure exerted by that detritus, until it had jaggedly split vertically, from the wall's base to its summit, like a wound, angled to the right, and exposing lopsided, un-cemented bricks layered beneath its concrete carapace. As though to accentuate that fissuration, a concise graffiti-inscription had been placed alongside it, by the hand of an asylum inmate (since, apart from a few prefabricated towers erected at its edges, nobody inhabited that sub-city, other than the mad, and their keepers), in the form of a letter 'v', either as part of a longer, envisaged inscription that had been unwillingly abandoned due to a lack of paint, or in an attempt to visually trigger the cracking-open of a further fissure from the boundary-wall's pressurised base, this time angled to the left. The architect who built Berlin's sub-city of the mad, over the period 1900 to 1914, Ludwig Hoffmann, had created two asylums, rather than one, since Berlin had by then become such an overloaded megalopolis of sensory turmoil that an excessive amount of madness could confidently be anticipated (especially in the form of mad young men), beyond that which would fill the first, albeit vast, asylum, constructed from 1900 to 1908, in an architectural style resembling an English Tudor palace, with endless pavilions stretching out behind the main building. The second asylum, built from 1912 to 1914, to a more austere design, but still with multiple annexes over a vast expanse, would soak up the first's psychotic overspill. Hoffmann's overreaching architectural ambition also mirrored that of Blankenstein, the creator of Berlin's colossal sub-city of slaughter. A railway line, used for the delivery of Berlin's mad to their new homes, bisected the space of the two asylums, heading north-eastwards towards the Baltic port of Stralsund (in time, that line would be extended, in order to serve Hitler's 'Berlin-by-the-Sea' vacation-city of Prora, on the Rügen island), its trajectory directly mirroring that of the wall-fissure at the asylum's boundary. But Hoffmann had miscalculated, since the mass-slaughter of the First World War, commencing in the year of the second asylum's completion, erased swathes of that asylum's awaited inhabitants, so that it became de-populated at its origin. That second asylum never filled with the mad, and after decades of mismatched attempts to re-purpose it, for paediatrics and other usages, it fell into abandonment. By contrast, the first asylum seethed with madness, including a clientele driven to psychosis by two wars' worth of traumas, and by hallucinatory lives in the GDR; a windswept back-pavilion of the

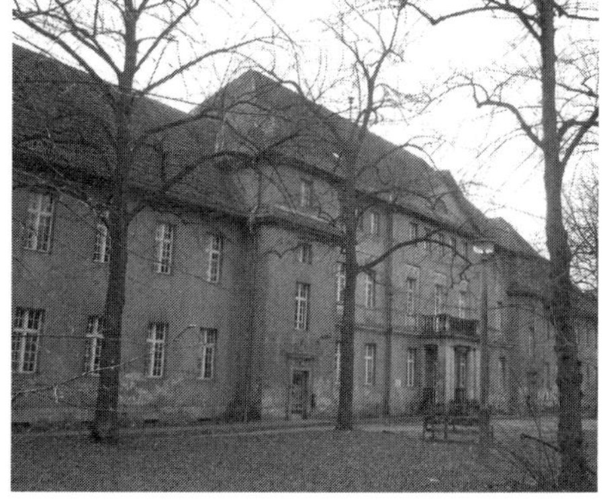

asylum became the site, in the winter of 1928, of Biberkopf's catatonic incarceration, in intimacy with death and slaughterhouse visions, in Döblin's *Berlin Alexanderplatz*, before his expulsion back into Berlin. In seizing and projecting madness, from Berlin and back again, the two asylums adopted the seminal form of the Skladanowsky projector's dual lens (one lens closed, to allow the other to function), with one asylum virulently operating a full-tilt regime of psychotic transmission, and the other lens silent and foreclosed, by its unforeseen dearth of madness.

Between the neglected pavilions of the second asylum, a tangible absence of Berlin's distinctive urban madness, with its awry elations and phantasmatic manias, inhabited that void terrain. As though as a merciful historical consolation-prize for their abandonment, the pavilions' walls still bore the multiple bullet-impacts of fierce fighting, indicating that, despite their integral redundancy, those surfaces had been contested during the Russian army's incursion into Berlin, in April 1945; subsequently, one of those pavilions' ephemeral re-purposings had been as a Soviet forensics-laboratory used for Hitler's autopsy. The psychoses and madness-traces usurped from Buch's second asylum had been retained in the heart of Berlin itself, and installed there on an indefinite basis, to be intermittently revealed by its urban surfaces, in the form of obsessional graffiti inscriptions, and through the corporeal imprintation of traces of ecstasy and exhilaration into those unhinged facades, where all habituating sensory ordering falls apart.

In Ludwig Meidner's series of paintings of madness-engulfed Berlin, dating from the same period as Hoffmann's construction of the second Buch asylum, the inhabitants of the city run wildly to escape mysterious eruptions at the edge of the image; the facades of elegant apartment-houses endure bucklings and fissurations like that of the Buch boundary-wall, and the black-furrowed sky over Berlin boils from the impact of vertically-projected detonations. The city, rather than its inhabitants, has gone irreversibly mad (as though in pre-

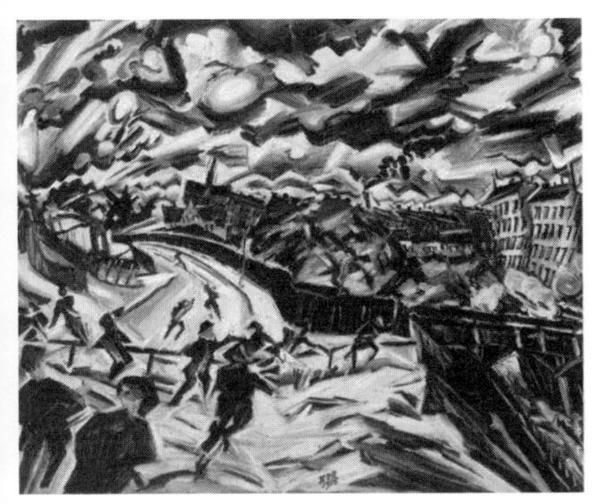

emptive response to Kracauer's formulation of Berlin-streets that 'scream'), and emitted its delirium, thereby precipitating secondary psychoses on the part of those inhabitants. Meidner accorded each of that series of rapidly-painted images the encompassing title *Apokalyptische Landschaft* (*Apocalyptic Landscape*), but their location-specific sub-titles intimate that Berlin's surfaces are erupting at its most banal, well-ordered sites, such as 'by the Halensee S-bahn station' or 'by the Spree docks'. Even the location of Meidner's Berlin studio formed an innocuous one, in the becalmed Friedenau district; overcome there by bouts of heat-exhaustion, in the summer of 1912, he began to paint frenziedly. By the next year, as a terminal annex to his apocalyptic outburst – and before the sustaining psychosis abruptly drained out of his work – he drew images of manically overpacked, seemingly slaughter-intent crowds amassed in the Potsdamerplatz (at the same, pre-war moment when Kirchner became absorbed in the sexual obsessions projected by that plaza's population), and used both sides of the canvas for his dual painting, *Die Brennende Stadt* (*The Burning City*), as though one face were not enough, and both surfaces demanded an immersal in urban madness.

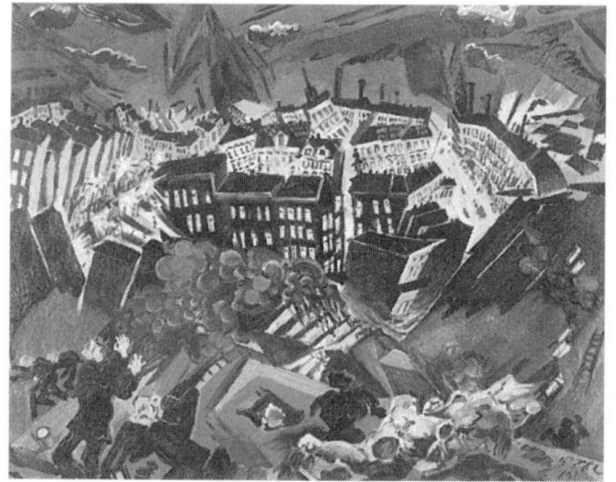

Cartographic journeys between Berlin's pivotal, extreme 'sub-cities' – such as that extending from Blankenstein's sub-city of slaughter to Hoffmann's two-fold sub-city of the mad, or from Meidner's apocalyptic Halensee station to the Spree docks – form propulsive, image-generated trajectories across the city, using that city's essential fissurations and subterraneas as their media of transport, and leading to the instigation of volatile Berlin-mappings that may run counter to its more linear, uni-dimensional cartographies. Berlin is a city in which the ecstasies of urban madness thrive, especially in its covert interzones and on its corporeally infused surfaces, though those ecstasies remain perpetually subject to the inundations and liquefactions which Werner Heldt envisioned for Berlin, in his drawings and paintings of an urban 'sea of ruins'.

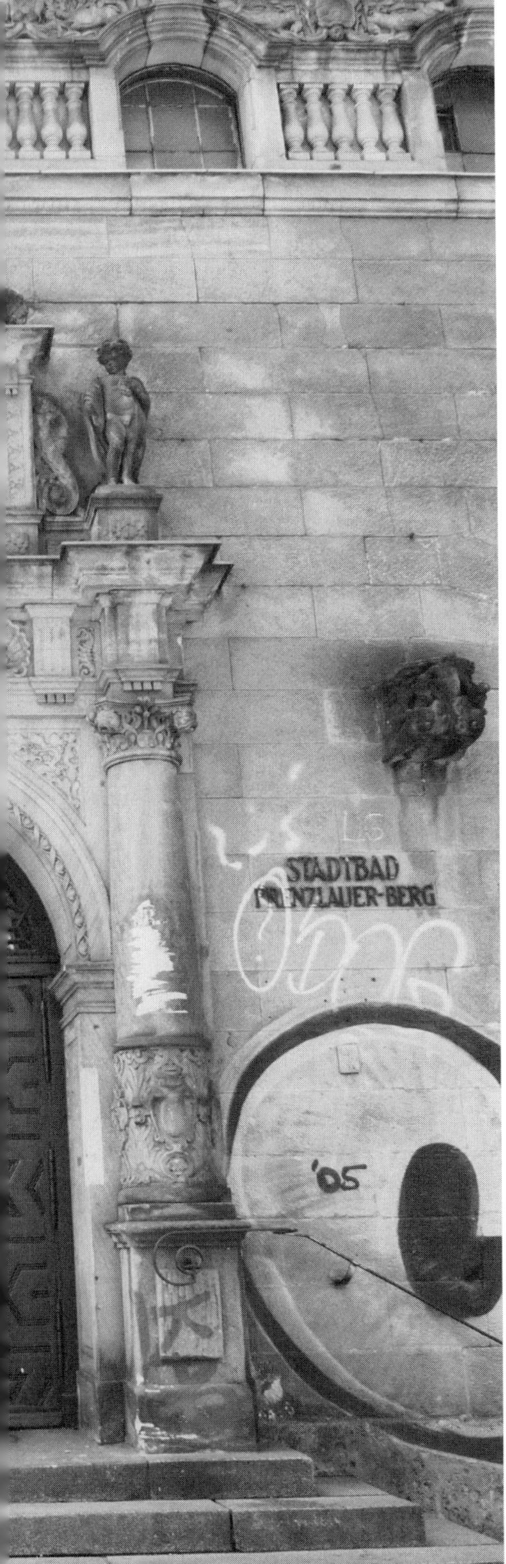

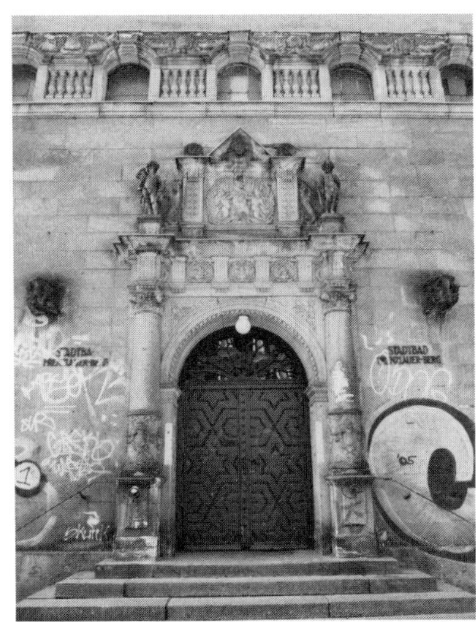

29

The seminal preoccupation in Berlin with an internalised, marine urban-landscape, stranded and depopulated following uncontrollable inundations, materialises on the graffiti-imprinted stone facade of the Stadtbad Prenzlauerberg, a phantasmatic urban swimming-bath constructed in the form of a palace, designed by Hoffmann at the same moment as he envisioned the first of his great sub-cities of the mad, and completed in 1902 in what was then an impoverished workers' tenement-district of breweries and factories, located in close proximity to the rooftop vantage-point from which the Skladanowsky Brothers had shot the first Berlin film-image, eight years earlier. While the facade of Hoffmann's first sub-city of the mad, on Berlin's periphery in Buch, was aberrantly mediated via the form of an English Tudor palace, his ornate swimming-bath for the families of urban brewery-workers constituted an equivalently perverse projection, resonating with the form of an Italian Renaissance palace, as though the swimming-bath's waterborne occupants, driven irreversibly city-mad by their inhabitation of the haywire megalopolis, could be ecstatically propelled northwards by a force of inundation that relocated them directly from palace to palace, from the Stadtbad Prenzlauerberg to the Buch asylum. During the era when the swimming-bath was constructed, few or none of the inhabitants of the surrounding, smoke-blackened tenements had any alternative access to hot running water, so the swimming-bath served also to momentarily erase the enveloping industrial dirt and detritus of the city. Around the great metal portal of the swimming-bath, figures of water-gods and angels burst out through the building's facade, to entice passers-by inside, promising a subterranean immersal in another medium from that of the abrasive ground-level city outside: a hallucinatory moment of exception and respite. But that portal into the swimming-bath had closed even during the GDR's final years, in the mid-1980s, since the neglected building had developed profound fissures in its vaulted ceiling after a shoddy concrete chimney was built alongside it, so that the building threatened to fall upon the heads of its occupants. Eventually, the abandoned swimming-pool was drained, and the lavishly tiled shower-rooms accumulated a layer of syringes, beer-bottles and indeterminate detritus, discarded by nocturnal infiltrators into that ruined space. Plans to turn it into a cinema or art-venue lapsed, and, voided of its defining medium of water, it immersed itself into its new status as one of Berlin's pivotally stranded sites, its portal now leading into infinite urban suspension.

Waterborne transits across Berlin's space, via its intricate network of canals and rivers, formed an essential element in the city's accelerating development over the final decades of the nineteenth century, doubling the trajectories of the vast railway network that brought inexhaustible human and material cargoes into the city. Through the outlet of the Spree docks, which Meidner transformed into an urban-apocalyptic axis of Berlin, in his 1912-13 sequence of deranged cityscapes, goods manufactured in the city's factories could be transmitted outwards, across Europe and towards the Baltic seaports, and the city was able simultaneously to absorb whatever could not be created within itself. Berlin was also surrounded on all sides, and especially at its south-western and south-eastern perimeters, by forest-edged lakes, many of them intersecting with its rivers, and which served a disparate purpose to that of the industrial, cargo-bearing canals, since those lakes constituted a merciful destination-point for human suspensions within the space of Berlin, through the medium of transitory escapes from the velocity of the city's propulsions, into madness, conflict or routine.

In Robert Siodmak and Edgar G. Ulmer's film *Menschen am Sonntag* (*People on Sunday*), from 1931, four young Berliners undertake a Sunday journey by suburban train out to the Wannsee lake, on the city's south-western edge, eluding the momentum of their habitual lives by improvising an ecstatic suspension, that takes the form of swims in the lake, full-tilt chases through the adjacent forest, and a sexual act between two of those escapees. In the film's opening sequences, which minutely scan Berlin's tenement-facades and its streets, the city's space is visualised as one impeded by the engulfing presence within it of dirt and debris: immense quantities of animal-excrement and earth have accumulated in its gutters, in mysteriously profuse quantities, along with discarded banners and paper wrappers which block all passage through the streets; those thoroughfares need to be hosed with great jets of water to clear them, and children's dirt-engrained faces must urgently be cleansed with water from the streets' fire-hydrants. The four young Berliners can only elude those habitual urban obstacles, and conjure bliss and elation, by heading for the city's perimeters. But even when two of the escapees, Wolf and Brigitte, after their headlong rush through the forest, find an optimum location for their sexual act, apparently exempt from all human or urban

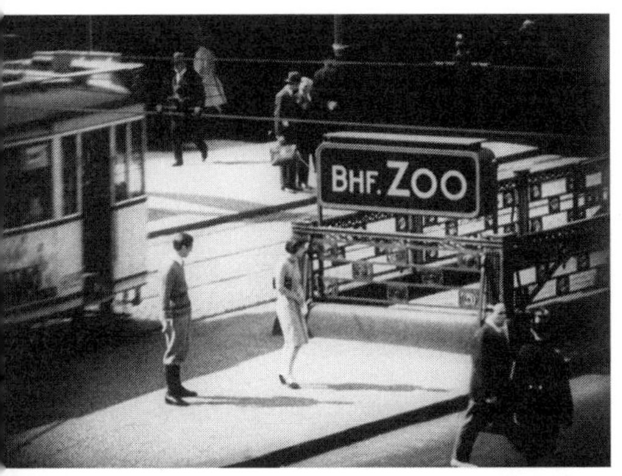

presences, the camera pans from their conjoined bodies to an array of jettisoned urban debris (cans, buckets) directly alongside them. Only those young Berliners' corporeal immersal within the lake, and their skimming movement over its surface, on a pedal-driven raft, provide a sensory respite from the city. In *Menschen am Sonntag*, the escape from Berlin is defined by its ephemeral duration and near-immediate return: the young Berliners, who all have jobs, will be back in the heart of the city by the end of the day. By contrast, in Dudow's *Kuhle Wampe*, from the following year, 1932, the filmic escape by suburban train from the corrosive city (whose poverty and unemployment have already caused one of the escapees' brother to plummet to his death from an apartment-window) forms a more desperate, semi-permanent one, that heads in the opposing direction, south-eastwards, towards the Müggelsee lake, where those escapees join a left-wing workers' camp of shacks and tents at the lakeside.

Berlin's film and art works seize vital moments of suspension, poised within the urban momentum towards calamity or engulfment; the existence of the young Berliners in both *Menschen am Sonntag* and *Kuhle Wampe* is one about to vanish, with the urban mutations and strictures precipitated by Hitler's imminent rise to power, and through the internment and eradication of all left-wing groups in Berlin, such as those occupying the 'Kuhle Wampe' camp. To escape the enveloping dirt and stasis of the city, the young Berliners of *Menschen am Sonntag* immerse themselves in the lake at its edge; but that medium of water, with its capacity to engender elation and desire, is itself intimately allied to the compulsive inundations which serve to propel Berlin's inhabitants through perilous and multiple trajectories, in which the city becomes torn apart, or unrecognisably displaced and rearranged; those unstoppable transits through Berlin leave behind the drained, marooned sites whose surfaces project urban oblivion, as with that of the Stadtbad Prenzlauerberg's palatial swimming-bath portal.

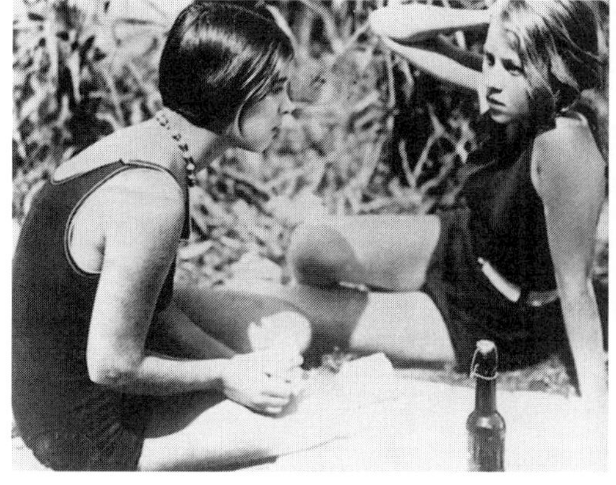

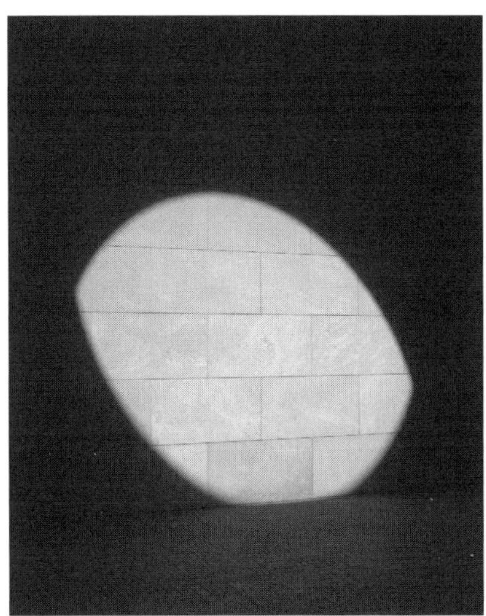

30

Against the back-wall of the Neue Wache memorial guard-house on the Unter den Linden avenue, the light of Berlin was projected through the medium of an overhead oculus, incised into that building's roof, to form a perfect eye-image, held in suspension like the waterborne bodies of the young Berliners in *Menschen am Sonntag*, and emanating an illuminated concentration of the city's memory, of its woundings and erasures, so dense with sensation that it could overturn at any instant into utter oblivion; the eye-image existed momentarily, before clouds closed that portal. The guard-house's cavernous interior had been re-assigned as a room for the dead of Berlin, and on the reverse side of that back-wall, facing outwards towards the city, an urban map of vertical, fire-imprinted striations had been inscribed. The transmission of light onto the room's back-wall resonated with that of a filmic projector beam which continued obstinately to exert its illumination, even when the film being shown had vanished, or been destroyed, so that only the act of exposure survived, in excess of any image's content which failed to seize urban memory, or whose tainting by the dirt of the city annulled it. In that room of Berlin's dead, all that could subsist was the apparition of an illuminating eye, as though that ocular form, its ovular configuration projected slightly askew as though as the result of a malfunctioning technology, could effortlessly exit the room of the dead and transit the entire city at will, phantasmatically liberated by its status of having passed beyond the constraints of urban life, and able exhaustively to archive every surface of Berlin, together with those surfaces' corporeal and urban imprintations, and their multiple sensory charge: an eye of death collecting the life of the city. The stone slabs which formed the back-wall screen for that eye appeared impassive and impervious, but their pivotal role was to absorb that determining light of Berlin, allow it to pass through their medium, while transforming it into the mutable map of Berlin that was then projected from their exterior surface.

For the first century or more of its existence, the Neue Wache's roof had been unpierced, and it was only in 1931 that the architect Heinrich Tessenow was assigned the work of overhauling that room into one of the dead, pre-eminently by creating the oculus in its ceiling that allowed it the status of an ideal urban cinema, in which all projection equipment, seats, insignia and other cinematic artefacts were rendered superfluous, reduced to nothing, and all that remained, through the projection of Berlin's light via the circle cut in the room's roof, was the seminal act of a human eye engaged with an urban eye, within a uniquely void room that mediated nothing but the compacting of all urban memory into death. In Berlin, the eye, film and art, and death, together form an essential urban amalgam for every act of vision and every projection, pre-eminently those seized, or irresistibly seeping, from the city's surfaces and facades. The momentary eye-image on the Neue Wache's cinematic back-wall screen formed a suspended point of origin for all transits across the face of the city designed to amass its urban illuminations.

The area around the Neue Wache building had also comprised the sensitised site of origin for cinematic exhibition, and for the filming of the centre of Berlin, across the decades before Tessenow cut his oculus into that building's roof. While the Skladanowsky Brothers had been based in the industrial north of the city, in Pankow and Prenzlauerberg, and had made only rare incursions into the commercial and memorial core of Berlin, above all for their projections at the Wintergarten Ballroom in November 1895, other film-pioneers had primarily inhabited the Unter den Linden avenue and the teeming streets between the Alexanderplatz and the Brandenburg Gate. The film-entrepreneur Oskar Messter ran Berlin's first cinema, opened in April 1896 and known under a multiplicity of names including the 'Biorama', located in the back room of a restaurant at 21 Unter den Linden, only a short distance from the Neue Wache building. Since he was a competitor of the Skladanowsky Brothers (whose improvised 'Bioskop' projector was, in any case, liable to malfunction), Messter used an 'Isolatographe' projector designed by the Algerian, Paris-based Isola Brothers, Emile and Vincent, which itself constantly malfunctioned, and was soon replaced by a new projector, conceived by the Berlin engineer Max Gliewe, which, following modifications, became the 'Model X' projector, as though named to intimate the negation at urban film's heart. Messter also operated Berlin's first film-studio, opened in the Friedrichstrasse, the same avenue in which the Wintergarten Ballroom was located, and while the Skladanowsky Brothers had filmed panoramas of industrial northern Berlin, Messter's own films of 1896 scanned the central avenues and monuments of the city, such as the Brandenburg Gate. In that same year, the Lyons-based Lumière Brothers, travelling through Europe for their film-screenings, shot a film from a vantage point adjacent to the Neue Wache building, of the Unter den Linden avenue's expanse, in which Berlin's inhabitants, standing in the image's extreme foreground, stare in compulsive fascination at the film camera; other,

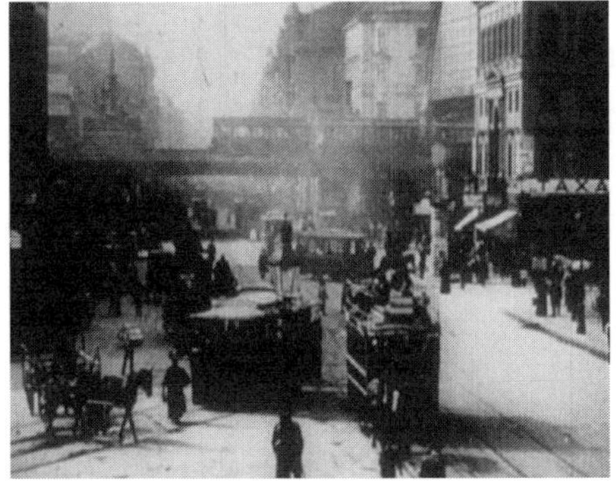

anonymous city-filmmakers focused on the central zones of Berlin that possessed a maximal concentration of human and mechanical movement (ever since the very first film, shot in 1888 by Louis Le Prince, of traffic and human figures crossing Leeds Bridge in industrial northern England, filmmakers had understood that dynamic urban film-panoramas needed to focus on intensive transits), pre-eminently the area stretching between the Alexanderplatz and Friedrichstrasse train stations, with their amassings of horse-drawn trams and ghost-presence passers-by, so that the traces of early film's hold on Berlin (apart from the Skladanowsky Brothers' originating aberrations) have their principal topographic axis in the Unter den Linden avenue and the Neue Wache building.

By the moment when Tessenow ocularly incised the Neue Wache's roof and transformed it into a vitally reduced, filmic room for the light-projection of death, in 1931, central Berlin's main conglomeration of cinemas had shifted eastwards, away from the Unter den Linden and Friedrichstrasse area, relocating itself alongside the Alexanderplatz, in the Münzstrasse, where Kracauer observed both the intricate cinematic rituals and the slow-moving street-crushes in his essay of that time, *Kino in der Münzstrasse*; as with the grandiose film-palaces of other cities, such as those of Downtown Los Angeles' Broadway, during that year when silent films (such as *Menschen am Sonntag*) were abruptly rendered redundant and sound-synchronised films (Fritz Lang's Berlin-set *M*, and *Berlin Alexanderplatz*) became ascendant, the Münzstrasse held a tightly-packed sequence of adjacent cinemas that mirrored the street's dense corporeal concentrations. All film mediates death. But by reversing cinematic time, and voiding it, together with its technologies, back to the moment before the Skladanowsky Brothers first conjured-up the film-projector, Tessenow's oculus-lit space of memory and death formed a uniquely stilled arena for the momentary suspension of the human eye, within its own image of urban illumination.

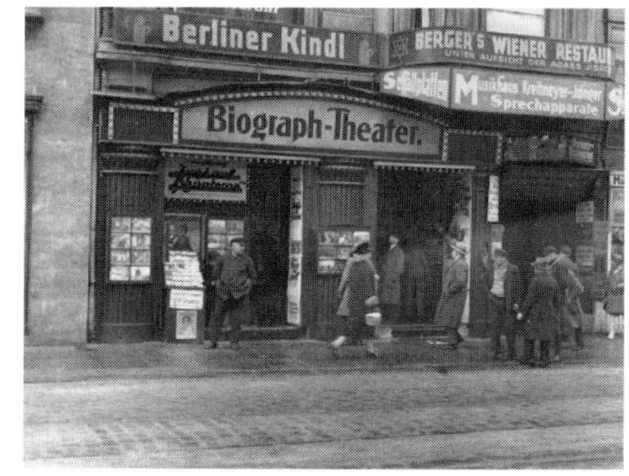

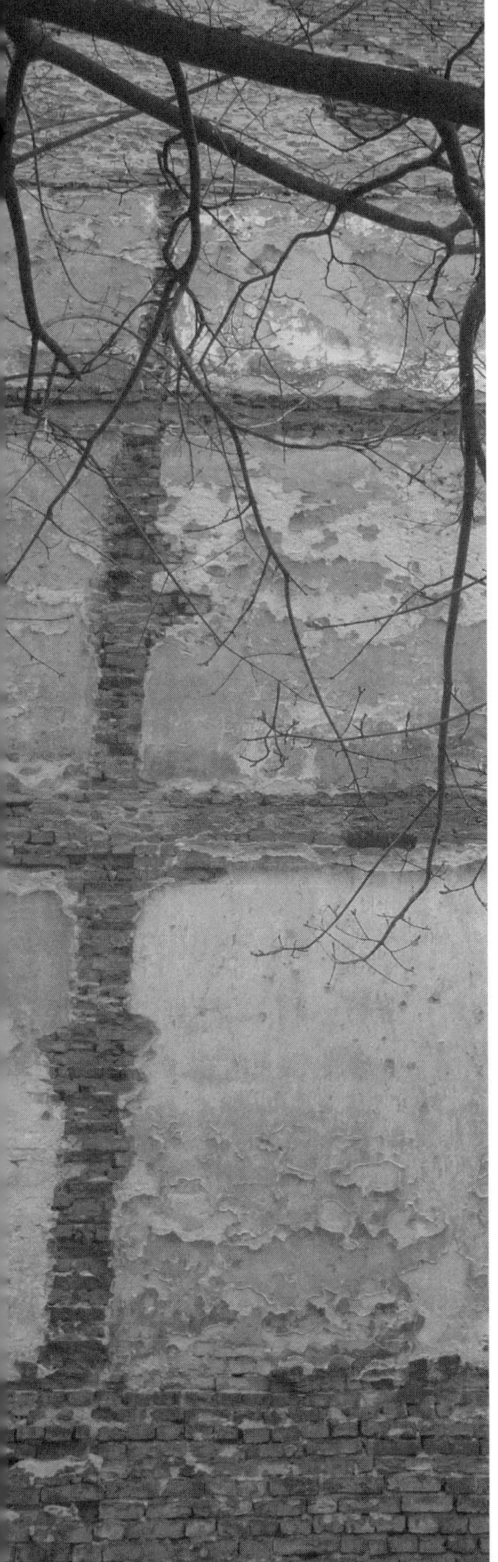

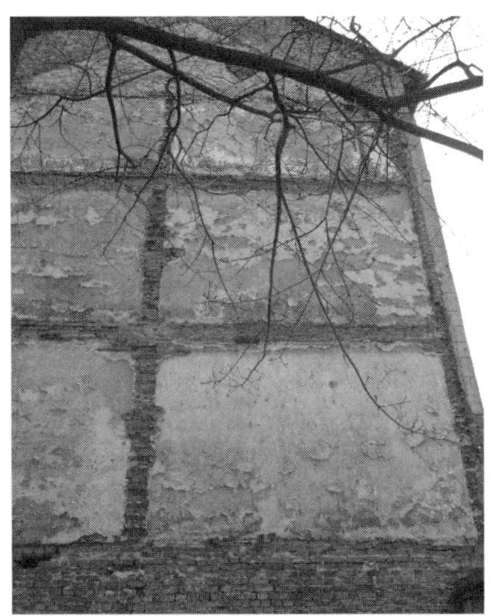

31

An entire house had unaccountably disappeared in one of Berlin's peripheral streets, as though confiscated by some omniscient urban hand and extracted from that street, so succinctly and completely that all that remained were the exposed imprintations of six interior walls on the adjoining house's facade. Each once-intimate room, now revealed to the eye, had been painted in a different colour, from blue to red; the tearing-open of those interior walls must have taken place decades ago, since the paint had gradually peeled into intricate decay-constellations, its layers turning in on themselves, like death-closed fists. The house's clean excision, as though sliced with a knife, indicated that it had vanished not through a firestorm's impact, or a destructive caprice of the GDR's planning authorities, but out of an irresistible urban desire to create six equally-sized cinematic screens for the simultaneous projection of six sequences from a film of urban disappearances: a seminal, now-forgotten urban event from which that excoriated wall enduringly constituted the petrified residue, awaiting a new filmic resuscitation. But those six screens also mediated their own sense of intent, rawly exposed by their house's vanishing, but possessing, too, the overriding compulsion of all of Berlin's interior spaces, such as that of the Neue Wache building's oculus-illuminated back-wall, to transform themselves into exteriors, and thereby project themselves, together with their engrained inscriptions and awry markings, to all urban eyes. Alongside those six painted screens, between which intervals of grey brickwork formed the perimeter separating their surfaces, a closed wooden door, with its handle still intact, was suspended at third-storey level, as though positioned there with a correspondingly cinematic intent, so that its next unwitting traversee, from the building's interior, could effortlessly plummet through elating or lethal space, mirroring the figures falling in *Germany Year Zero* and *Kuhle Wampe*. Every portal in Berlin forms a medium leading directly into thin-air, and the contours of the ensuing fall (into sensory exhilaration, or inversely, cast into terminal, deathly space) remain unknowable until the instant that portal has been crossed. The eroded door, poised in space like the six screens of the building's facade, formed a sensitised aperture ready to project the results of its own corporeal traversals.

In 1946, at a denuded moment when he evidently had access to no other medium for his visual obsession with Berlin, Werner Heldt used an entire wooden door, its handle removed and its hinges gone, for a painting of the city's facades and phantasmatic human figures. As in all of Heldt's imageries of Berlin from that moment, his figures are subject to a propulsive marine environment now instilled in the once-inland city, the sea-water coursing rapidly between tenement firewalls and majestically domed buildings, in order either to engulf or strand

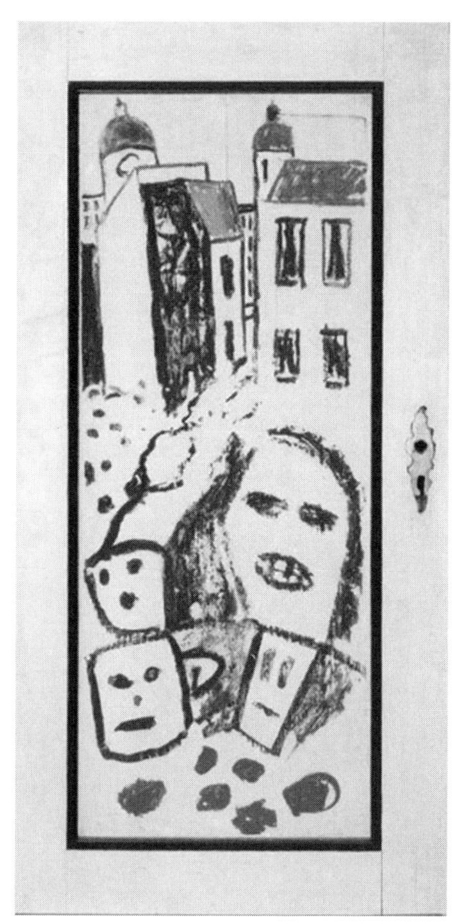

those figures. The painting's four disembodied figures have been reduced-down to their clenched-teeth and oblong-angled faces, and arranged in such a configuration that those amassed faces resemble the near-emptied rooms of a house whose infrastructure has vanished; directly in front of those figures, a scattering of arcane red marks has accumulated, as though forming the detritus from that house of faces, or else the ghost-traces remaining from other, now-submerged Berlin-figures. Heldt's reduced title for his painting – *Tür* (*Door*) – indicates the crucial status of his improvised, last-ditch medium, scavenged from Berlin's ruins, in conjuring-up an image of the city directly from its own flotsam.

All transits across Berlin's urban surfaces reveal the unstoppable transformation of interiors into exteriors, and the mutations endured by secrets, intimacies and covert sensations when they are re-processed for undifferentiated ocular exposure. Many of those urban intimacies have been unwillingly torn-open, through conflictual apertures in the face of the city like that created by the abrupt disappearance of the six-screened house, to disclose an infinity of traces of private lives; other intimacies are intentionally divulged, like the graffiti inscriptions of sexual acts or the visual embedding of mysterious memory-residues, in such forms as family photographs, within urban surfaces. Whenever an internal urban surface becomes inverted, and made momentarily external (as within Berlin's innumerable building-site upheavals), the projection of its contents entails an aberrant act of revelation, able always to transfix the eye that scans it. Film and art works of Berlin's urban facades serve to incise the city's interiors in order to gather-up its most hidden strata and sensations, and then to expose them in such a way that their intimacies permeate to the surface.

In Fassbinder's *Berlin Alexanderplatz*, a moment after Biberkopf, consumed by a sudden rage, has abruptly beaten his lover

Ida to death on the kitchen floor, his landlady, Frau Bast, terrified by Ida's screams, pulls opens the apartment's door and enters to gaze at the scene, her traversal of that portal immediately revealing the act of murder that has just been accomplished, in which domestic intimacy has mutated, from moment to moment, into 'public' horror; later, in the film's epilogue, as though the carapace of Biberkopf's apartment has been ripped-away to release her, Ida is resuscitated, as a wounded Berlin-ghost – like those populating the ruins of Heldt's sea-engulfed megalopolis, on his detached door-painting – to wander through the city's streets, and to haunt and taunt Biberkopf with the memory-traces of his act. After being incarcerated for several years, Biberkopf hesitates at the metal door of Berlin's Tegel prison, torn between an enticing but impossible return to the prison's interior, and his compulsory liberation, expelled towards the urban exteriors of Berlin, which will propel him into a further immersal in murder, and into madness. In Berlin's films and art-works, all portals from interiors to exteriors form apertures that reveal and enact urban tearings. The peeling wooden door, suspended in space alongside the six-screened post-cinematic facade left behind by the vanished house, signals both the volatile mutability of Berlin's transits between opposed urban zones, and also those spaces' vital interpenetrability: between memory and oblivion, between elation and erasure.

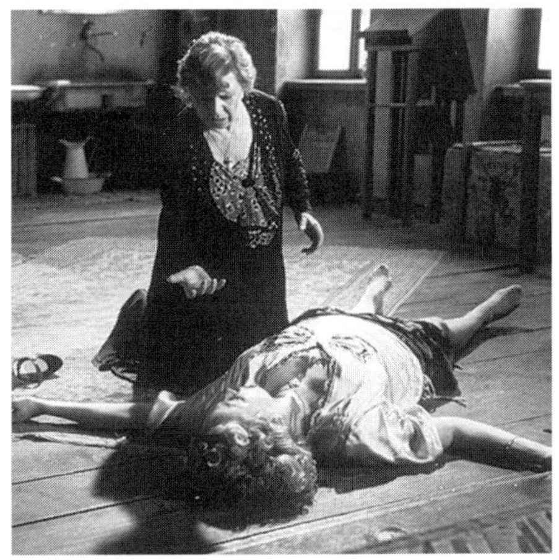

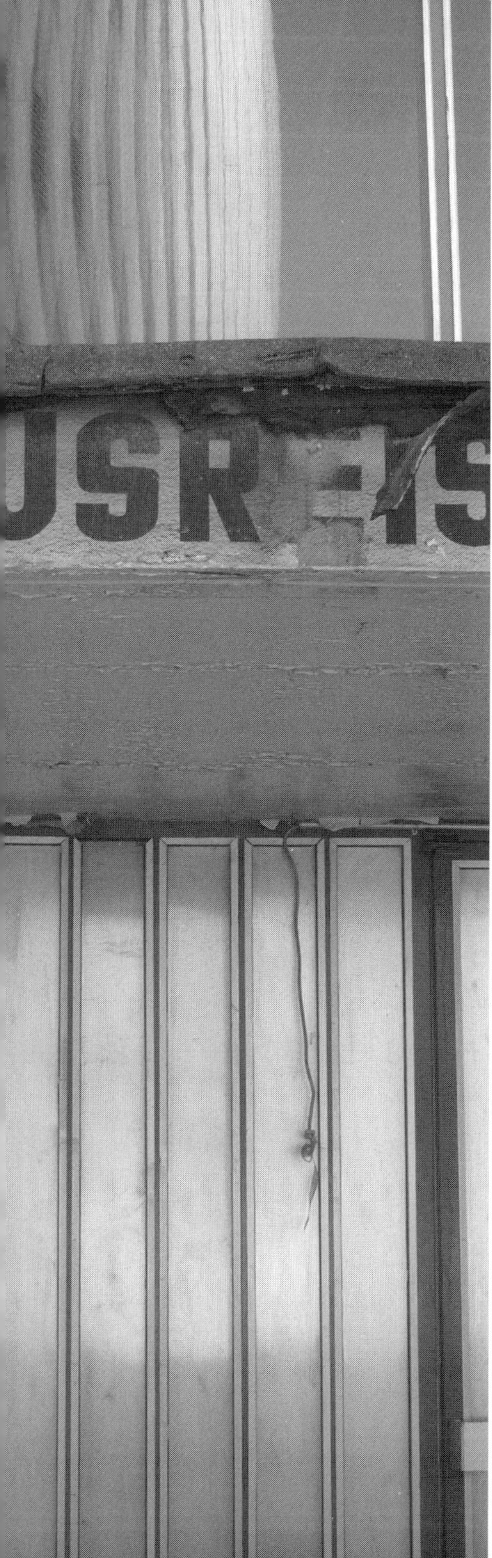

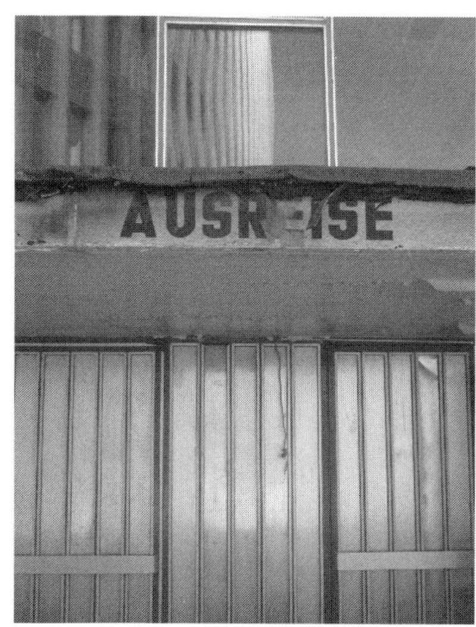

32

Stranded between the Friedrichstrasse station and the river Spree, within a zone that had been devoted to the construction of mirror-facaded corporate towers, a vast shed, assigned during the GDR era for crossings out of the phantasmatic space of East Berlin, had been abandoned in a morass of mud and red earth; since only crossings from east to west were permitted through the shed's portal, it had become known as the 'Tränenpalast' ('palace of weeping'), from the excess of sensory tearings-apart that had amassed around that door marked 'Ausreise', since the figures swallowed into it were vanishing into nowhere, travelling outwards and beyond, from a state of urban-hallucination into an unknown, potentially terminal and death-inflected orifice: an eye engulfing everything (corporeal, sensorial) that came its way, its opaque omniscience accentuated by the fact that nothing ever re-emerged from it. Immediately beyond that door, its entrants had headed into invisibility, lost from sight as they descended into an infernal subterranea, within which they would be perpetually stalled and minutely scanned, before being jettisoned into the urban-beyond. The aluminium doors of that denuded palace now appeared irrevocably closed as it awaited erasure, or its architectural amending as a corporate annex, and the windows directly above the portal distortedly mirrored the business towers constructed alongside it, but its one-word text still intimated a last-ditch act of transition, and an urban mutation via disintegration into a new visual configuration, with its letters peeling away (the 'e' almost gone) and obscured by strands from the crumpled tarmac-roofing directly above it, which appeared to have melted-down, as though that outlandish urban eye had spontaneously incinerated itself, in tears of fire, in despair at the absence of the weeping bodies which had once been sucked into it. Even in its obsolescence, the damaged insignia on the palace's surface, signalling a one-way corporeal vanishing into its interior, still constituted a seminal trace of urban conjuration.

In contemporary Berlin, digital data-screens and image-vectors comprise urban-media corporeal transmissions that generate equally comprehensive human vanishings and erasures to those signalled by the Tränenpalast's orifice, and in which all abrasive or intrusive perceptions of the city are mercifully lost, to be supplanted by an undifferentiated sensory expansion, into a digital medium of elation and oblivion, far beyond the city's layered arena of scarified memory. The axis of traversal for those flights from urban space is invariably screen-located (a corporate image-screen, a cellphone-screen, or a laptop-screen) but it is simultaneously an invisible boundary, whose crossing is performed in disembodying stasis, and entails an exemption, of indeterminate duration, from all coruscating ocular contacts, ignited by transits across the city, with the multiply image/text-embedded projections of Berlin's urban surfaces. That

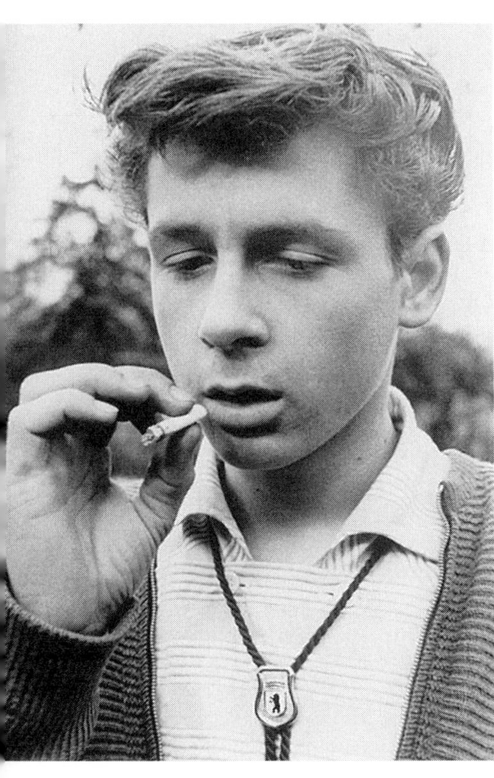

oblivious stasis resonates with the one-way swallowing, into nowhere, exacted by the Tränenpalast's voracious eye.

In Gerhard Klein's 1957 film *Berlin Ecke Schönhauser*, one of the disabused East-Berlin street-gang rebels who shatter the streetlight beside their archway dancing-site, Dieter, has fled into West Berlin, after becoming entangled in acts of identity-theft and murder, but soon discovers that he has entered an infernal nowhere-zone; along with his co-escapee, Kohle, he is detained in a brutal transit-house, and endlessly interrogated for information which he does not possess. If those escapees attempt to leave the house's grounds, they are beaten by a club-wielding guardian at its gate; they lose all hope of liberation, and fall into lassitude. In an attempt to precipitate a fever which he believes may lead to him being released from the detention-house, Kohle swallows cigar-tobacco mixed in water, which unexpectedly poisons and kills him, so that he transits between inter-urban limbo and death. That event finally incites Dieter to return to East Berlin, and he runs at exhilarated speed back across the near-invisible boundary (at that moment, in 1957, the perimeter between East and West Berlin is marked only by wooden placards), regaining his corporeal presence in the city. Klein's films of that moment are preoccupied with the crucial invisibility of the boundary separating the two mutantly-conjoined half-cities; in his film of the previous year, 1956, *Eine Berliner Romanze*, a young couple (the girl from East Berlin, the boy from West Berlin) agonise about their future urban location, and endlessly cross-over the invisible boundary, until those traversals congeal into an entranced stasis: West Berlin is full of neon-inscribed cinemas and avid eyes, East Berlin comprises haunted, skinned-alive urban facades. In the final sequence of the film, that indecisive couple appear almost to have evanesced within the city; but in *Berlin Ecke Schönhauser*, Dieter's determinedly headlong re-emergence, across the invisible boundary, generates a near-miraculous self-expulsion from his infernal interzone, even though that emergence directs him into new urban exigencies and dilemmas.

Berlin's traversals constitute journeys into transformational, violent or vanishing space, with unforeseen consequences, unless they are performed in static oblivion. At the rear of the marooned Tränenpalast-shed, a mysterious and long-rusted steel door lay half-concealed within a terrain of churned mud and decades-old debris, its frame enticingly prised-open by a narrow hairsbreadth, as though that now-stranded palace of urban disappearance possessed an alternate, two-way portal, enabling its entrants to momentarily pass through it, in either direction, and then emerge unscathed, instead of being engulfed indefinitely by its one-way subterranean propulsion. Crowbar-bucklings, like those exerted by history-thieves on the lead plaques of the Schönholz memorial-site, indicated intensive attempts to peel-open that resistant steel door, and enable a vitally aberrant, wrong-way-round entrance into that space. Through the resulting fissure, the box containing the shed's electrical wiring-system was visible, and behind that, illuminated by elevated windows, its tile-walled waiting-space also appeared, containing the cracked-glass hatches, booths and counters through which its stratified occupants had once been minutely scanned and channelled. Instead of being erased, or re-purposed as a corporate annex, that abandoned shed-palace could instead be jump-wired and ephemerally transformed into a monument to the virulent projections of Berlin's surfaces, and their capacity infinitely to absorb imprintations, woundings and charges of memories, and simultaneously expel them, for seizure by urban eyes.

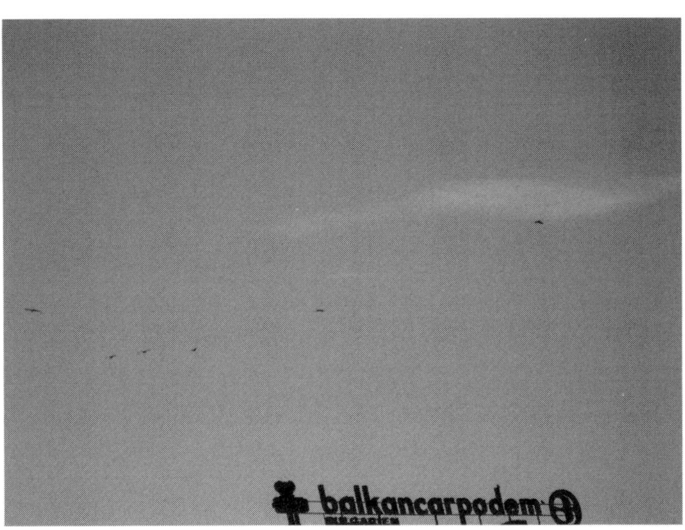

33

On the roof of an apartment-complex close to the Alexanderplatz, a hoarding had been installed against the sky, in thin-air, the transparence of its letters and insignia drawing the eye vertically towards its aerial configuration, as an urban text of Berlin designed to restrain the city's final disappearance, by anchoring its flight, as though that city were itself now attempting to escape its own excessive memory and history by capriciously vanishing through one of its innumerable eye-portals, like those of the 'Tränenpalast' or the bunker by the Friedrichstrasse station, thereby leaving behind the scorched-earth anti-city, cleared of all constructions and converted into farmland, which Churchill, Stalin and Truman had initially discussed as a future option for Berlin, during their meeting at the Cecilienhof villa in Potsdam, shortly after the city's 1945 fall, as a counterweight to the grandiose, world-engulfing future city of 'Germania' formulated by

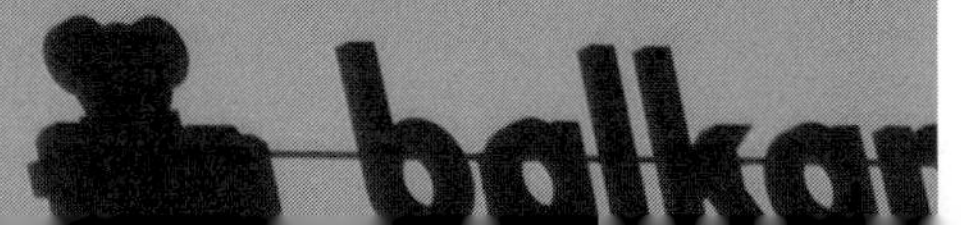

Hitler and Speer, before that all-powerful trio elected to leave the city to the course of its future transmutations, rather than erasing it. The mid-air hoarding, announcing the supposed existence of a Bulgarian crane-construction company, as though it were an enigmatic hallucination which, if seized, would deliquesce, had replaced previous generations of roof-top hoardings, on that site, lauding the chemical industries of the GDR, but that hoarding-variant appeared almost indistinguishable from its now-supplanted predecessors, its content negligible, and serving solely to intimate that, by positioning itself at an extreme urban perimeter, against the immense sky of Berlin, it constituted a final trace of the city before its presence lapsed, at the moment when vertically-directed ocular trajectories, which overridingly configure and map Berlin, surpassed it, to envision a site beyond the city. As the terminal trace of Berlin in its process of evanescing, that roof-top hoarding formed a tenacious, last-gasp exclamation of the city, inciting the eye in movement caressingly to scan its contours, before moving upwards, into the post-urban void.

Berlin possesses an infinity of perimeter-sites, at which the terminal traces of its relentless, excoriating self-transformations may momentarily be seized. Pre-eminent among those sites are those which bring Berlin's urban surfaces into proximity with the images or locations of art and film. On the city's northern perimeter, at Weissensee, in 1913, a 'Film-Stadt' ('film-city') was created, by the entrepreneur Paul Köhler (whose previous specialism had been that of a demolition-expert), as though to form a trio with the sub-city of slaughter inaugurated by Blankenstein in 1881 and Hoffmann's twin sub-city of the mad, whose construction was being completed in Buch at that same moment. But rather than a sub-city, Köhler's 'Film-Stadt' indicated its capacity at least to duplicate, if not supplant, the remainder of Berlin; as well as shooting-stages, that 'film-city' also incorporated chemical-laboratories for the developing and printing of film-footage, so that the entire filmic process could be undertaken within that one site, which, from nothing, emitted completed films

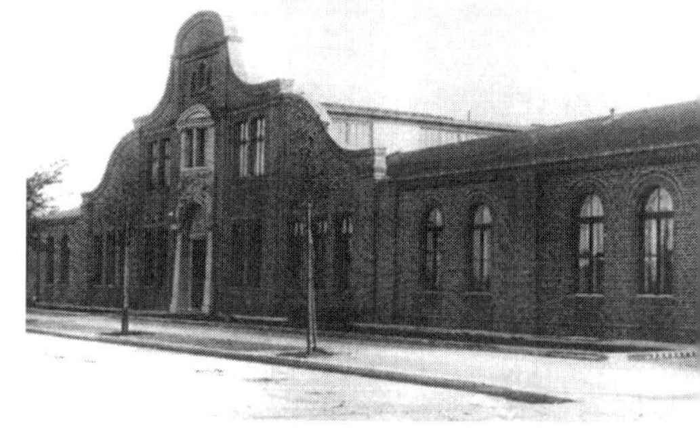

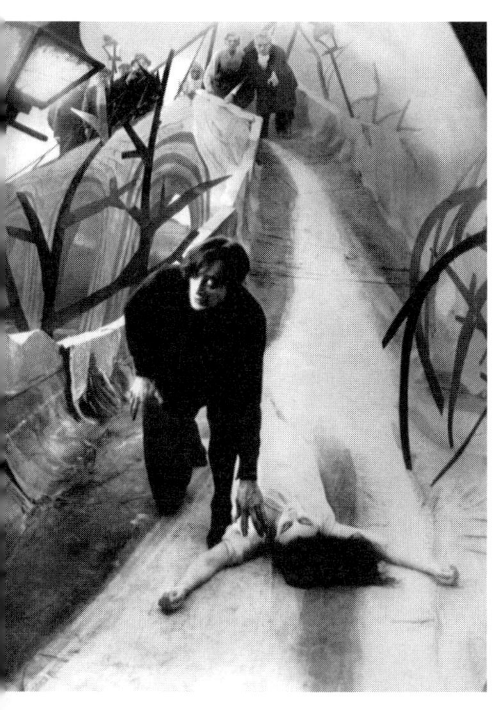

ready to be distributed for cinema-projection. Over the sixteen years of its existence, the Weissensee 'Film-Stadt' held multiple, perpetually-amended names: Lixie-Atelier, Vitascope, Greenbaum, among others. It generated Berlin's seminal films of that era, above all Wiene's *Das Cabinet des Dr Caligari* (*The Cabinet of Dr Caligari*) (1920), which was mass-advertised, in advance of its first projection, by exclamatory street-posters plastered across the entirety of Berlin's urban facades, bearing the mysterious invocation: 'You must become Caligari!', and whose asylum-sequences appeared to have had their location transplanted from Hoffmann's nearby sub-city of the mad, in Buch; the first film-appearances of Berlin's sexually-incandescent blue star, Marlene Dietrich, were shot at the Weissensee film-city, a quarter-century before she returned to the ruined, burnt-out Berlin for *A Foreign Affair*. The 'Film-Stadt' overspilled into the adjacent district for its outdoor-shoots, reconfiguring parts of Weissensee into locations such as the gladiatorial chariot-arena, the Circus Maximus. The studio-buildings of the 'Film-Stadt' were earmarked for vast, 'Germania'-style expansion, but that film-city began to experience financial difficulties only eight years after its inauguration, and the global meltdown of the late 1920s ended its operation. The interior of the film-city was then inhabited for decades by a dye-factory, before becoming a semi-abandoned terrain of workshops, with one of its adjacent buildings used as a car-windscreen installation-shed. In its filmic dereliction, it emanated the terminal traces of Berlin's originating film-industrial urban surfaces and imageries.

Alongside the voided, seminal urban-sites of film-production in Berlin, many of the films which intently interrogate the city's surfaces also exude an aura of belonging to a last-ditch moment, poised before that city's imminent evanescence. Gerhard Klein's final film, *Berlin um die Ecke* (*Berlin Around the Corner*) was shot in 1965, almost a decade on from his two explorations of the city's invisible boundaries, *Eine Berliner Romanze* and *Berlin Ecke Schönhauser*, but was prohibited by the GDR authorities (during that regime's accelerating petrifaction) as a spurious depiction of the city and its inhabitants, and rendered unviewable even before its first projection; the film's raw footage was re-assembled only in the early 1990s, after the GDR's erasure. The film envisages East Berlin as a disintegrating and exhausted entity, so profoundly riven and scarred that only sexual acts and nocturnal motorcycle journeys at speed, through its avenues, can dispel that terminal aura. Klein's city is populated by antithetical, dual populations: elderly figures, ailing and acutely burdened-down by their history and memory, and alcohol-driven younger figures, of around twenty (born out of a moment of urban apocalypse, many through the furore of mass-rape instituted by the Soviet army on its arrival in Berlin), consigned to repetitive factory-work, desperate and politically nihilistic. In that intractable state of urban and human stasis, the gestures of street-gang rebellion which activated *Berlin Ecke Schönhauser* have lapsed: only a comprehensive urban and sensorial razing will allow the city to resuscitate itself.

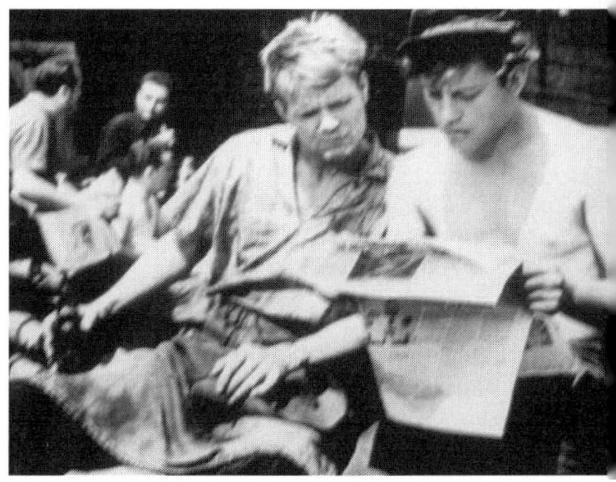

At pivotal moments, the filmic history of Berlin and its urban surfaces mesh revealingly, as vanishing traces. In 1995, Wim Wenders made a film about the Skladanowsky Brothers, *Die Gebrüder Skladanowsky*, as an amalgam of documentary and fictional sequences. In that film's final sequence, a black ghost-carriage (like that of Murnau's *Nosferatu*), carrying Max Skladanowsky's long-dead daughter, Gertrud, and his brother, Eugen, who have come alive and now want to view contemporary Berlin, enters a road leading into a sprawling, dead-end urban wasteland (the then re-emerging Potsdamerplatz) of endless cranes, debris and gouged-out earthworks, inundated by great pools of water; the two filmic ghosts gaze at that engulfing, transformational landscape, in a mixture of elation and horror, until their carriage has disappeared into it. Through all of its terminal images and texts, Berlin always projects, welded-together, both its ecstatic vanishings and its deeply memory-churned immersals.

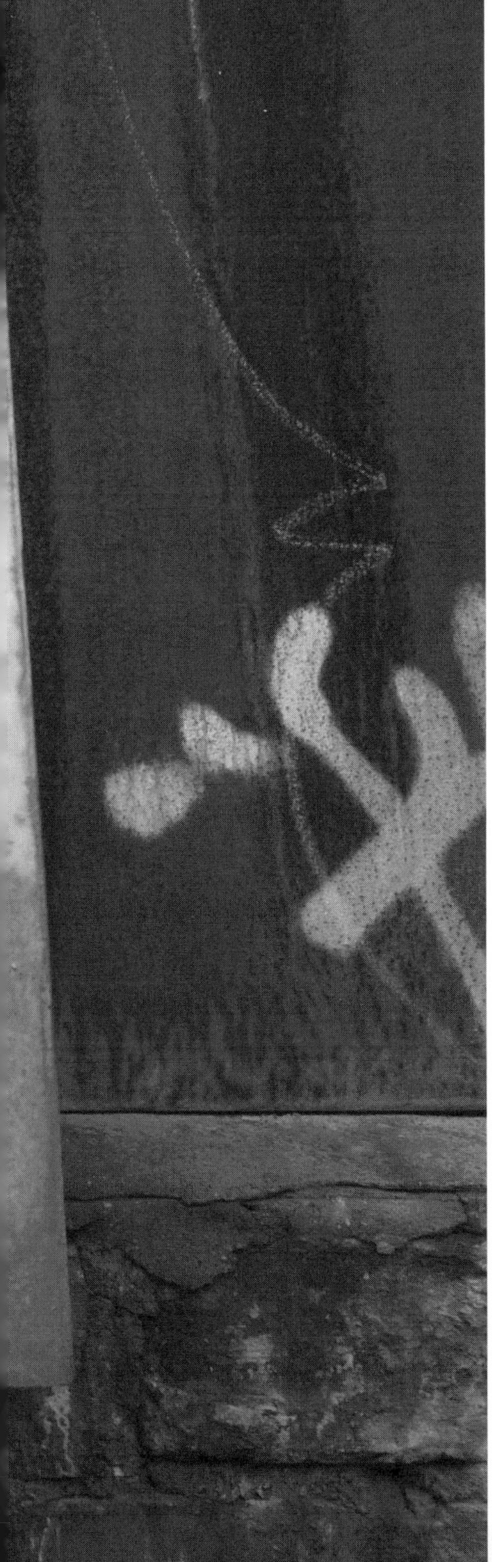

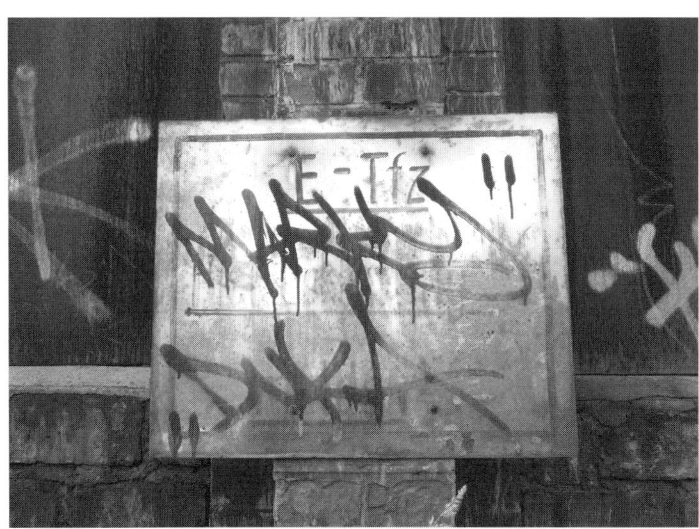

34

Alongside its surfaces' intimation of an urban vanishing which is imminent, or constrained only by its hoardings' determining hold upon the city, Berlin also possesses its innumerable excessive facades, on which the simultaneous presence of irreconcilable moments and traces becomes compacted-together, in dense projections, so that for every signalling of an out-going urban disappearance, an implosive concoction of volatile image and text insurges into the city. On the facade of an abandoned railway building in the Pankow district, a placard carried its conjoined interlayering of archaic and contemporary texts. The placard's original inscription, once black-bordered as though enclosing an enunciation of death, had mostly eroded into illegibility, with only the hand-painted statement 'E – Tfz' still present; the line of text directly underneath had been underscored, to reinforce its importance for whoever viewed that placard, but the line's content had faded-out into the engulfing medium both of urban dirt, and of obliterating rust which seemed to have encroached across the placard from its lower edge, in a vertically-directed incursive movement, so that only the emphatic underscoring remained intact. Beneath the second line, a final line was also composed only of its underscoring, with the lettering annulled into invisibility. At some recent point, a graffiti-inscription had been layered over that text, the acrylic-dripping letters closely following the spatial configuration of the original text, so that the dual underscorings now enhanced the graffiti content, which was enclosed by citation-marks, at its upper-right-hand and lower-left-hand points; the upper citation-marks appeared alongside the final letter of the still-legible original inscription, 'E – Tfz', thereby allowing it retrospectively to be accorded an ambivalent, half-citational status, as though it constituted an algebraic formula for the deciphering of urban space which could only ever be half-valid, and all cities envisioned according to that formula would necessarily be consigned to the divisive status of a dual entity, in which one half-city functioned perfectly, like a film-projector's fully-operative lens, and the other half cast itself into urban disintegration, in self-abandoning caprices. But even that contemporary graffiti-text had irreparably faded in the interval since its inscription, so that it appeared near-interchangeable with the original text, both texts, each in black lettering, now equivalently immersed, and in the process of being gradually dissolved, within that urban surface's aura of corrosive time and memory, which also inhabited the facade directly behind the placard, composed of fissured black bricks and rusted metal-coverings positioned over voided windows.

In intermittence with Berlin's vanishing traces, the city projects its assaults of excessive urban components, so that they accumulate in amalgams, veering across time, reconciled only by half-

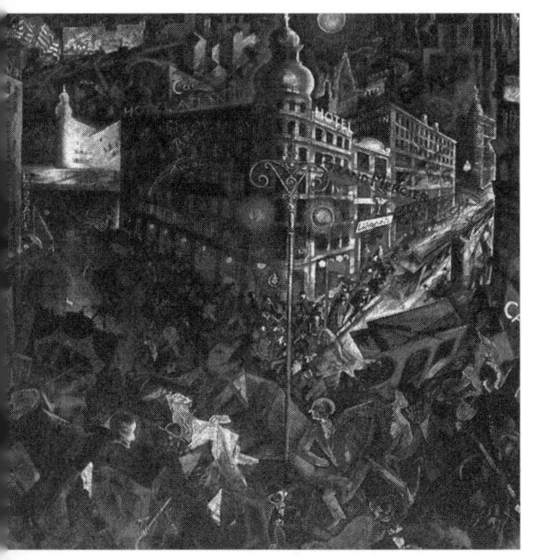

collapses into erasure, like that of the Pankow placard. The transmutatory excess of those projections occasionally takes on such elaborate compactings of visual and textual elements that the facades holding them appear to become autonomously detached from the surrounding urban strata, to phantasmatically float-free in space, like the so-called 'false facades' once constructed by Prussian emperors, often in the form of grandiose gateways, designed to conceal covert terrains, in militarised environments such as that of Potsdam, on the edge of Berlin: palatial, ornate, but free-standing and 'false' portals, leading into nowhere, and divided from the remainder of the city by a narrow but never-cohering gap. Once such 'false facades' become detached from the sustaining furore of the city, they constitute urban ghost-presences, excessive but terminally stultified, so that whatever new transmutations occur in the surfaces that surround them, they will never move again.

In George Grosz's painting *Metropolis*, from 1917, Berlin's saturated avenues are overwhelmed by a medium of maleficent red light, as though the entire city had been inundated by blood, as an alternate propulsive medium to Heldt's sea-water, thirty years into the future; that propulsion activates both the corporeal amassings of the painting, with its scrambled, heaped-up bodies in full-tilt flight across the city, each face monstrous, and also ignites the insignia of Berlin's central avenues: hotel-signs, advertising-hoardings, flags, and indeterminate inscriptions, many of them semi-detached from the buildings' surfaces, or else wildly veering across them, as though possessing an aberrant life of their own. In the preceding years, Grosz had made drawings of the far peripheries of Berlin, with their improvised encampments of tenuous populations, displaced by poverty or conflict, unable to adhere themselves to the city. In *Metropolis*, he paints, instead, the heart of the city, in its sensorial self-abandonment, focusing on the junction of the Friedrichstrasse and the

Georgenstrasse as an axis for the onrushing confrontations of opposed human presences, as though they were approaching an urban precipice. The painting's axis of vision allows it flexibly to warp the city's terrain, so that the remainder of Berlin is concertinaed and propelled vertically, re-located directly above and behind the street-junction, so that its peripheral tenements stretch upwards towards the image's upper surface, poised to crash down on that street-junction axis. Grosz's painting itself comprises a 'false facade' of Berlin, though with a revelatory compulsion, rather than a concealing one: so dynamically excessive, in its sensory and urban invocations, that it abruptly freezes itself, and generates its own petrified autonomy, as an infernal and unique vision of Berlin, while the city it depicts continues relentlessly to transmutate, and half-misfire, around it.

In the art and film images which attempt to seize Berlin's infinite transformations, and thereby accumulate an excess of urban traces and projections, the intention may always be to screen voids: to deflect the viewer's eye from the endemic fissurations of the city, and from its elements' rushings into disappearance, by creating multiple points of focus, able to preoccupy and entrance that eye with imageries of the city's incandescent attractions, its layerings and illuminations. Grosz's visualisation of a repulsive, blood-lit slaughterhouse-Berlin, powered by corporeal and urban mutation, is simultaneously a compelling, enticing one, welded to the following decade's worldwide obsession with the ascendant exhilarations of awry metropolitan space. But Berlin's excesses can also, conversely, be stripped-down, through its surfaces, films, and art-works, to sparse enumerations of urban acts and abysses.

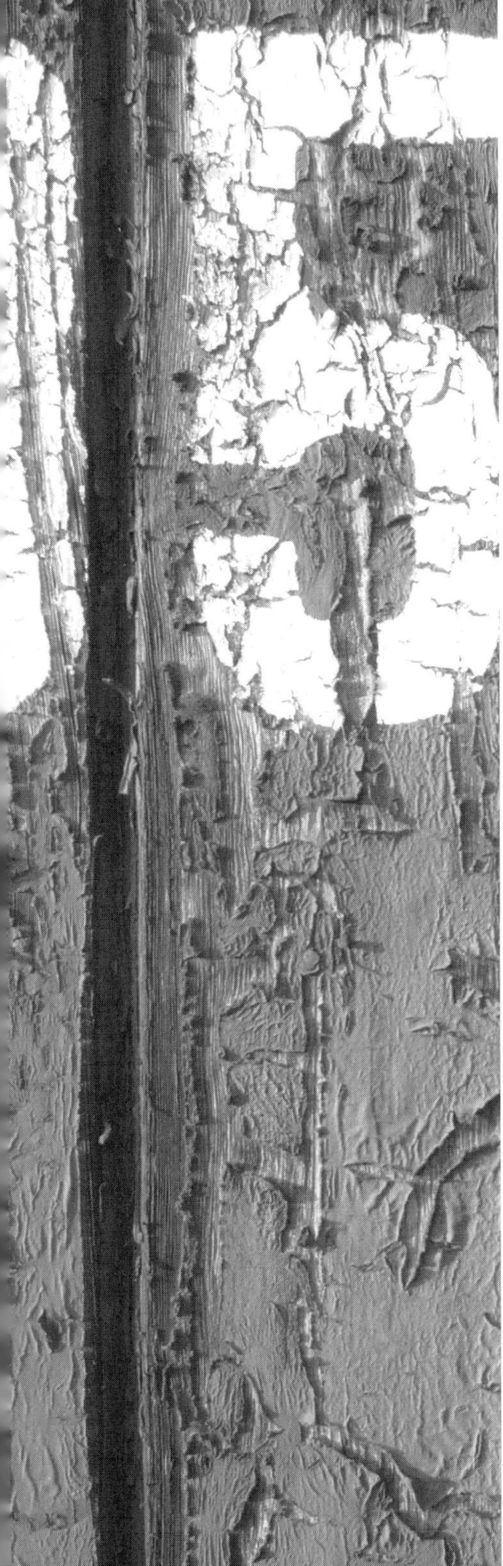

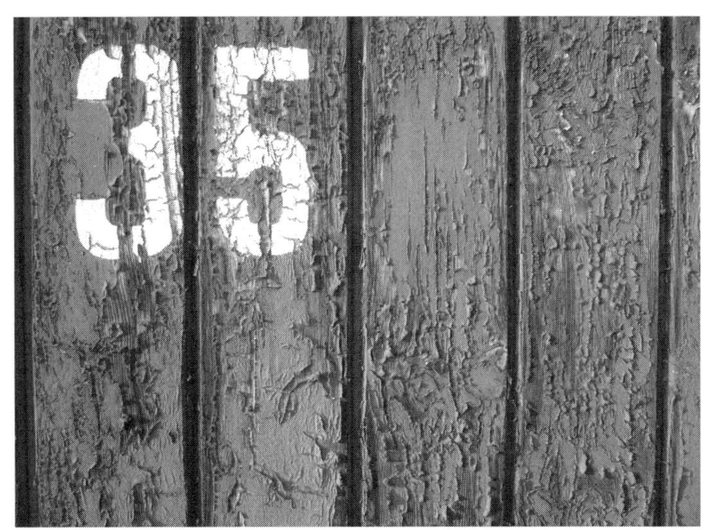

35

Berlin's surfaces form compulsive screens for the imprintation, often in multiple variants, of a mysterious urban numerology, permeated by the obsessive marking of the city's acts of slaughter, and of its human scannings and amassings, alongside more mundane numberings. The enumeration of urban surfaces indicates the presence of a power which always seeks to appropriate, often for purposes of human or urban elimination, but which also exposes itself, through its numerological mania, to disintegration. In the grounds of the Pankow district's Schönhausen palace, close to the sex-instilled, graffitied facade of the abandoned hotel that once housed entourages of the GDR regime's official guests, an immense terrain of now-voided garages retained their enumeration, the paint-peeled doors inscribed with an almost-infinite numbering. In all communist regimes, cars possessed a pre-eminent status which overruled all urban space and time; at the moment of Stalin's death, at his villa on the periphery of Moscow, the first act of his would-be (soon-executed) successor, Beria, was immediately to yell for his chauffeur to bring his car, to transport him into the city's heart, where he could seize power. Whenever the GDR regime's leaders made their fast-moving transits through East Berlin, in black Volvo limousines, to their centrally-located governmental buildings, either from Pankow or from their Kurtz-style collective-compound outside the city, in Wandlitz, the avenues' inhabitants and their vehicles were methodically swept aside, disappearing into thin air, all eyes averted, so that the motorcade could traverse the city at maximum velocity, in invisibility, like a ghost-carriage. The massed garages in the Schönhausen palace-grounds housed both the leaders' primary fleet of luxurious limousines, and also the multiple sub-cars of their entourages and bodyguards, necessitating a rigorous enumeratory collation of every garage-door. Once those sweeping transits through the city were abruptly stilled, at the GDR's own vanishing, the garage-terrain became instantaneously emptied-out, and derelict, its doors' intricately compiled numerology now rendered redundant, but remaining intact, to erode across time, within the spectacular decay of the surfaces projecting it.

Berlin's expansive enumerations extend from the proliferating imprintation of its urban facades, such as the number '13' inscribed on the multi-storey Marzahn tower alongside the Sojus cinema, to the seminal numerology of death and calamity, recorded and archived with precision by such bodies as the city's Nazi bureaucracy, and the East and West Berlin secret-police authorities: the number of the dead, excised from the city during the Nazis' deportations, and propelled towards Europe-wide concentration-camps, via the portals of the Grünewald and Plötzensee railway marshalling-yards; the number of animals, of all species, butchered in Berlin's sub-city of slaughter (those quantities painstakingly transcribed by Döblin, in his novel

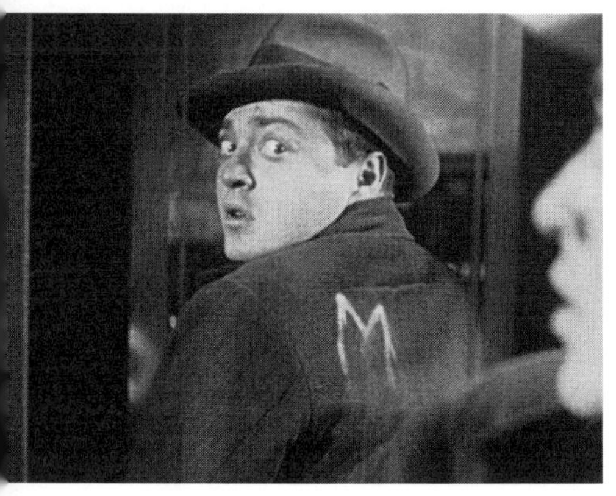

Berlin Alexanderplatz), and the number of the urban insane consigned to Berlin's sub-city of the mad, in Buch, most of them never to return; the number (vastly excessive, as though indicating an ocular malady) of human eyes orchestrated by the secret police, as a banal routine, to exhaustively scan potential acts of aberrance, in GDR-era East Berlin, and the number of that same era's ocular scannings of protesters, anarchists, ecologists, squatters, and exiles, in West Berlin; and the number of contemporary Berlin's human and urban suppressions, infinitely engendered by the two-number code integral to digital media, to facilitate sensory coercion and regimentation.

In films of Berlin, the compulsive enumeration of urban facades can extend to corporeal surfaces, and metamorphose from numbering into lettering. In Fritz Lang's studio-shot film *M* (1931), the criminals of Berlin decide to assume responsibility for overseeing the capture and execution of a child-killer, Beckert, played by Peter Lorre, who is capable of conjuring young girls into invisibility from the streets, while the bovine police, in their Alexanderplatz headquarters, enmesh themselves in dossiers containing innumerable half-clues. Berlin's beggars construct a city-encompassing ocular network of surveillance, which locates Beckert as he escorts his latest victim on a slaughter-trajectory, towards her imminent death. Beckert's overcoated body is then imprinted from behind with the letter 'M', transferred via the medium of chalk-crayon from the palm of his locator's hand, and then onto Beckert's shoulder, in an act of 'rear-projection', similar to that used pervasively in the early years of cinematic exhibition, whereby the projector was located directly behind the screen, the film-images transmitted first to the screen's rear face, before traversing it, to reach the film's audience. The letter 'M', imprinted on Beckert's shoulder, glows luminescently; he catches its reflection in a shop-facade mirror and is captivated, wide-eyed, by that inscription, which remains resistantly present even when his intended victim tries to erase it with her handkerchief. As Beckert begins to move rapidly, in increasing panic, through the Berlin streets, aware that he is being multiply scanned, his imprinted body forms a mobile entity of urban-projection, mediating death, allowing him to be tracked through those streets by their peripheral inhabitants, stalled and cornered, then taken down into a subterranean space, to be judged by the city's elite criminals.

Berlin's numerological urban surfaces are subject to relentless transmutation, across time, and exposed to capricious amendments. Their forms may be located at precarious boundary-zones, oscillating between the status of urban art-works mediating entrenched preoccupations with numerological mysteries, and that of surfaces which simply demand incessant acts of numerical supplantation. On an apartment-tower facade, a section of primed wall had been expansively numbered, firstly with a stencilled '1', then beneath it, with a smaller, stencilled '3'; the number '4' had then been inscribed at a tangent to the two initial numbers, and alongside it, a '5' had been rapidly hand-imprinted, before an all-engulfing, terminal '8', enumerated in red paint, had annulled all of the previous numbers. Equally, that sequence could be scrambled, set into reverse order, or re-arranged in any alternative sequence of its components. Berlin's numerology intimates the simultaneous existence, on its surfaces, of irreconcilable urban enumerations, along with the intensive ocular work required to reinforce or else void them, as though, if a perfect numerical sequence could ever be created, to embody Berlin's urban surfaces, it would instantaneously be returned to zero.

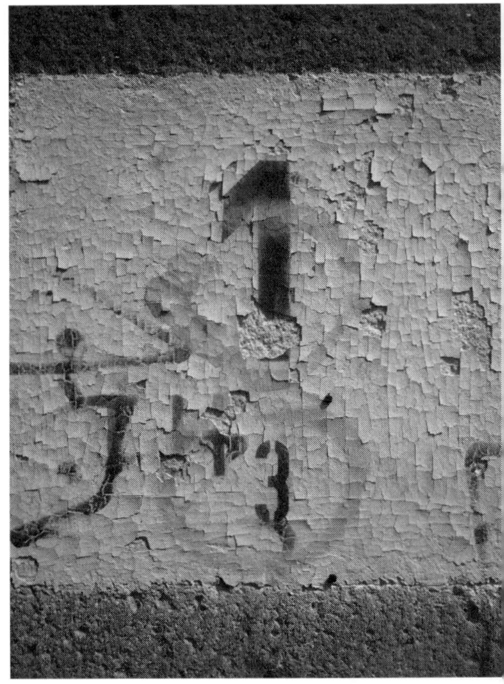

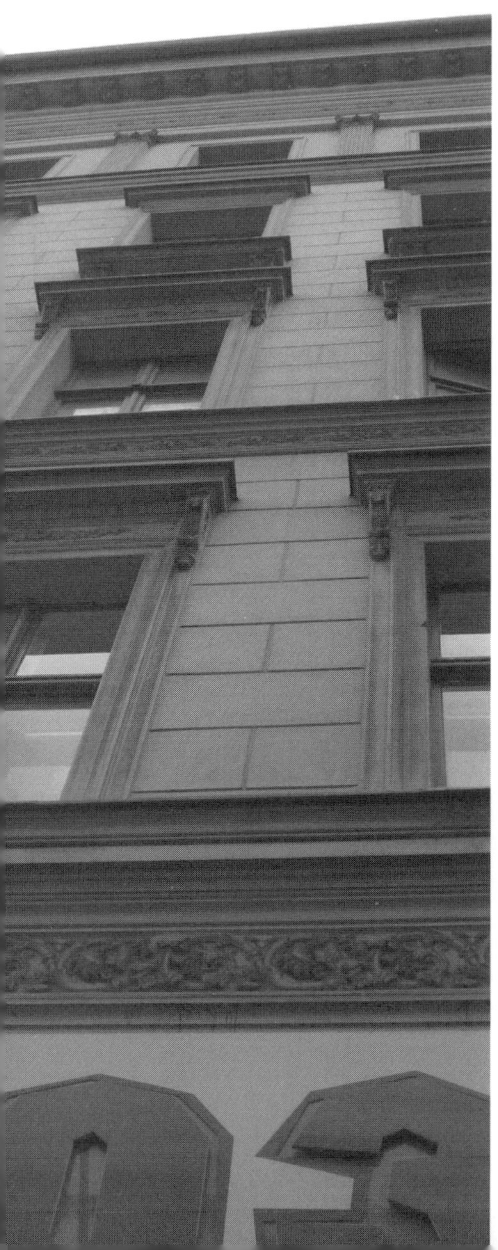

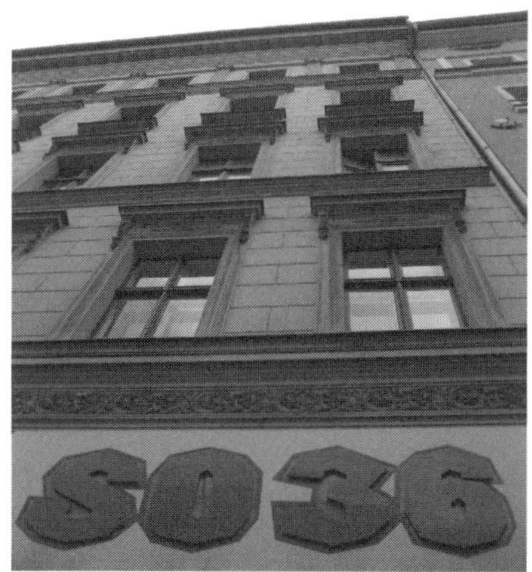

36

Berlin's numerological manias possess a sonic, insurgent dimension, with its own history of furore, embedded within the city's urban surfaces in intimate, confrontational proximity to their visual and textual contents, that amalgam forcibly projected outwards from Berlin's surfaces through (as Kracauer imagines) a 'scream' of the streets. Pre-eminent among those sonically-charged urban surfaces is that of the SO36 – the legendary punk-rock club in an avenue of the Kreuzberg district, immersed from the end of the 1970s, and through the following years, within a perpetual sonic uproar that spilled-over onto the surrounding streets, many of them inhabited in that era by militant squatters, autonomous anti-property communes, exiled and uprooted populations, filmmakers and artists, hidden-away terrorists and dissidents, and experimental-noise factions. The naming of the SO36, from the district's former post-code ('Standort 36': 'Location

36'), resonated with a concentrated enumeratory sparseness that implicitly annulled West Berlin's inverse numerological preoccupations, with accelerating Cold War weapons-quantities, property-speculation profits, terrorist-arrests, and other accumulations. At the same time, the club's name explicitly located its filmically-inflected space: a single long room originally constructed, over a century before its transmutation into the SO36, as a beerhall, that passed through multiple spatial incarnations – as a cinema, slaughterhouse, supermarket, squatted art-space – before coalescing in 1978 as a punk-rock club. The metal-gated facade, with its frequently-amended numerical insignia and battered portal, inhaling and expectorating cacophony and a deranged corporeal detritus, was positioned at the base of a five-storey nineteenth-century tenement. For its fanatical clientele, many of them young artists and filmmakers, the numerological dimension of the SO36 focused specifically on the sequence of dates, notably those of its first period of existence, on which seminal events (by West Berlin-based performers, as well as from British and American cities) had erupted from that club's space, in ephemeral instants of negation and exhilaration, delineating the future-city's askew films and art-works. Occasionally, the space was utilised for festivals of allied events, such as performances by Japanese 'ankoku butoh' choreographers. West Berlin's other punk-rock venues rapidly disappeared, while the SO36, though intermittently shut-down for long periods by the Berlin police, or self-abandoned by its proprietors, persistently resuscitated itself, in aberrant indestructibility.

An artist-habitué of the SO36, Helmut Middendorf, transpierced the club's exterior-facade to expose its darkened, urban-instilled interior, in his 1979 painting *Grossstadteingeborene* (*Those Born in the Metropolis*). Middendorf's rapidly-painted image, spanning two panels which were subsequently adhered-together, is

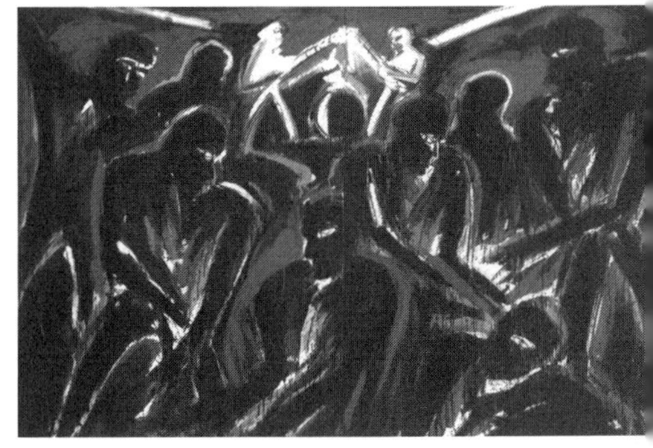

permeated by the extreme cacophony which its figures inhabit: those identically-dancing figures are occupied by gestural manoeuvres, arms contorted or outstretched, as though executing acts of violence, and each possesses one immense, excessive eye, as though, in that light-voided space, new strategies of envisioning Berlin's urban parameters are being formulated, involving corporeal as well as ocular mutations. The two musicians on stage, located far behind and beyond the frenzied audience, as though in a parallel spatial dimension, appear as undifferentiated as the audience's figures, both playing identical instruments, though one musician possesses a vivid red mouth, either streaming with blood or lavishly lipsticked.

Even under the GDR's constrictive, ailing regime of the 1980s, with its inhabitants' obsessional mass-scanning of one another to detect traces of social anomaly, and the perpetual threat of summary jettisoning into asylums or prisons for its deviants, punk-rock clubs resistantly operated in East Berlin, often occupying the spaces of run-down or overlooked youth-clubs, notably in the deteriorated Prenzlauerberg district of excoriated, dirt-encrusted urban facades and secretive back-courtyards. During the last-gasp moments of GDR-era East Berlin, punk-rock performances lost their covert dimension and often took place outdoors, in those courtyards, as though in accord with the skinned-alive vocal performances undertaken a decade or so earlier by Bruno S., in West Berlin's rear-courtyards, filmed by Herzog in *Stroszeck*. East Berlin's utterly raw, compressed punk-rock was conjured with near-zero technological means, and attracted devotees from cities across Europe, who entered the GDR's hallucinatory urban space via the portal of the Friedrichstrasse station (and then exited, before midnight, through the 'Tränenpalast' shed), where the guards were too hard-pressed by the traversing human crush to devote capricious time to refusing them entry. The Duncker club operated from 1983, in an outbuilding of a community school, emblazoned with animals and insects, and built by Hoffmann, in 1913, at the same

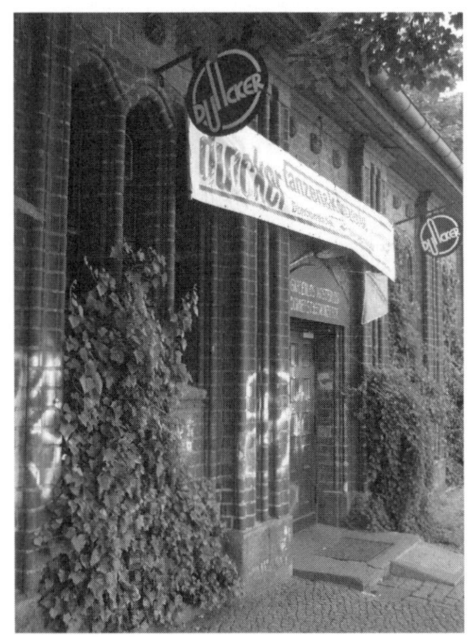

moment as he was completing the second of his great sub-cities for Berlin's mad, in Buch, as though that architect, in one of the city's temporal and topographical warpings, had been presciently compelled to map-out direct movements, backwards and forwards, between his Buch asylum-pavilions and his school-outbuilding's psychotic sonic-furore, seventy years into its future existence. The oblong box-shaped space of the Duncker club, possessing minimal dimensions alongside such immense terrains as Hoffmann's sub-city of madness and Blankenstein's sub-city of slaughter, along with those of the Weissensee 'Film-Stadt' (also constructed in 1913), appeared as though phantasmatically conceived by Hoffmann as the haywire control-room designed to synchronise and interconnect all of Berlin's sub-cities, across their pasts and futures, thereby sparking electrified, malfunctioning urban-transits, between madness and film, between slaughter and madness, between film and slaughter. As with the SO36's varied spatial usages before it eventually became a punk-rock venue, the Duncker club's darkened interior space, behind its fissured red-brick facade, had previously been used as a horse-stable, gymnastics exercise-room and salt-depot, so that it exuded a profoundly compacted olfactory, as well as sonic, presence.

Even in the enduring survival of those spaces, the facades of Berlin's sites of urban cacophony, such as its punk-rock clubs, form haunted, half-disappearing surfaces, upon which the sonic outbursts of insurgence and negation, projected from those spaces' interiors, conjoin with the multiple images and texts that also constellate those surfaces, as scarifications and marks of elation, and become amassed within those visual traces, along with Berlin's other aural presences, such as its innumerable voices of the dead, its mysterious nocturnal exclamations, as well as its suppressed or violently erased cries, finally forming surfaces from which urban ghosts appear simultaneously to be screaming at maximum volume, and held in silence.

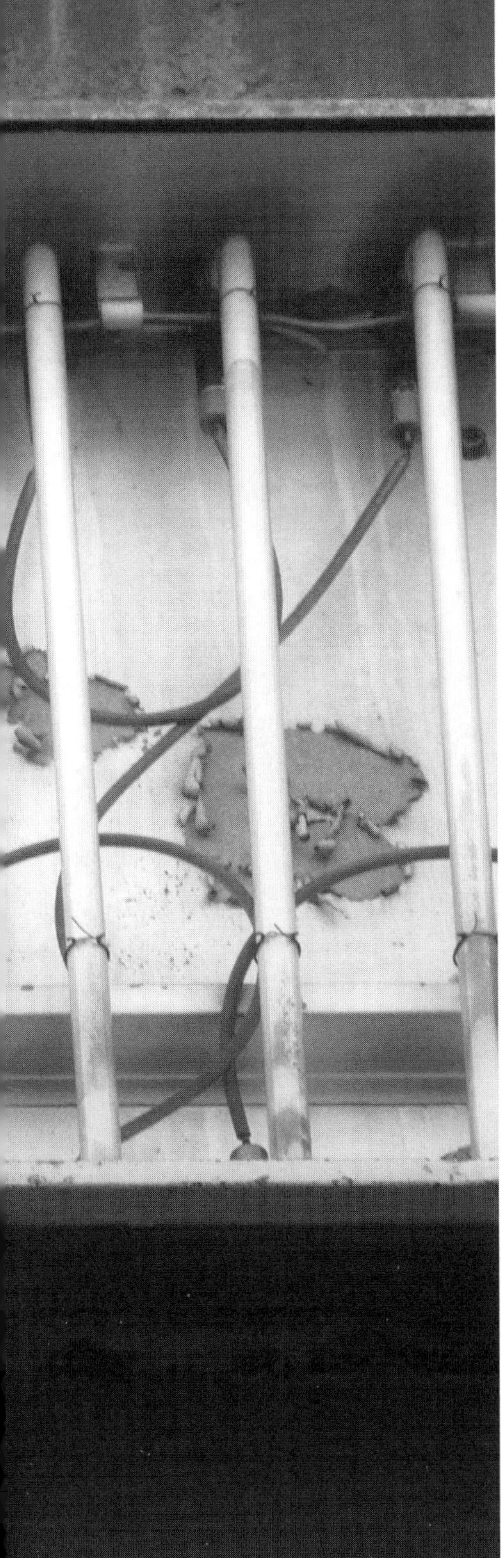

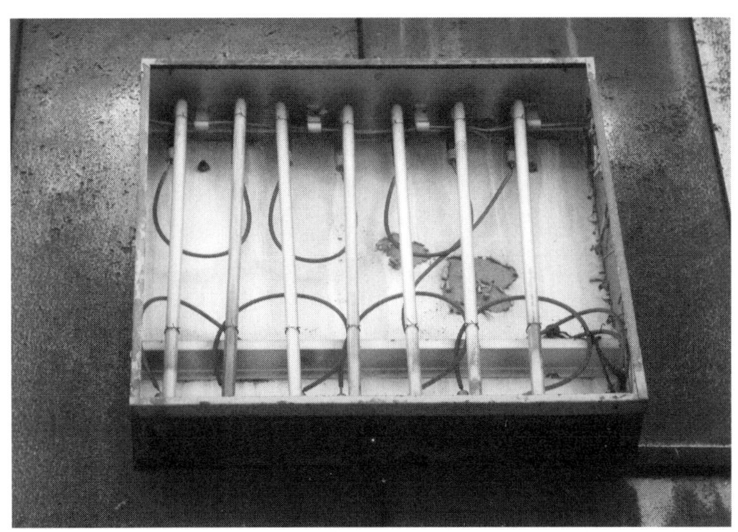

37

Whatever amasses on Berlin's urban surfaces becomes an eye, and the city can perform no more essential act than to deploy its infinite ocular capacities to scan and mark its human inhabitants, instilling the memory-lacerated contents of those facades into their skin and into their own eyes. At the same time, Berlin's urban surfaces appear also to gaze at and into themselves, exposing and excoriating their fissures and traces of ecstasy, rendering them open for seizing, by art-works and film images. On the facade of a building nearing its moment of demolition, or its comprehensive re-surfacing through renovation, the configuration of an urban eye had transmutated from a once-illuminated oblong box, that appeared to comprise a still-further miniaturised variant (ideal, for the digitised city) of the Duncker club's control-room, operated posthumously by the architectural ghost-presence of Hoffmann, to bring Berlin's urban surfaces ever more intimately into contact with madness, slaughter and sonic insurgence. That box, poised against a dirt-encrusted wall of concrete slabs, contained seven vertically-directed neon tubes, apparently installed in order to transmit Berlin's scorched-earth images and mappings up from ground-level, in trajectories towards its sky, like all vital urban transits, and revealed when their casing had been ripped-away, like the lens-cap of a film-camera, as an unforeseen prelude to their erasure, so that, for that indeterminate interval of survival, they had been conjured into a seminal eye, gazing outwards and inwards, able to absorb and project every corporeal and urban trace that entered their ocular arena. The power-supply to that eye's neon tubes appeared to have malfunctioned, but the cabling remained intact, with seven wire-loops corresponding to the seven tubes, primed for immediate re-illumination. Although that eye seemed recently to have been painted yellow, with a near-intact layer of that colour along its lower edge, its original coloration had evidently been metallic blue, glimpsed through two patches of corrosion on the corneal facade behind its seven tubes, and also beneath the yellow paint's eroding, so that it formed a blue eye, conjoined with Berlin's filmic blue stars.

Throughout the GDR era in East Berlin, phenomenal exertion was devoted to the ocular scanning by its inhabitants of one another, under the supervision of the secret police, in order to pierce habitual screens of normality and allegiance, and illuminate any evidence of deviance (from offhand sonic mutterings against the GDR regime, to explicit visual declarations by its punk-rock factions and dissidents); the numbers of inhabitants engaged in that glacial scopophilia extended into the hundreds of thousands, depending on whether the numerical calculation encompassed both 'official' and 'unofficial' collaborators of the secret police. In extreme cases, those who had negated the GDR regime were consigned to the permeable zones of criminal incarceration and psychiatric confinement, and covertly executed, guillotined or shot in the back of the neck; in the final years of GDR-era East Berlin, the hallucinatory system of ocular surveillance began to break-down, with a scarcity of recruitable new eyes, as though that system's own excess had driven it into backfiring sclerosis. With the GDR state's abrupt vanishing, after forty years of exhaustive ocular work, those hundreds of thousands of skilfully honed eyes, now shot with deterioration, turned from corporeal scannings to scannings of Berlin's urban surfaces, resulting, in its young population, in an engulfing, city-wide early-1990s graffiti-imprintation of those surfaces, performed as an inscribed extension of their over-active eyes, and, in its elderly population, in an invisible but tangible embedding, into those surfaces, of strata of urban memory, and of memory's tearing-apart. The textual, photographic and filmic documentation of the GDR inhabitants' ocular regime of obsessive self-surveillance, punitively compiled, had formed a near-infinite archive, part-shredded or burned in panic by its bureaucratic custodians during the regime's final days, but so sprawlingly vast that much of it survived that attempted destruction, and became a volatile, contested archive for the future years of recrimination and exposure.

Within the atrium of the Sony Center, inaugurated in 2000 alongside the Potsdamerplatz, and supplanting the bombed-out and voided wasteland, formerly occupied by luxurious hotels and cafes, into which the Skladanowsky ghost-carriage is swallowed in Wenders' film *Die Gebrüder Skladanowsky*, two immense digital image-screens transmitted sequences of corporate animations, far over the heads of the atrium's consumers. From time to time, those animations abruptly ceased, and the screens projected, instead, surveillance images fed simultaneously from cameras positioned around the Sony Center's exterior and interior, switching at set intervals from one to another, so that the building appeared multiply to be watching itself, and its own urban surfaces, while disclosing that act of surveillance, through the twin eyes of its digital image-screens, as though the excessive momentum of the GDR state's orchestrated ocular scanning, now utterly drained and obsolete, still demanded a transplantation, its focus invasively colonising the Sony Center's digital technology, and

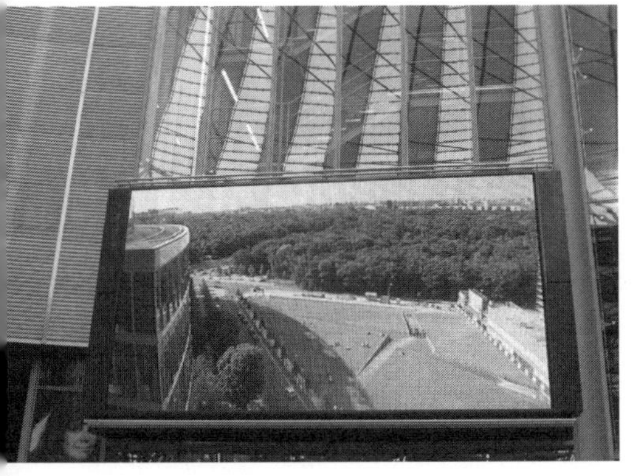

phantasmatically inhabiting those screens, projecting an urban rather than corporeal content, with one eye occasionally veering to a transmission of archival film-footage of the evanesced Potsdamerplatz of the late 1920s, while the other maintained its contemporary surveillance projection, so that those dual eyes appeared wrenched by memory, between the digital and the filmic.

In Guy Hamilton's film *Funeral in Berlin* (1966), the inept spy Harry Palmer flies unwillingly to West Berlin's Tempelhof airport to supervise the non-existent defection to Britain of a Russian officer; from that moment of arrival, he is incessantly subjected to multiple, contradictory acts of surveillance, from competing factions (of West Berlin, East Berlin, Israel, the USSR, and Britain) attempting to transform his bemused transits across the city into acts of power or death. Palmer's taxi-journey through the East Berlin cityscape is a counterfeited, mis-matched one, conjured by filmic back-projection, and as he passes the Brandenburg Gate, the film's sequence aligns itself exactly with that undertaken almost twenty years earlier for *A Foreign Affair*, in which a studio-located US army jeep transports its congressional delegation through pre-shot footage of ruined, incinerated buildings. Whereas that delegation compulsively gazed at, and filmed, the city around them, Palmer is oblivious to it, despite its close resemblance to that cityscape of decades earlier (all that has changed is that it is now shot in bleached colour); he looks straight ahead, in bleak disinterest, as though negating all ocular power-dynamics. His taxi is heading for an address in East Berlin's Marx-Engels-Platz, but Palmer arrives, instead, still in West Berlin, at the derelict, blackened facade of the Görlitzer railway-station in Kreuzberg, and is arrested there, as though the hardhatted controller of urban vision, operating from his plinth by the actual Marx-Engels-Platz, has irresistibly scrambled and inverted all ocular mappings of urban space, so that Berlin's eyes remain always aberrantly dislocated.

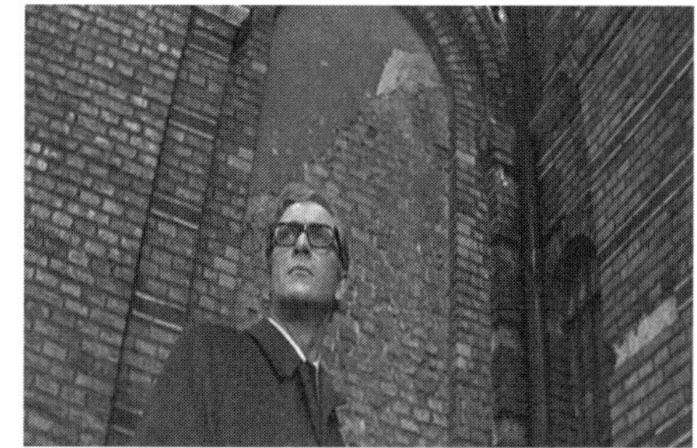

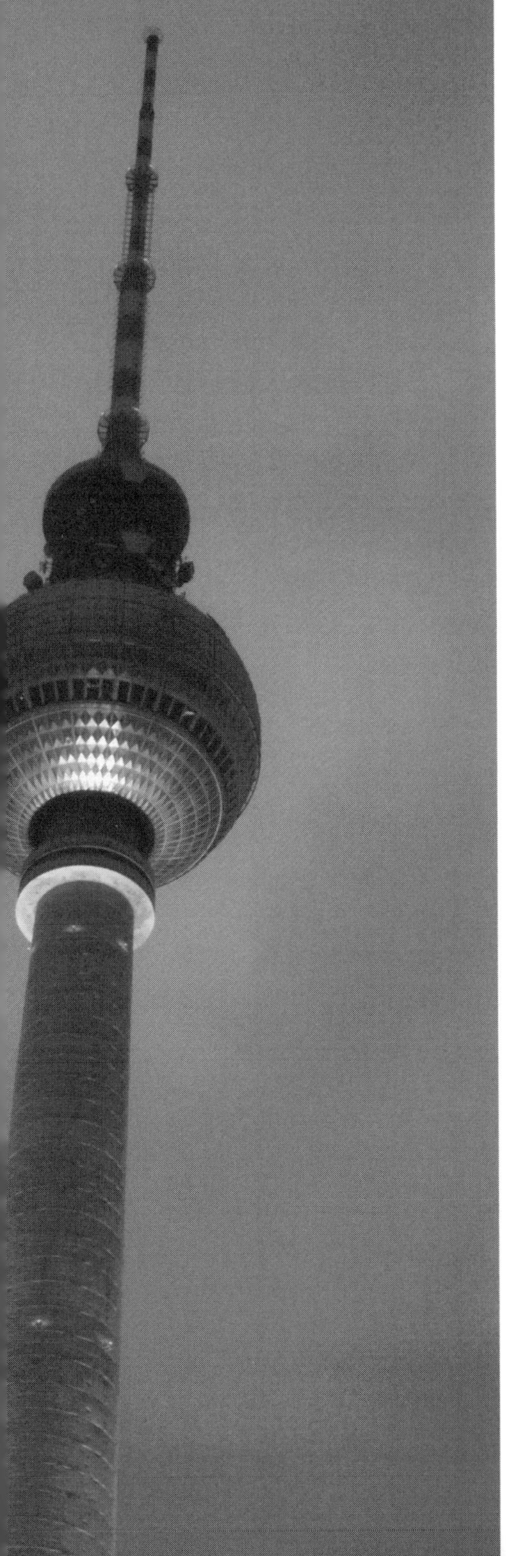

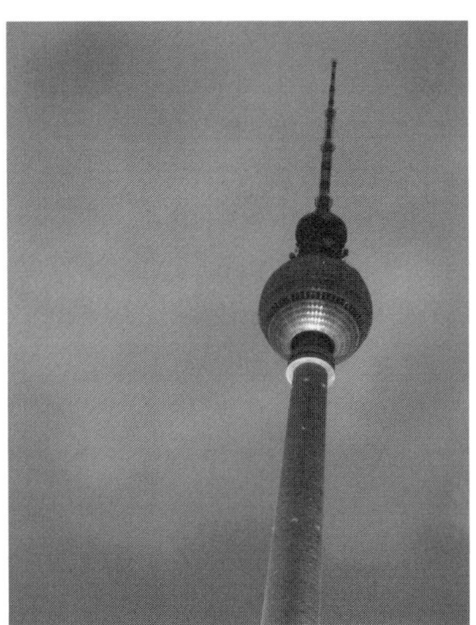

38

While the wall-fixed eye, conjured from seven neon tubes, had fused and malfunctioned, the concrete-faced stem of the Alexanderplatz's Television Tower, visible from almost every point in Berlin, remained illuminated at dusk, by multiple beams of light directed upwards from sites around that vast plaza, and also emitted from the stem itself, with constelled points of red light warning, or enticing, low-flying air-traffic. The Television Tower had constituted the pre-eminent hallucination of East Berlin, capriciously re-located into the area's 1960s redevelopment by the GDR's leader, Walter Ulbricht, from its originally planned site on the city's elevated south-eastern edge, as though to enable its stem to be gripped from above by some omniscient urban overseer, and used to spin the city into ever more vertiginous, haywire revolutions. The eyeball-shaped viewing platform at the stem's summit itself revolved; during the final years of the GDR era, that movement had been a jarred and uneven one, emitting sonic groans from the tower's neglected infrastructure, as though the exertion required to survey the entirety of Berlin precipitated ocular agony, and incipient meltdown, in empathy with the disintegration of the GDR's once-grandiose surveillance system during that same period. That revolving eye, its dual horizontal slits poised tightly together, and surrounded by outlandish configurations of diamond-shaped metal panels, appeared the result of an unprecedented but maladroit invention, like that of the Skladanowsky projector, as though its group of architects (notably Hermann Henselmann, who inherited an East-Berlin variant of Hoffmann's city-architect status, and also designed the Stalinallee's towers), on initiating construction in 1964 at Ulbricht's orders, had viewed plans for more streamlined, adept tower-constructions from the same era, such as Moscow's in-progress Ostankino tower, but had been so ocularly compelled by Berlin's vision-instilled surfaces that their own tower irresistibly took the form of an aberrant urban eye, poised on an elongated, tapering stem, as though stretched to enable that eye to see ever-further; to mark the tower's miraculous inauguration, on 7 October 1969, after several years of frequently-stalled construction in which it had resembled a colossal, raw nail, half-hammered into the Alexanderplatz, incandescent streams of light were shot directly at that eye, in order to activate its visions.

Viewed tangentially from ground-level at its moment of nightfall illumination, the Television Tower transects Berlin's sky as though forming a space-delineating fissure, like that of the Buch asylum-terrain's wall, and Berlin's other, infinite surfaces of urban fissuration, with the ocular configuration at the tower's summit comprising an accumulated axis-point, at which the high-tension process of fracturation has widened outwards, to form an eye which can only ever intimate its own movement through space, and the corporeal and urban scannings which result from that transit. All such processes of fracturation, in Berlin, issue from the city's sensitised

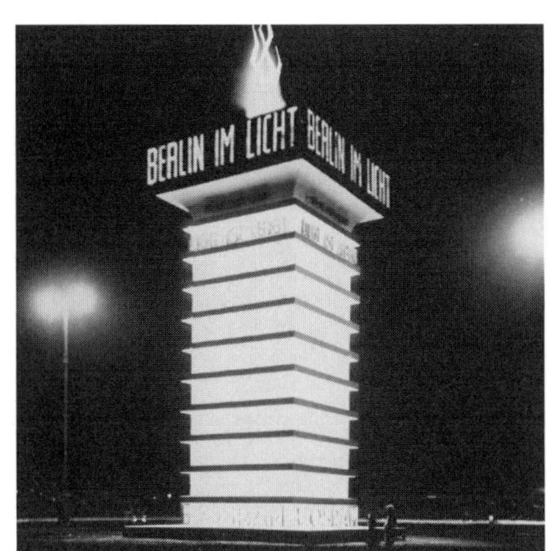

ground-level, and are directed upwards, towards the attaining of a status of visual blurring or disappearance, as though that movement were one in which the ground-level had become overheatedly seared, both by memory and by the transmutation of memory into oblivion, thereby instigating a vertical trajectory, compacting elation and erasure, whose escape-velocity itself generates a vital source of illumination – drawing the vision of all urban inhabitants towards it, and simultaneously throwing-out light – before tapering to zero, in the form of the Television Tower's transmission-mast, affixed directly above its revolving-eye, and finally deliquescing.

Berlin's cultural history, since the mass-electrification of its streets and transport networks, has been wired into its preoccupation with acts of illumination; embedded into that concern with illumination is the mutation from controlled light into all-consuming conflagration. The 'Berlin im Licht' ('Berlin in Light') festival took place from 13-16 October 1928, as a civic endeavour designed to promote Berlin's ascendant technologies, transforming all of its central avenues and plazas, such as the Potsdamerplatz, into incandescent urban spaces. The facades of nightclubs, department-stores and cinemas became emblazoned with multi-coloured neon, and many of the paint-inscribed texts on the city's billboards and firewall-hoardings were overlayered with neon strips that followed the contours of the original texts; similarly, the forms of blazing neon figures (human faces, consumer objects) were layered across the paint-imprinted figures on urban facades, both accentuating and annulling those original images. The 'Osramtürm', a tower lauding a light-bulb company, was created in horizontal strata of light, prefiguring the Television Tower's lateral bands of illuminated concrete, and positioned in the centre of a plaza to project both its inscribed text: 'Licht ist Leben' ('Light is Life'), and its vertically-directed ignitions of electronic fire. Journeys across Berlin, by public transport, became near-hallucinogenic transits through streets of blazing light, with the vehicles themselves re-surfaced as multiple light sources, to constitute mobile projectors of 'life' (inverse urban presences to that of the child-murderer Beckert's panic-stricken Berlin-transit, in *M*, in his rear-imprinted human projection of death). The festival was conceived as an immense public spectacle, with an integral sonic dimension (Kurt Weill composed music for the opening and closing events); much of its surviving documentation resulted from amateur film and photographic images shot by its witnesses, as with all of the city's subsequent acts of urban illumination and uproar, seminally recorded by their observers. Once the festival was over, the redundant neon strips, installed only days earlier across Berlin's facades, were immediately jettisoned; the apparition of the excessively illuminated city vanished, though Berlin retained the luminescent marquees of the 5,000 cinemas it held in that era. Five years later, insurgences of light re-appeared in Berlin, with the Nazi regime's 'architectures' and 'cathedrals' of light, many of them designed by Speer, propelled vertically into the sky, at night, in choreographed mid-air arrangements, from searchlights (rather than being materially projected onto, or from, urban surfaces), above open spaces where vast crowds could amass, such as the Tempelhof airfield (where Harry Palmer arrives in *Funeral in Berlin*), and at the 1936 Olympic games' closing ceremony. The intensive wartime destruction of Berlin, by incendiary bombing and then during the Soviet army's entry into the city, in the final week of April 1945, generated new acts of urban conflagration, whose residue was the mass-disappearance of the city's facades themselves, rather than of their media of illumination.

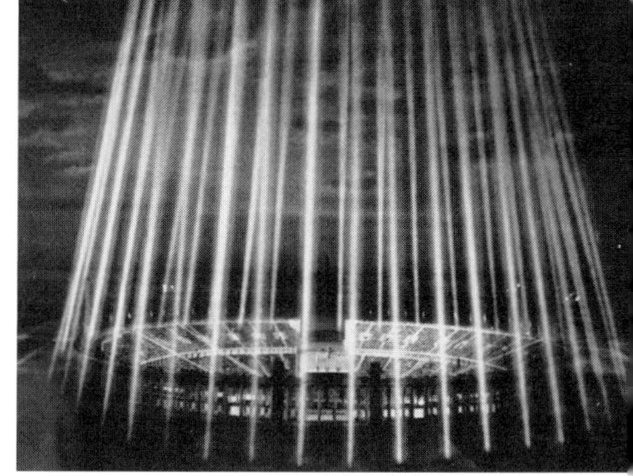

Berlin's illuminated digital-image screens, such as those of the Sony Center, form contemporary variants of such evanescing media of urban incandescence as the 1928 Osramtürm: screens prepared imminently to dematerialise, after projecting their surveillance-inflected content, but also resonant both of Berlin's ground-level strata of indistinguishably half-assembled or half-abandoned buildings, and of its innumerable monoliths, plinths and steles, with their integral fissurations.

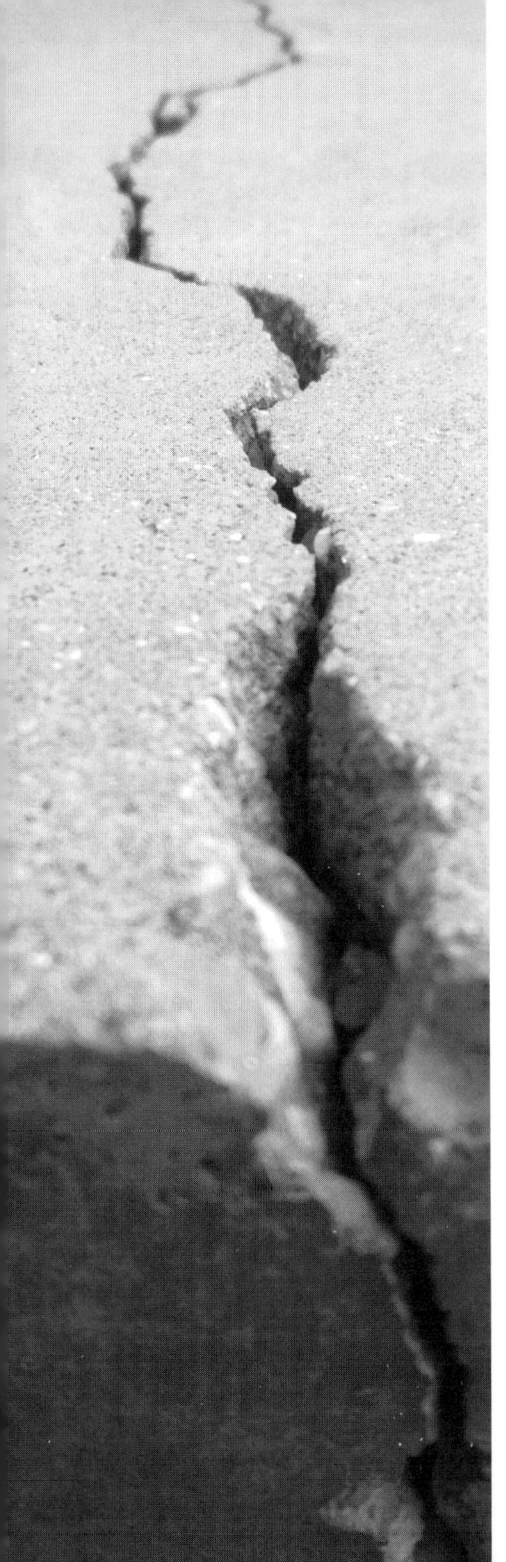

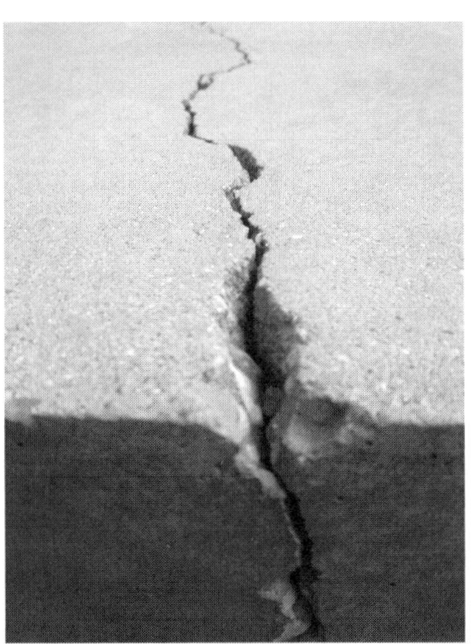

39

A profound fissure was created, on and within the urban surface of an unmarked memorial construction in Berlin, and that fissuration possesses its own history, exactly equivalent to all histories of memory-projections emitted from the city's surfaces. That fissure originates with a minuscule flaw, of mysterious provenance, in the concrete which holds it; although that concrete's memorial status has been explicitly prioritised by the great expense entailed in its installation within the city, and has been 'cured', as part of its casting process, and coated with a chemical substance designed to withstand Berlin's climatic assaults and corrosion, as well as its graffiti imprintations, those strategies have all misfired, and the concrete's crack gradually widens, as years pass by and acute fluctuations in temperature, resulting in immersals of its surface in ice and heat, place strains on the concrete's capacity to maintain that surface intact, and never to split open. But the concrete splits, wider and wider, and reveals its interior; although those concrete innards appear undifferentiatedly identical to the exterior, apart from the absence of the surface's chemical sealant (which is itself invisible and intangible), it simultaneously constitutes an outpouring, of death and memory. The fissure forms a raw, jagged line, like that surmounting the Television Tower's exposed concrete stem, in documentary film-footage in which it appeared semi-abandoned during its extended construction period; but, unlike that half-built, mid-1960s Television Tower, the fissured monument's construction is already 'ended', years earlier, and its self-willed tearing-open, as an outburst of irrepressible urban viscera, forms a posthumous, phantasmatic act. The process of fracturation gradually inscribes a vertical trajectory up the concrete's surface, so deep that adjacent splinters become detached, and fall to the ground; when the fissure encounters a right-angle in the concrete's form, it adeptly shifts from a vertical to a horizontal direction, and simply keeps going, now illuminated by sunlight, infinitely, like the courses of European rivers, scanned from above and followed towards Berlin, in the opening sequence of Riefenstahl's film *Olympia*. The fissure marks that transition from vertical to horizontal movement by exacting an accumulation of damage around its trajectory, then occasionally adjusts its course in order to secure an optimum transit across the flawed concrete terrain, adroitly dividing its course at one point into two channels, as though to conjure Kiefer's art-work *Zweistromland*, or Berlin's own river-enclosed Museuminsel; it maps its own aberrant itinerary, ever deeper, endlessly, across and into its concrete surface.

The remainder of the other 2,710 concrete memory-steles of that monument, the Memorial to the Murdered Jews of Europe, together with the terrain on which it stands, appear engulfed, to vanishing-point, into that seminal fissuration of Berlin's memory: a fissure which both absorbs, and projects. The monument's construction

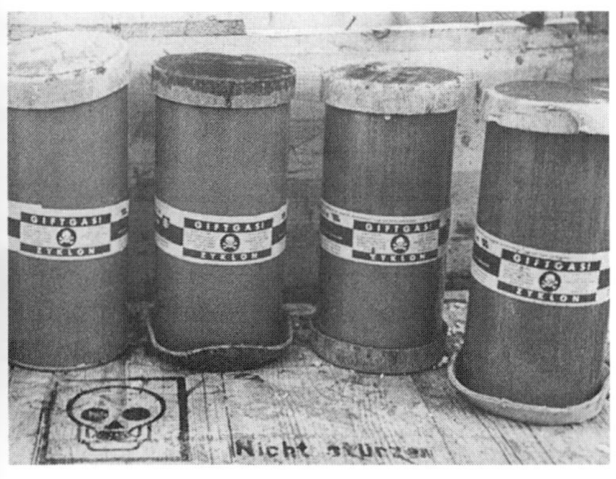

possessed an intricate, contested history, of budgetary disputes and rejected prototypes, even before the eight-year period, 1997 to 2005, between its commissioning and completion. Archival film-footage of the selected terrain, between the Brandenburg Gate and the voided sites of Hitler's Chancellery and subterranean bunker, immediately before the start of construction, shows an expansive, grass-covered wasteland with two large pools of water; the architect, Peter Eisenman, actively precluded the presence of all text and image from the monument, apart from several inscribed plaques at ground-level, their surfaces densely striated by sharp objects, as though through repeated acts of attempted erasure, and detailing regulations for human entry into the steles' otherwise un-boundaried compound: such entries must always be performed 'slowly', with no 'loud noise of any kind'. During their factory-stage process of construction, the steles were cast upside-down, and heat-'cured', their surfaces coated with the sealant 'Protectosil', against water-leakages, corrosion, and graffiti, before they were installed on their assigned site, in Berlin; despite those precautions, the city's history insistently leaked-in. The 'Protectosil' sealant had been manufactured by the thriving chemical conglomerate, Evonik-Degussa, whose 1940s incarnation had operated a subsidiary company, Degesch, which was the principal distributor and promoter, over several decades, of the extermination-medium 'Zyklon-B' (its name derived from an acronym of the names of its components, of which the main element was hydrocyanic acid; the resulting name also intimated a level-'B' 'cyclone', as though the pre-eminent, level-'A' cyclone was still to come), in existence in that form since 1922, processed as pellets and widely used for pest-control, but deployed from 1941 in concentration camps, including Auschwitz-Birkenau, for human eradication. The Degesch subsidiary company worked in close collaboration on 'Zyklon-B' manufacture and distribution with the IG Farben conglomerate, which ran a forced-labour factory adjacent to the Auschwitz-Birkenau site; the predecessor company to Evonik-Degussa, known in the 1940s simply as Degussa, also used forced-labour and became a primary processor, at its Berlin refinery, of gold from the teeth of Jews murdered in Polish ghettoes, such as that of Lódz. In mid-construction of the monument, that industrial history became unearthed, and its governmental funders and sponsors debated whether, even before its completion, the monument had now become so pre-contaminated that it were better to abandon its construction, erase all traces of the in-progress building-site, and begin again from zero; finally, the monument's completion went ahead as planned, but its own distinctive history, as a seminal urban surface of Berlin, became instigated – in autonomy from its sponsors' desires, and beyond its 'ending' – only from the precise moment when its irresistible process of fissuration welded itself with those of Berlin's other, infinitely cracked urban surfaces.

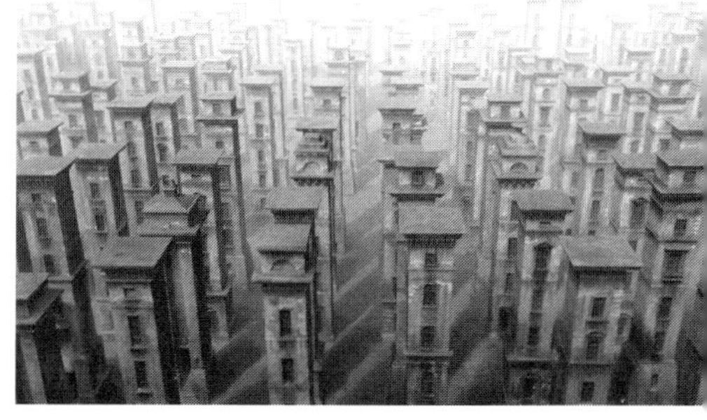

Integral to that monument's non-aligned, post-'completion' urban history is its transmutation through art-works. In 2007, two years after the monument's inauguration, Stefan Hoenerloh's painting *Stelenfeld* (*Field of Steles*) reconfigured the memorial-terrain as one of an autonomous city, formed entirely of equidistant tenements, each storey holding only one room. As with the memorial steles' contoured terrain, the tenements' elevations fluctuate, as though positioned on seismic ground, but they are otherwise almost identical; they cast oblique, dark shadows onto the intervals of wasteland that intersect them, but in the distance, those tenements are vanishing into incandescent light. All of Hoenerloh's other cityscapes, though inspired by his first ocular contact, in 1980, with the disintegrating facades and rear-courtyards of East Berlin, form entirely imagined urban spaces, as with his painting of 2001, *The Knarz House, Ten Years Later*. But that resistance to the absorbing of his internally-conjured, film-inflected images, as sub-cities within Berlin's excessive, over-determined arena, became momentarily cracked-open in *Stelenfeld*, as though contaminated by the monument's sealant, which promised an impermeable protective layering against unwanted inscriptions and acts of corrosion, but inversely instigated an autopsy-wide opening in Berlin's urban and corporeally-ashen space.

Hoenerloh's *Stelenfeld* embodies the manifestations of urban memory which, through their proliferation and vanishing into thin-air, are transformed into a status of oblivion, which possesses a pre-eminent aura of elation, even though the exact moment of that transformation – spatially located at the dividing boundary between memory and oblivion – may precipitate an extreme urban laceration, whose imprintation into the city's surfaces can revealingly be seized in its art-works and filmic images. Berlin's urban memory negates its archival homogenisation, numerological formulation, and its enclosure in regulated compounds; even terminally annulled, beyond its 'end', it perversely moves in flux-impelled and ghost-haunted transits, via urban fissurations, between pivotal sites on the city's surfaces, internally incising and simultaneously projecting, for ocular scrutiny, those surfaces' inexhaustible content.

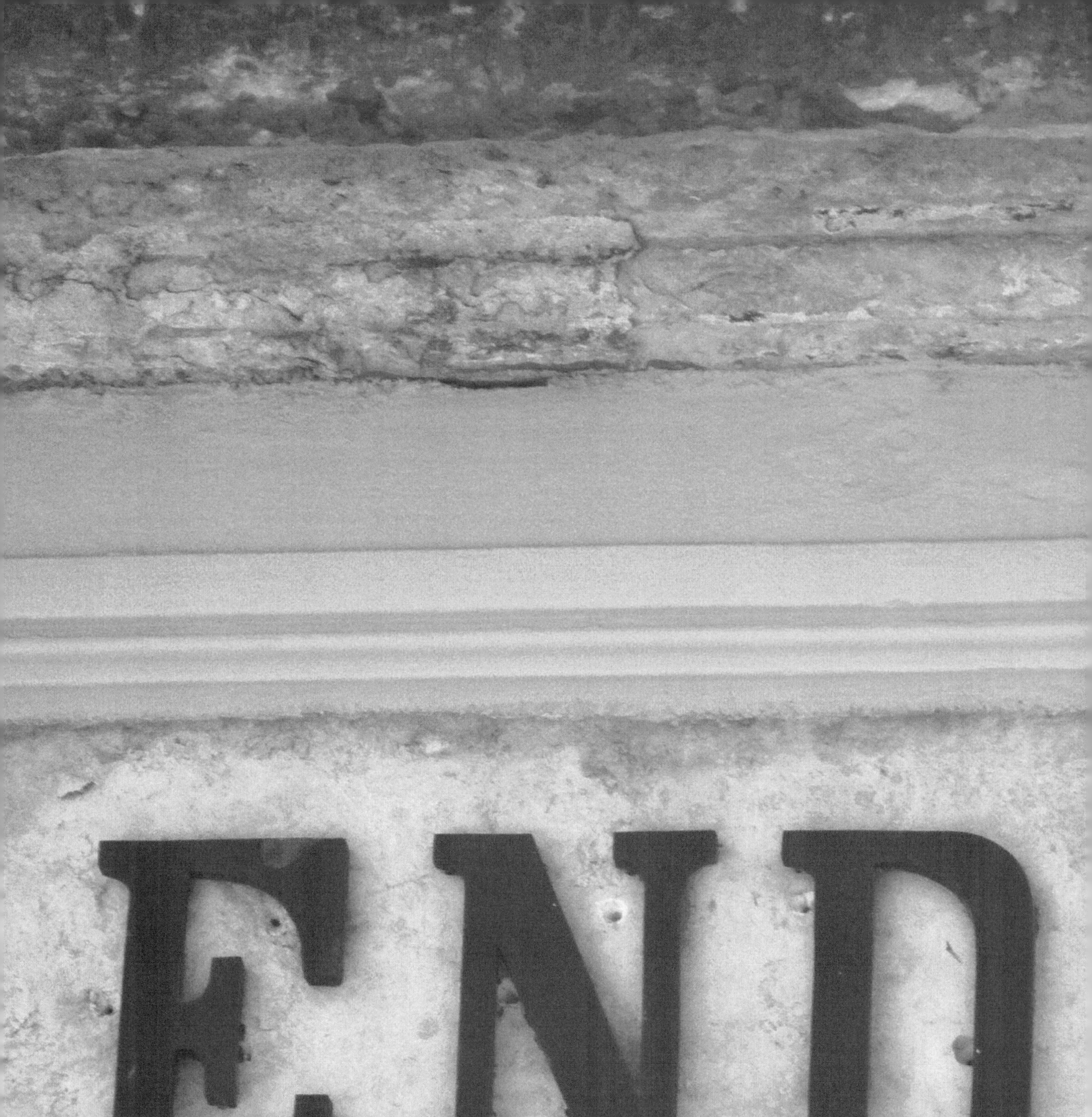
END

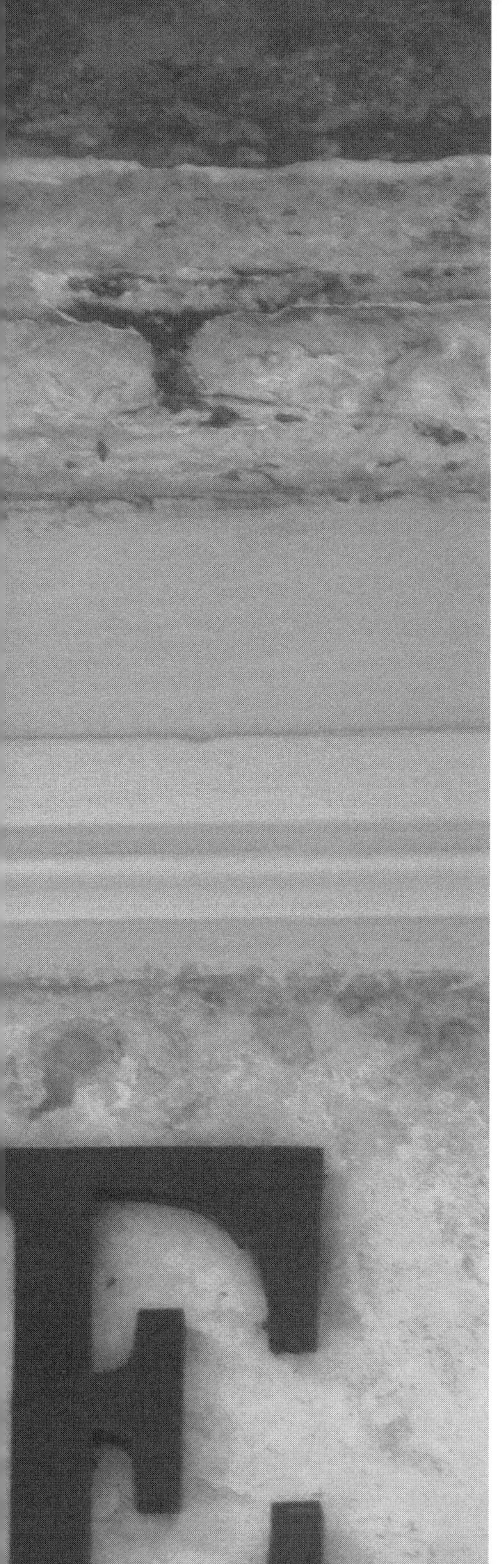

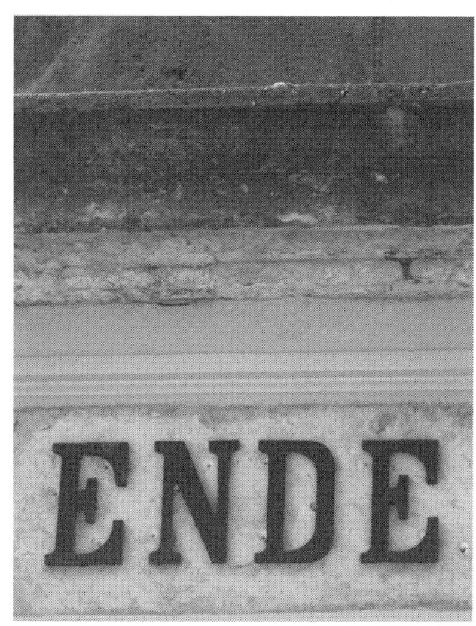

40

Final urban images and texts, from Berlin's walls, configure the 'end', together with the futures that move forwards from, but also backwards across, that terminal moment. In the long-abandoned, high-walled Georgen cemetery, in Berlin's Prenzlauerberg district, an originating tomb, one of the first installed in that cemetery, opened in 1814, was that of the family 'Ende': an ending to the family (like that negation of familial structure proposed by Brando in *Last Tango in Paris*), in a city whose Kreuzberg district was constellated in the 1970s by anti-familial, free-sex communes, but also a terminal indicator, for the terrain of that cemetery itself, which forms an extraordinary zone of the destruction of death's space: many of the majestic tombs torn-apart and opened-up by wartime bombing, their facades already inscribed in intricate erasure-languages from shrapnel impacts, before that death-terrain was fiercely fought-over, during the Soviet army's transit through the Prenzlauerberg district in the final week of April 1945, in machine-gun battles that left its surfaces marked by veering bullet-trajectories like that held by the Baltic wall; the ruined cemetery was then closed-up altogether in 1970, during the GDR era, with many lavish, nineteenth-century 'wall-tombs' voided of their inscriptions, rendered nameless surfaces, either through disintegration or looting, and other, smaller gravestones ripped-up from the earth and piled in colossal heaps; tombs became scrambled-together or simply vanished (like that, in the Invaliden military-cemetery across Berlin, of Heydrich, assassinated by Czech partisans shortly after the 1942 Wannsee conference which instituted the 'Final Solution' for Europe's Jewish population, and whose provisional grave-location, earmarked for a future memorial-stele to be sculpted by Breker, was obliterated by the Soviet army on its arrival in Berlin), as though exhaustively documented into oblivion, in one of Berlin's innumerable corporeal re-archivings; in the 1990s, the cemetery opened again, but the traces of resurgent activity only served to exacerbate its facades' capacity to emanate an extreme variant of the terminally gouged, incineration-imbued aura, projected by the entirety of Berlin's urban surfaces.

An urban-surface 'end'-point in Berlin, while disclosing terminal auras, from the profound fissurations of memory embedded in its monuments and other edifices, always simultaneously holds, and incites, future reconfigurations of the city. Berlin's futures are instilled in its art-works and films, but those formulations also take on a distinctive architectural medium, of pre-abandoned urban-planning, as though all conceptions of the future of Berlin compulsively erupt into hallucination, then implosion. The city's architectural archives contain countless scale-models for unused or untenable future imaginings of Berlin, dating from every decade of the city's existence, but accumulating towards the contemporary moment, and into which great investments of planning-time and expense are swallowed-up, as though the conceiving of Berlin's future spaces were itself a profligate act of urban perversion. A determining point of origin for the city's architectural cancellations is the envisaged transformation of Berlin into the colossal, future-city of 'Germania' (a transformation necessarily effacing the existing Berlin's traces, down to its name), prepared to minuscule scale-model detail, in collaboration between Speer and Hitler. Architectural plans may fracture after completion, as well as at their planning or scale-model stages, as with the seminal act of in-built self-destruction, in 1980, of the 'Haus der Kulturen der Welt', which exhilarated Berlin's young punks. The moment at which an all-encompassing architectural urban-future, lethally striated by the past, is summarily cancelled, as with that, in June 2010, of the scheme to overhaul the core of the city, by reconstructing the austere Prussian city-castle which had been dynamited in 1950 to make way for the GDR's illuminated Palast der Republik, always forms a revelatory one, as though all rational urban coherence becomes overruled, by the excessive overlayering of Berlin's spaces, with the outcome that such immense architectural schemes are invariably assigned, for nonchalant annulling, to the hardhatted controller of urban vision, scanning his multiple screens of Berlin's potential futures, from his metal plinth on the Marx-Engels-Forum plaza. A resultant wasteland, inhabited by incidental and seminal fragments of memory, at the heart of the city, forms an integral Berlin-future space.

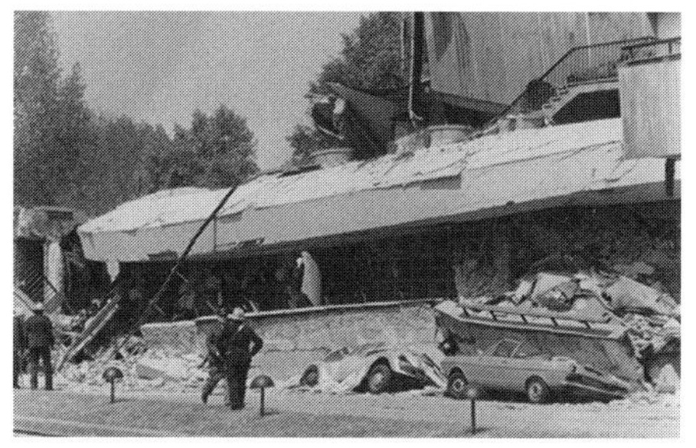

Berlin's future, generated from the interrogations and projections of its urban surfaces, is simultaneously digital, archaic, and apocalyptic, as though no upshot could be found for the city other than to compact its dynamics of memorial erasure with those of its memorial saturation. The contemporary digitised city – extending from the large-scale static image-screens self-scanning the Sony Center's space, to minuscule sub-screens directing corporeal transits of the city, and to invisible, intangible non-screens of data (which, operating like a contaminating layer of 'Protectosil', immerse and contain a city prone to cracking-open) – is inhabited both by its entrenched memory-woundings and by its capricious desire for elation-provoking disintegrations, with that contrary amalgam visualised and transmitted, across Berlin's space and time, by its art-works and film-images.

A vital urban film-image always precipitates a new act of vision, incorporated in infinite trajectories across the face of the city. At the 'end' of *Menschen am Sonntag*, once the film's four figures have dispersed – two of them perched at the rear of a rapidly moving vehicle, heading eastwards through the Tiergarten towards the Brandenburg Gate, then urgently overtaken by the still faster-moving vehicle that is filming them, as though its film-camera were now compelled immediately to transpierce that urban portal, in order to conjure, decades into the future, the film-images (of bodies spatially dislocated from the city) of the US delegation's jeep-tour in *A Foreign Affair* and Palmer's *Funeral in Berlin* taxi-transit, shot against the Brandenburg Gate – the terminal intertitle's one-word inscription, reinforced with a full-stop, intimates, at the same moment, that the city's momentum and its temporal unfolding cannot stop, and will transport those caught in its haywire acceleration, beyond the 'end', into ever more concentrated sensorial spaces, layered between the urban and the corporeal. That act of urban transporting can also possess an aberrant, inundating velocity, able to seize and uproot the eyes that scan Berlin, to propel them towards one or other of its sub-cities – or out of its space.

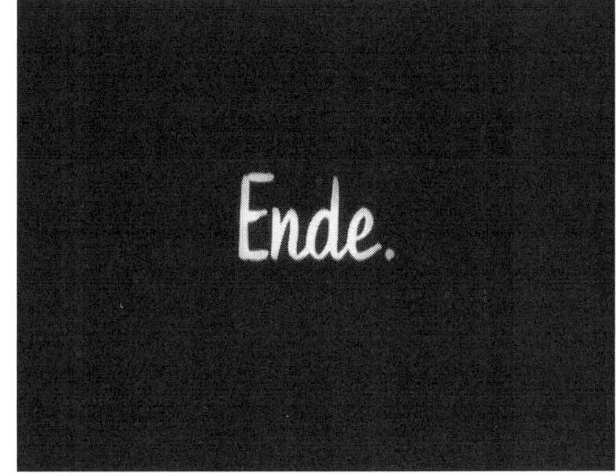

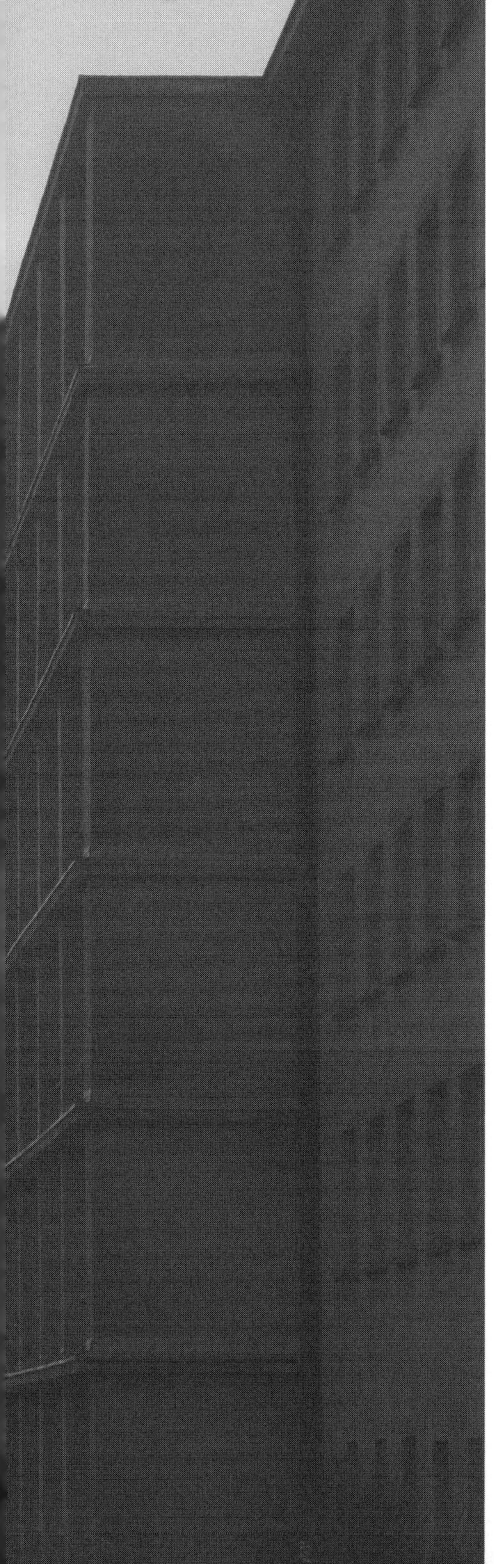

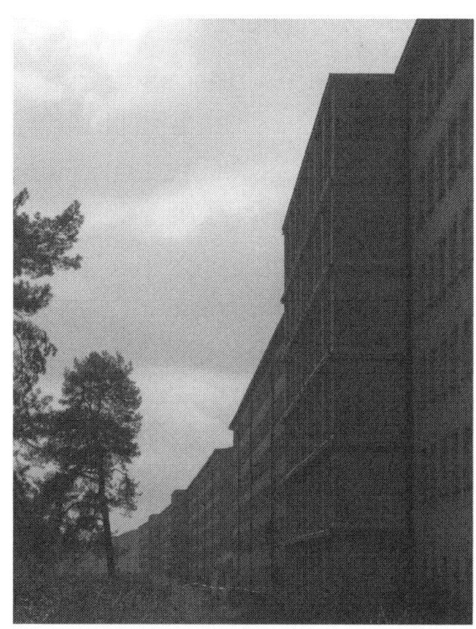

Berlin-by-the-Sea

Once the forty walls of Berlin – ocularly conjured from the medium of the Skladanowsky projector's dual lens, in the Potsdam Film Museum, and oscillating between those urban surfaces' interconnections with visual art and film, between memory and erasure – had vanished into thin-air, I took a train northwards out of Berlin, back towards the Baltic, propelled by the inundating momentum which that instant of the evanescing of all images generated, moving away from Berlin, but simultaneously through and towards an engulfing terrain of its sub-cities. From a departure point at the Ostkreuz station, I passed directly alongside the slaughterhouse sub-city inaugurated by Blankenstein in 1881, with the enduring remnants of its ornate metal-facaded pavilions for the extermination and processing of untold numbers of animals, for Berlin's consumption; I then travelled past Hoffmann's minuscule, control-room annex to his 1913 Prenzlauerberg community school-building, transformed in the 1980s into a sonic-furore sub-city of cacophony, as the Duncker punk-rock club, perched high above the railway-cutting on the route out of Berlin; finally, I headed northwards from the city, via the dual zones of Hoffmann's sub-cities for Berlin's mad in Buch, those zones transected both by the railway tracks and by the fissured boundary-wall which resonated with all of the city's innumerable, cracked surfaces. But once at the Baltic coast, as though that journey by train had been directed by an afterimage coda of the Skladanowsky projector, still phantasmatically conjuring-up residual images even after its extinguishing, I discovered I had arrived at Berlin's final sub-city: Prora: Berlin-by-the-Sea.

The immense Prora resort-complex, abandoned but ineradicable, ran endlessly along the eastern coast of the Baltic island of Rügen, directly north of Berlin. Hitler himself, along with Speer, had been the devisor of Prora, as though they had needed to formulate an equivalently maniacal counterpart for their vast re-envisioning of Berlin, as the future-city 'Germania'. The Prora sub-city of Berlin, never inhabited, possessed multiple, curtailed urban-histories. One of a number of Berlin-by-the-Sea sub-cities planned for mass-orchestrated leisure, and assigned by Hitler to Robert Ley, who ran the Nazi-regime's KdF – 'Kraft durch Freude' ('Strength through Joy') – organisation for their realization, Prora was the only one built. Four to five kilometres in length, Prora was designed to accommodate a population of 20,000 inhabitants, in 10-day relays, within identical, sea-facing rooms in six-storey concrete blocks. That sub-city would be reached directly by train from Berlin (and other cities), or via ocean-liners, crossing the Baltic to Prora from the railway-ports of Stralsund and Warnemünde, from vast, specially-built jetties; the Prora jetty was intended to channel the resort's new inhabitants directly into an immense assembly hall, able to hold the sub-city's entire population at once, and where they would immediately receive the exhaustively enforced itinerary for their vacation. The Prora sub-city was an elongated, streamlined one, its breadth that of its narrow concrete blocks, and distanced from the white-sand Prora bay by a strip of pine-forest; its first batches of inhabitants were intended to arrive in 1941, and construction-work extended from May 1936 to the outbreak of war in September 1939 (construction accelerated in the final year), before abruptly ceasing, with the reallocation for combat of its workforce. The colossal complex, undemolishable and unmanageable in its excessive urban dimensions, was then largely left to disintegrate, barriered from access during the following decades, with several blocks maintained and used for training-exercises by the GDR army; after the GDR's erasure, Prora's disintegration deepened, although property speculators sporadically announced that its now-eroded, deeply-fracturated blocks would imminently be renovated into holiday-apartments as an 'ex-KdF beach-resort', their promotional placards affixed to the blocks' surfaces, entirely covering their expanse, and showing animated images of the digitally transformed, luminescent future-blocks, once finally inhabited.

I walked the entire length of that Berlin-by-the-Sea sub-city, along its landward and seaward faces, and then entered its ruined interiors, with their precarious stairways ascending into infinite corridors of vacation-rooms, left as raw shells by their Nazi-era builders but partly installed, during the following decades, with the GDR military's shoddy fittings and artefacts which, rendered suddenly obsolete, had accentuated the original interiors' abandonment, taking the form of a dense, ground-level layering of shattered-glass, buckled ducts and discarded, sodden archives; ventilation outlet-pipes had been gouged from the facades' concrete walls, creating eye-shaped orifices, for transits in and out of those spaces. The property speculators' wall-sized hoardings, many of them shredded by Baltic winds and immersed in dirt, their digitally-pixellated visualisations of a resuscitated future-Prora now corroded, only served to exacerbate that sub-city's aura of exacting a determined strategy of de-population, and of corporeal erasure, as though it had been conceived solely to fulfil its own urban obsessions, as a site of seminal abandonment and extreme dereliction, through the summary pre-expunging of every generation of its potential inhabitants, even before their first arrival at that site. One block's crumbling facade held a large-scale, painted image of the emblematic Berlin bear, now prone on the Prora beach and sunbathing, as though, having lost consciousness and fallen backwards, after receiving a slaughterhouse electric-shock or hammer-blow to the skull, and plummeting from his original site on the rusted cattle-market pavilion-facades in Berlin's sub-city of slaughter, that cerebrally-voided bear had been obliviously transported, for edenic relaxation, to the hallucinatory Berlin-by-the-Sea sub-city.

In Werner Heldt's painting *Berlin am Meer* (*Berlin-by-the-Sea*), executed in 1946-47, in several variants, as though through compulsive re-statement of an obsessional urban preoccupation, but in many ways a unique, and solely adequate, art-image for Berlin's urban surfaces, the inundated, drained city is located simultaneously within the space it once occupied, and is also displaced to a beyond-space, of its own cataclysmic self-expulsion. Heldt's marine-Berlin has been depopulated, like the Prora sub-city, rendered still and ashen, but is imprinted with the traces both of a power-mediating past existence, in the forms of palatial structures and statues of eminent figures, and also with the prescient traces of its urban future, in the form of a zigzagging urban-surface screen, ready for filmic projection, vividly illuminated but already fissured and part-blackened, and flickering between the alternating appearances of a blank-facaded housing-complex and a Berlin Wall prototype. 'Berlin-by-the-Sea', existing beyond the city, as a terminal-image annex, and conceived within the spaces both of the Prora sub-city and of Heldt's Berlin urban-surface art-image, forms a site of seminal ocular inundation, inhabited – in its human vanishing – by irresistible projections and absorbings, by precipice-terrains and quicksand-zones, and by infinite acts of transmutation, instigated via the intervention of eyes and through the instituting and ecstatic annulling of boundaries.

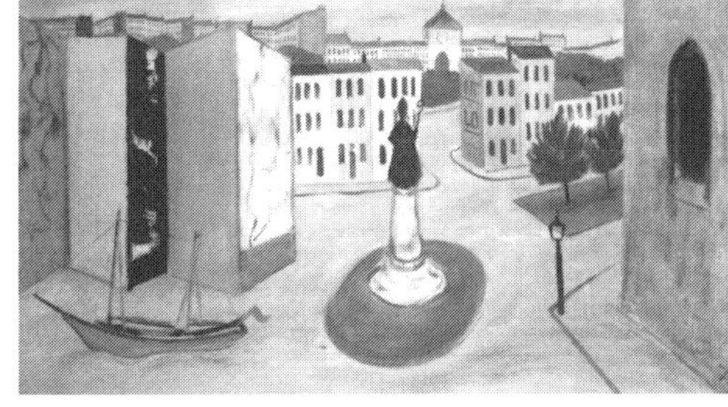

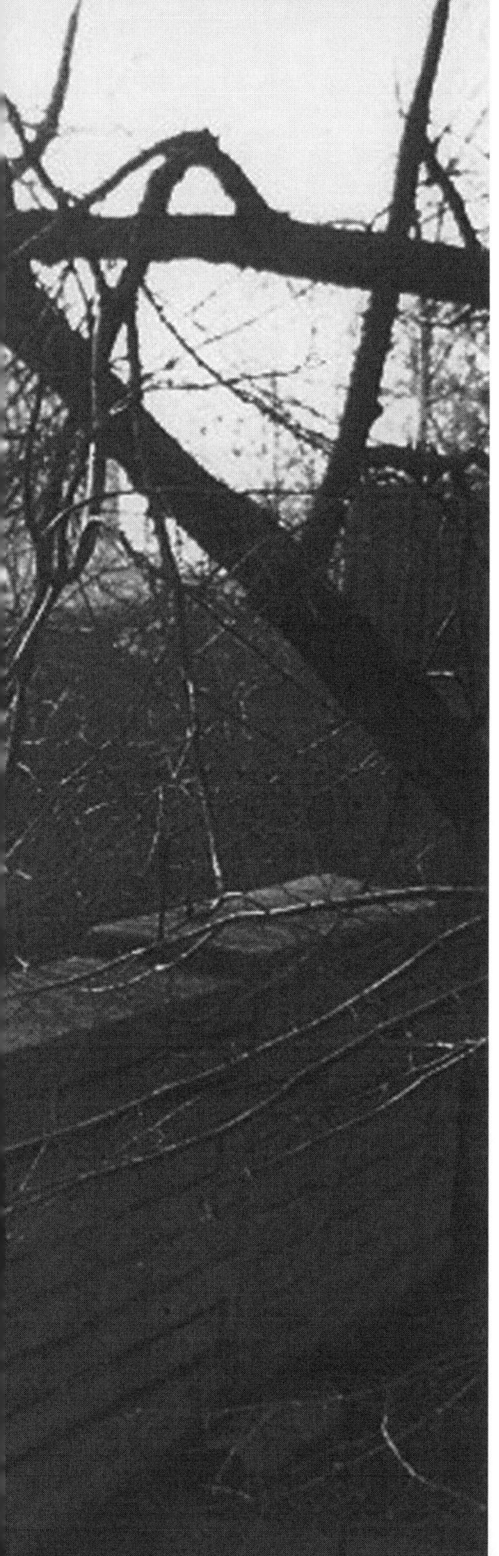

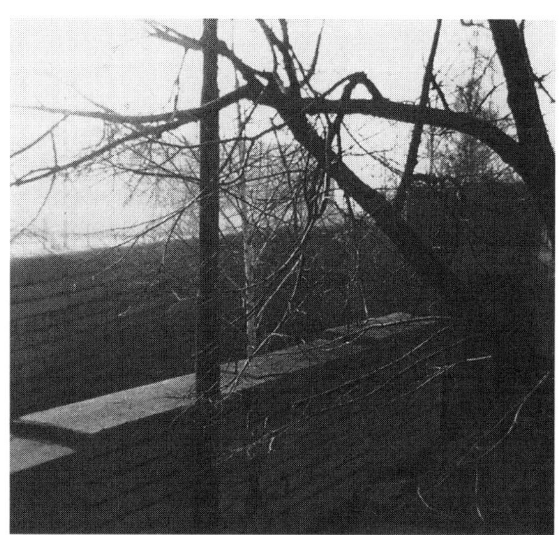

A 'Wall' of Berlin

There was once a 'wall' of Berlin...

On all of the journeys I made to Berlin during the 1980s, relentlessly transiting west to east, and east to west, through the then-operative portal-eye of the 'Tränenpalast', I took only one photograph, in February 1980, as though seized by a compulsion for images which otherwise immediately negated itself, so that it took the form of only one image, in solitude, of Berlin's urban surfaces. That photograph was taken in the Bernauerstrasse, which ran directly between East and West Berlin; at that time, the street's one-storey facades, on its eastern side, simultaneously formed urban-surface fragments, and also constituted the Berlin Wall itself. From the moment of that death-delineated boundary's materialisation, in 1961, until 1965, the five-storey tenement facades of the Bernauerstrasse's eastern side remained intact, and unwilling inhabitants of East Berlin would periodically throw themselves from their tenement windows, those movements infused by film-imageries of Berlin tenement-window plummets, from *Kuhle Wampe* and *Germany Year Zero*. It could appear, to an accidental urban observer, as though, as with Prora's resort-blocks, with their pre-emptive strategy of obsessional de-population, that those window-plummeting figures had been forcibly expulsed, by their own buildings, and sent flying. Several of those thin-air falls, from the tenements' upper storeys, to the West-Berlin pavement below, became lethal ones, so that the escapees were killed by their impacting contact with the terrain they desired. The tenement-windows were eventually bricked-up, their interiors corporeally voided; then, in 1965, those interiors were demolished, their emptied-out facades reduced to one-storey residues, and reinforced, in their dual role as urban-surfaces and Berlin-Wall components (behind which further obstacles and death-strip spaces accumulated), by laterally-assembled concrete blocks. The photograph was taken from the Bernauerstrasse's pavement, at an awry angle, at the point where it intersected with the blocked-off Strelitzstrasse; the facade of the tenement-building, Bernauerstrasse 22, had been cut-down to its ground-storey remnant, formed by the facade of a shop, with the name of its owner, Erna Schüssler, inscribed over the bricked-up doorway. Winter sunlight over-illuminates the background of the image, and over more than thirty years, the photograph gradually faded-out, the objects and surfaces within its frame bleaching to rust-hued forms, the background's urban elements (the Television Tower, the brick-firewalls of the Strelitzstrasse) evanescing, as though into a conflagration. The urban surfaces recorded within the image were also about to vanish: at that site, two months later, in April 1980, the GDR regime implemented its 'Grenzmauer 75' ('Borderwall 75') plan, instigated in 1975 but only belatedly applied to the Bernauerstrasse,

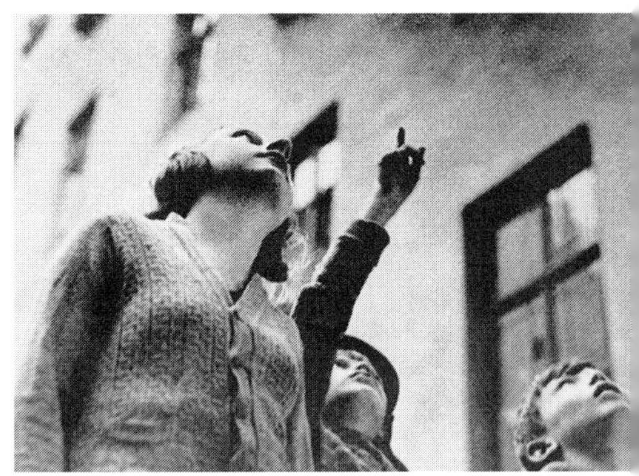

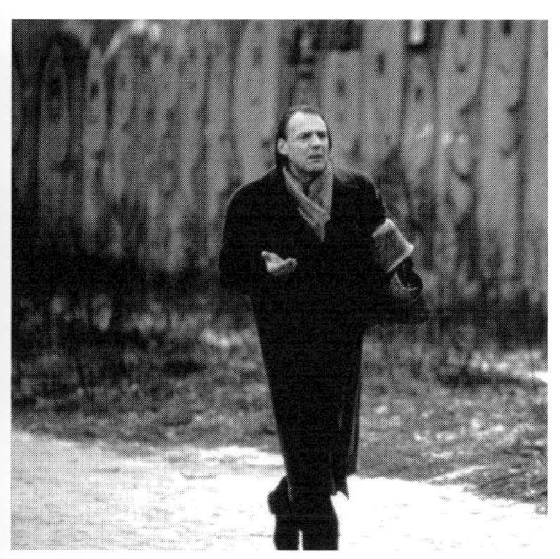

designed to homogenise the construction standards of the Berlin Wall, to a much higher elevation, rounded at its summit, and more easily subject to surveillance. The urban residues in the photograph were erased through a three-month process of demolition, the first day of which, 1 April 1980, was documented by a West Berlin television station, as well as from within East Berlin; by June, the entire contents of the urban site I had photographed were totally obliterated, and that photograph became a surviving trace of a vanished Berlin-'wall' variant. The disappearance, or permeability, of the Berlin Wall became a future focus for filmmakers, especially through its course's topographical ocular-scanning, either by air or from ground-level: in Cynthia Beatt's *The Invisible Frame* (2009), a bicycle-journey follows the grass-grown trajectory left behind by the uprooting of the boundary's final manifestation, and even several years before that 1980s-era Berlin Wall disappeared, it had already begun to appear outlandishly friable, as in Wenders' 1987 *Der Himmel über Berlin*, whose two angels effortlessly transect that boundary in either direction (though they are unable, so easily, to traverse the city's resistantly dense archival data, or the infinite voices of its dead). By 2010, at one end of the Bernauerstrasse's course, the multiple apparitions of the Berlin Wall had been amalgamated, and rebuilt, at great cost, across a vast terrain, as an officially sanctioned monument-spectacle. But, for my excoriations of Berlin's urban surfaces, that 'amateur' photographic image formed the vital, terminal – and only – image of a Berlin 'wall'.

Urban obsessions may be embedded, and belong to, Berlin's surfaces themselves; equally, such obsessions may be assigned to, and originate from, the corporeal, or the ocular, thereby resulting, when propelled headlong, in ocular aberrations within the act of envisioning the city. Such obsessions can also mutate into sonic urban-pathological manias, extending across corporeal and city-surface domains, as with

Kracauer's proposal for a 'scream' emitted by the Berlin streets, and necessitating dual incarcerations, for that urban vocal-tract, within both Hoffmann's Buch asylum and that same architect's cacophonic punk-rock club building. Urban obsession, though volatile, has already reached an extreme, optimum status, and can ascend no further; but, in every instance, it may imminently be downgraded, or transformed, through the annulling or erasing of its sustaining traces, into a passion, into a banal preoccupation, and then still further downwards, into indifference, and finally into extreme oblivion. But there remains always a last trace of an urban obsession, even if all other images, media, and inscriptions, are now erased; there remains, too, a final trace of an urban obsession, even when all residues of memory are subjected to a wipe-out gesture, or an irreversible overturning into oblivion. What remains then possesses a seminal urban mystery, like that of the photographic image of a Berlin 'wall', recorded on an icy winter morning in 1980, its own image-surface and the urban surface it holds both eroded and deliquescing, as though that image now wanted to vanish into the city.

I returned to Berlin by train, from the white-sand beach of Prora's Berlin-by-the-Sea sub-city, and the frozen Baltic, taking a journey backwards across time via its other successive sub-cities, of madness, then cacophony, then slaughter, to that photographic image's site, over thirty years on in time, at the right-angle junction of the Bernauerstrasse and the Strelitzstrasse, from which the first street veered downwards towards the river Spree, and the second street descended towards the Television Tower. The site remained an interzone wasteland, now of sand-soil, grass and embedded debris, as though poised in the drained aftermath of a compulsive inundation, like those of Heldt's paintings, with no trace of its former surfaces, either those of the urban facades eradicated shortly after their seizure in the photographic image, or of the upgraded Berlin Wall which supplanted

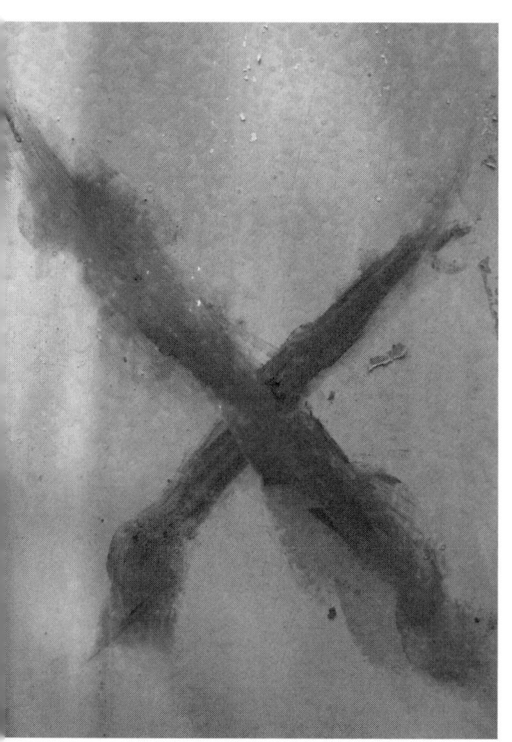

them; at the same time, those previous surfaces remained glaringly and phantasmatically present, with their voided traces and their ineradicable presence welded-together. But no tangible surface endured, into which the photograph could vanish. At nightfall, I took the photograph and walked northwards towards the Pankow district, to the abandoned railway-shed portal, which intimated an exit from Berlin. I set fire to that photograph of a 'wall' of Berlin, and it burned-up, in an instant, releasing a sudden toxic-outburst of its chemicals, along with its image's conflagration, expulsed into ashes. I then assembled the small heap of ashes, and inscribed them in dual, rapid hand-gestures across the surface of the railway-shed portal, into an 'x'-configuration, and photographed them, in the last light, to finally annul that obsessional urban image, and conjure from it, as an act of resuscitation, a new image of Berlin's urban surfaces.

There was once an image of Berlin....

Main Images

The Baltic Wall
The Skladanowsky Projector

40 Walls of Berlin:

1. Railway shed, Berlin-Pankow
2. Plinth, Berlin-Mitte
3. Photographic graffiti, Berlin-Prenzlauerberg
4. Archive, Berlin-Heinersdorf
5. Celluloid facade, Berlin-Friedrichshain
6. Transparent hoarding, Berlin-Friedrichshain
7. Hotel entrance, Berlin-Pankow
8. Meistersaal, Berlin-Kreuzberg
9. Rear-courtyard, Berlin-Prenzlauerberg
10. Ruination, Berlin-Friedrichshain
11. Stone screen, Berlin-Mitte
12. Filmic aperture, Berlin-Mitte
13. Transparent time, Berlin-Friedrichshain
14. Blue star, Berlin-Pankow
15. Red star, Berlin-Marzahn
16. Stalin's name, Berlin-Schönholz
17. Stalin's tongue, Berlin-Mitte
18. Slaughterhouse insignia, Berlin-Friedrichshain
19. Displaced fist, Berlin-Prenzlauerberg
20. Celestial fist, Berlin-Köpenick

21. Bunker eye, Berlin-Mitte
22. Execution shed, Berlin-Mitte
23. Incised steles, Berlin-Charlottenburg
24. Moss-grown surface, Berlin-Pankow
25. Eroded urban-language, Berlin-Kreuzberg
26. Re-facading, Berlin-Marzahn
27. Map, Berlin-Mitte
28. Crack, Berlin-Buch
29. Swimming-bath, Berlin-Prenzlauerberg
30. Oculus projection, Berlin-Mitte
31. Multiple screens, Berlin-Mitte
32. One-way portal, Berlin-Mitte
33. Last urban traces, Berlin-Friedrichshain
34. Placard, Berlin-Pankow
35. Garage, Berlin-Pankow
36. Cacophonic facade, Berlin-Kreuzberg
37. Neon eye, Berlin-Mitte
38. Tower eye, Berlin-Mitte
39. Fissuration, Berlin-Mitte
40. 'End', Berlin-Prenzlauerberg

Berlin-by-the-Sea
A 'Wall' of Berlin

Acknowledgements

I'm very grateful to the Gerda-Henkel-Stiftung, the British Academy, and the DAAD, for the grants which enabled me to write this book. I'd like to thank Berlin's archival curators of urban cultures, visual art and film, as well as Matthew Gandy and Mark Shiel, for their invaluable support, and everyone who helped me in Berlin, especially Verena von Stackelberg, Sharmaine Reid and Sara Piazza.